The Author

J. Edwin Orr, an internationally re-
spected authority on church history,
holds degrees from Oxford University
(Ph.D.), the University of California
at Los Angeles (Ed.D.), and Northern
Baptist Seminary (Th.D.). His studies
of recent evangelical awakenings have
gained wide recognition for their thoroughness and accuracy.

In collecting material on the subject
of evangelical awakenings Dr. Orr has
traveled to more than 150 of the
world's 160 countries. He has lectured
on countless college and university
campuses around the world and has
authored scores of publications as well.
His most popular book is *Full Surrender,* which has been translated into
fifteen languages and has been steadily
gaining readers since its initial publi-
cation fifteen years ago.

THE EAGER FEET

THE EAGER FEET

Evangelical Awakenings, 1790-1830

by

J. EDWIN ORR

moody press
chicago

ISBN: 0-8024-2287-X

The author acknowledges with gratitude a generous research grant from National Liberty Foundation of Valley Forge.

Printed in the United States of America

CONTENTS

INTRODUCTION

EVANGELICAL AWAKENINGS

An Evangelical Awakening is a movement of the Holy Spirit bringing about a revival of New Testament Christianity in the Church of Christ and in its related community. Such an awakening may change in a significant way an individual only; or it may affect a larger group of believers; or it may move a congregation, or the churches of a city or district, or the whole body of believers throughout a country or a continent; or indeed the larger body of believers throughout the world. The outpouring of the Spirit effects the reviving of the Church, the awakening of the masses, and the movement of uninstructed peoples towards the Christian faith; the revived Church, by many or by few, is moved to engage in evangelism, in teaching, and in social action.

Such an awakening may run its course briefly, or it may last a lifetime. It may come about in various ways, though there seems to be a pattern common to all such movements throughout history.

The major marks of an Evangelical Awakening are always some repetition of the phenomena of the Acts of the Apostles, followed by the revitalizing of nominal Christians and by bringing outsiders into vital touch with the Divine Dynamic causing all such Awakenings—the Spirit of God. The surest evidence of the Divine origin of any such quickening is its presentation of the evangelical message declared in the New Testament and its re-enactment of the phenomena therein in the empowering of saints and conversion of sinners.

It is more than interesting to compare the characteristics of the Awakenings of various decades with the prototype of evangelical revivals in the Acts of the Apostles, a perennial textbook for such movements.

Our Lord told His disciples: 'It is not for you to know the times or seasons which the Father has fixed by His own authority. But you shall receive power when the Holy Spirit has come upon you; and you shall be My witnesses . . . to the end of the earth.' Thus was an outpouring of the Spirit predicted, and soon fulfilled.

Then began extraordinary praying among the disciples in the upper room. Who knows what self-judgment and confession and reconciliation went on? There were occasions for such. But, when they were all together in one place, there suddenly came from heaven a sound like the rush of a mighty wind and it filled all the house. The filling of the Holy Spirit was followed by xenolalic evangelism, not repeated in the times of the Apostles nor authenticated satisfactorily since.

The Apostle Peter averred that the outpouring fulfilled the prophecy of Joel, which predicted the prophesying of young men and maidens, the seeing of visions and dreams by young and old. He preached the death and resurrection of Jesus Christ. What was the response? The hearers were pierced, stabbed, stung, stunned, smitten— these are the synonyms of a rare verb which Homer used to signify being drummed to earth. It was no ordinary feeling; nor was the response a mild request for advice. It was more likely an uproar of entreaty, the agonizing cry of a multitude.

Those who responded to the Apostle's call for repentance confessed their faith publicly in the apostolic way. About three thousand were added to the church. Then followed apostolic teaching, fellowship, communion and prayers.

What kind of fellowship? Doubtless the words of Scripture were often used liturgically, but it is certain that the koinonia was open. What kind of prayers? There are instances of individual petitions of power and beauty, but there are also suggestions of simultaneous, audible prayer in which the main thrust of petition is recorded, as in the prophet's day.

The Apostles continued to urge their hearers to change and turn to God, which they did by the thousands. And no hostile power seemed for the moment able to hinder them. Persecution followed, but the work of God advanced.

The events recorded in the Acts have been repeated in full or lesser degree in the Awakenings of past centuries. From the study of Evangelical Revivals or Awakenings in cities and districts, countries and continents, generations and centuries, it is possible to trace a pattern of action and discover a progression of achievement that establish in the minds of those who accept the New Testament as recorded history an undoubted conclusion that the same Spirit of God Who moved the apostles has wrought His mighty works in the centuries preceding our own with the same results but with wider effects than those of which the apostles dreamed in their days of power.

1

REVOLUTION AND INFIDELITY

It is difficult to explain why the capture by the people of an old castle-prison, defended by a few pensioners, should mark the downfall of the old order of France and the upsurge of revolution all over the world. The fall of the Bastille on 14th July 1789 was the signal of revolt in France and the forerunner of revolution far and wide.

On 27th August 1789, the National Assembly of France declared the Rights of Man, based upon the American declaration of 1776. The Americans first established modern democracy, but their breach with Britain was not with the British tradition of government. It was the French who set in motion the revolutionary forces of democracy, nationalism and social reform which changed the face of Europe.

In France, one of the unhappy by-products of the Roman Catholic persecution of the Huguenots was the fact that hundreds of thousands of the best-educated people in France, compelled to violate their consciences to conform outwardly to a religion that their souls abominated, laid themselves and their children open to scepticism and infidelity. Much of the free-thinking which preceded the 1789 French Revolution was derived from perjuring Huguenots,[1] whose antagonism to forced religion was intensified by the fact that it was a Catholicism of the poorest spiritual type that had triumphed, one of shameless immorality among the clergy and of limitless arrogance among the bishops. When the Revolution came, the people of France revolted against French Christianity. Voltaire denounced as 'L'Infame' the whole system of ecclesiastico-political oppression.

When the explosion of the French Revolution scattered its fire all over Europe, the enfeebled Christian countries nearby were unable to offer resistance. And the fire inside France was so intense that nominal Protestants as well as Roman Catholics melted into the new infidelity, and so apostasized. As early as 1765, there was an almost universal contempt of all religion, among both sexes and among all ranks.[2] Voltaire held that every sensible man, every

1

honorable man, must hold the Christian sect in horror. No exception was made for the Reformed minority.

When the storm broke in France, it struck the Roman Catholic Church with full force. The National Assembly ordered the sale of ecclesiastical lands, closed monasteries and nunneries, declared freedom of conscience, and tried to reorganize the Church.[3] The reaction of the clergy left France with only four diocesan bishops and half its parish priests. In 1791, the Pope condemned the civil constitution of the clergy, and many such fled the country.

Bishops and clergy agreeable to the new constitution were elected, precipitating trouble with those loyal to the Pope.[4] When fear of foreign invasion arose, the masses attacked the clergy under suspicion and massacre followed. A wave of anti-Church feeling swept the country, and the radical revolutionaries became frankly anti-Christian. A popular Parisienne was crowned goddess of reason in the cathedral of Notre Dame; Divine worship ceased in many metropolitan and provincial parishes; a majority of the constitutional bishops either apostasized or abdicated; and when the Reign of Terror erupted, many of the clergy were guillotined. The end of the terror brought little comfort to the Church, and, while increasing numbers of clergy agreed to obey the government, persecution continued and the cause of religion languished.

On the eve of the Revolution, there were half- a-million adherents, more or less, of the Reformed faith in France. About a hundred and eighty pasteurs cared for Reformed flocks. By 1793, all the churches in Paris were closed and many pasteurs abandoned their charges for the heady life of political action.[5] Abjurations were common and abject.[6] In the historic Huguenot South, half the pasteurs abjured. In all of France, almost every last Protestant church was shut up. In 1798, France annexed Geneva, and a landslide into infidelity followed. D'Alembert was delighted to report that in the citadel of Calvin there were pasteurs who no longer believed in the deity of Jesus Christ.

Jean Frederic Oberlin, a Reformed pasteur in the Vosges mountains of France, maintained his witness in the remote area of his ministry, preaching and teaching, supporting a school, introducing economic helps to a poverty- stricken community.[7] He survived the hardships of the times and lived many years of selfless service—almost sixty of them. His was a ministry to the faithful remnant.

The third quarter of the eighteenth century had seen the rise of sophisticated sceptics in England, men such as David Hume and Edward Gibbon tickling the ears of upper-class dilettantes with their infidelities. Their influence was, of course, limited to the intelligentsia. Hume died in 1776, a year noted in Britain 'as belonging to the period most marked by infidelity and laxity of doctrine'[8]—according to Trevelyan. The events of the last quarter of the century were to scare the infidelity out of the aristocrats.

During the last decade of the eighteenth century, the progress of revolutionary republicanism in France served to corrupt the middle and lower classes in England. Tom Paine was in England during the French Revolution, and his writings 'deluged the land with blasphemy and ribaldry.' His prosecution for libel increased the influence of his opinions even though he fled the country for France in 1791.[9]

The outbreak of revolution in France evoked sympathy at first among British people. But the prevalence of distress and the spread of republican opinions brought the nation to the verge of rebellion, and disposed people to receive with eagerness any allegation of oppression.[10] An observer noted of that time:[11]

> Never before, in the modern history of Europe, did any country present such an arena of conflict between light and darkness, revealed truth and infidel error, as did Britain during this time. . . These circumstances exercised a fearful influence on the faith and morals of England.

Latitudinarianism, which supported the episcopal form and catholic ritual of the Church but denied its divine origin, dominated much of the Church of England outside the revival societies, whether of Wesley, Whitefield or the Countess of Huntingdon. Deism influenced the Dissenters, wreaking its greatest havoc in English Presbyterianism, which slid into Unitarianism. Methodism was ill-prepared for the struggle against 'the unusual and baneful excitement'[12] produced by the French Revolution. But in the long run, the excesses of the French revolutionaries caused a backlash among British folk, working class and aristocracy alike. Horror of French atheism spread in the lower ranks of society, and helped the Evangelical cause after the death of Wesley in 1791. A new revival began almost immediately, but it had been preceded by a period of spiritual declension which cut it off from the earlier Evangelical Revival.

During the first half of the eighteenth century, there had been a marked decline in the religious life of Scotland. Both Deism and Arianism wrought a deadening work. As the century rolled on, even greater havoc was created by a system of lay-patronage, in which a patron without spiritual insight was free to inflict an unspiritual minister upon a parish. The General Assembly protested year by year against the infringement of the rights of the Church. Soon a greater and greater number of ministers in the General Assembly were found to be indifferent to evangelical religion, and the condition of Scotland at the close of the century was sunken low in spiritual lethargy. The catechizing of the people was shamefully neglected, and in many parts there was no parochial visitation. Parish ministers preached over and over again the same sermons, and schoolboys delighted to mimick them in reciting well-used prayers, of the most ancient vintage. Highlands, islands, and lowlands alike suffered a sorry decline in religion and morality which included parish ministers. The party supporting this state of affairs named itself 'the Moderates.'[13]

Across the channel, in Northern Ireland, conditions in the Presbyterian churches reflected the situation in nearby Scotland, more particularly concerning matters of doctrine. Most Presbyterian ministers took their theological training in the Scottish universities, particularly at Glasgow where the Moderate professors, John Simpson, Francis Hutcheson and William Leechman held forth. Their indoctrinated Irish graduates failed to corrupt their congregations; they simply put them to sleep with their homilies on self-improvement by noble aspiration.[14] Thus the Presbyterian Synod of Ulster maintained a largely deistic outlook during the latter half of the eighteenth century. The same was true of the Church of Ireland, an episcopal establishment in the country despite its minority status. Only the Methodist enthusiasts among them seemed to have spiritual life, and they were a tiny percentage of the Church. Baptists and Congregationalists and Moravians and Quakers were few in numbers, too few for significant influence in Irish Protestant affairs.

Conditions were better in the principality of Wales. A land of peasants, Wales was less moved by the currents of philosophical and theological speculation.[15] The charity schools of Griffith Jones and his successors had taught many Welshmen to read, but the limits of the national language cut them off from European thought.

In the German lands, the influence of the Pietist revivals had given way before the spreading Enlightenment, which—although it contributed much to the progress of civilization—became the enemy of evangelical Christianity. Ever since in 1706 Christian Wolff had been appointed professor of natural philosophy at Halle University,[16] his influence had spread from Marburg and Halle over the German States. His patron, Frederick the Great, aided the leaders of the Enlightenment which, while it helped science and philosophy, denied the supernatural in things religious. The result was the deterioration of evangelical Christianity in Germany. When the French Revolution erupted, the German States lacked the moral power to resist, and were overrun. From 1792, the French Republic was at war with one or other or all of the German States, decisively defeating Austria and Prussia in turn. Napoleon annexed whatever suited his interests, dominated the remainder of the States, humiliated Austria and Prussia. The Germans found that their vaunted enlightenment availed them little in the face of tyranny.

The Netherlands also suffered eclipse. For a generation, the Dutch suffered from the influence of English deists, German philosophers, and French sceptics. The French Revolution directly threatened the Netherlands, and in 1795 an invasion toppled the government and established the Batavian Republic as part of the French Empire. Even so, the leavening influence of the Evangelical Revival in Britain produced a resurgence in a minority of believers.[17]

In 1797, the French overran Switzerland and established the Helvetic Republic.[18] The Swiss also had been sabotaged by the counter-Christian philosophies of the times. In the Scandinavian countries, conditions were discouraging. In Sweden, the per capita consumption of alcoholic beverages exceeded that of every other country in Europe.[19] Likewise, in Norway, rationalism deadened Lutheran faith. Denmark was even more influenced by the continental infidelity. And Finland was devastated by war, suffering from a barren moralism in church life.

In Spain and Portugal, the militant Society of Jesus had been dissolved. Neither of the Iberian kingdoms nor the States of Italy could withstand the onslaught of revolutionary forces. Protestantism was practically non-existent in these Roman Catholic countries. Much the same was true of the rest of Europe. Even at the Cape of Good Hope, religion was moribund.[20] European Christianity was in eclipse.

The French Revolution affected all of the countries of Western Christendom, and other countries with whom its peoples had relations, especially the contiguous countries. It began in France, but there were much worse tyrannies in the world of 1789 than that of the French monarchy and aristocracy. It started in an absolutist Roman Catholic regime, but its philosophers shared ideas with those of the Protestant countries. It was resisted most in the English-speaking world, where also there were gross injustices, but where a progression of reformations and revivals of New Testament Christianity had provided a safety valve for the tremendous pressures building up.

Melville Horne, at Christ Church, Macclesfield, gave expression to the defiance of Britain against Napoleon, the iron fist of the French Revolution, before whom nations trembled and rulers were afraid:[21]

> At the head of this formidable body, we see a man, the wonder of his age, and whose name, feared and execrated, will never be erased from the pages of history. A foreigner, a needy adventurer, of mean birth, and of a contemptible nation, has found means to raise himself above his fellow generals, and to establish a military despotism among a people still delirious with theories of impractible liberty. Unprincipled, fierce, subtle, bloody, and remorseless, he tramples on all the laws of God and man. Hatred and revenge impel him to the desperate attempt of invading our island. The magnaminity of British counsel, the spirit and freedom of the British nation, and the successful valour of the British arms, frustrate his vast plan of empire, cherish the dying embers of freedom, and remain the last hope and asylum to the ravaged and intimidated continent.

In every great movement for social justice, the Enemy of men's souls is prone to take advantage of the turmoil to attack the guarantors of freedom, God and morality. The onslaught in the years between 1789 and 1815 set back the cause of evangelical Christianity frighteningly. In the careful words of Kenneth Scott Latourette,[22] 'Again it looked as though Christianity were a waning influence, about to be ushered out of the affairs of men.' At the time, Voltaire was predicting that Christianity would be forgotten in thirty years, and Tom Paine was gleefully repeating the assurance to English-speaking folk on both sides the Atlantic.

During the latter part of the eighteenth century, there came a general decline in morals and religion in the United States of America.[23] The unsettled state of society following a long-fought war and a revolution, the self-assertive feelings which accompanied independence, the changing social conditions, the lure of the western frontier, the rugged individualism of the frontiersman, the break-up of family and church relationships due to migration—all these were factors in the decline, but they were matched by the influence of the militant French infidelity which had swept the country.

The wartime alliance existing between the Americans and France, now moved by a more violent form of insurrection, brought a flood of infidelity to the United States which the moderates were unable to stem. Inevitably, hospitality was shown to the work of noted sceptics and political radicals, pro-French extremists capturing the place of evangelical moderates in the national life.[24]

The noble figure of Thomas Jefferson, father of the American republic, lent much aid to the rapid spread of rationalistic deism in the newly independent United States. Jefferson was a deist,[25] with a reverent attitude towards religion, and he claimed to be a Christian 'in the sense that Jesus wished anyone to be,' though he did not make it clear how he knew what Jesus Christ wished in this regard. In fact, Jefferson compiled from the Gospels those sayings and doings of Jesus which met his approval, leaving aside every trace of the supernatural and every claim to Deity.

In events, it had so happened that the objects of patriotic American deists and of patriotic American evangelicals coincided, and their efforts together so moved public opinion that the Revolution became possible and succeeded. If the matter had rested there, there would have been little clash between this gentle deism of Jefferson and the positive evangelicalism of the recently revived Churches.

But there was also the blistering Tom Paine, champion of American independence and French revolution, proposing rationalistic deism as the proper doctrine for emerging democracies.[26] Paine's writings were immensely popular and masses of restless people took hold of his ideas and abandoned orthodox Christianity.

George Washington received a letter from an intimate friend in 1796, predicting that national affairs were leading to some crisis, some revolution; and Washington agreed, saying that he was unable to foretell what might happen.[27]

George Washington, Patrick Henry, John Adams, and kindred spirits were much opposed to the new ideas, but other national figures were not, for Thomas Jefferson was a deist, Henry Dearborn an unbeliever and General Charles Lee a violent opponent of Christianity.[28]

Of a population of five million, the United States suffered three hundred thousand drunkards, and buried about fifteen thousand of them annually.[29] Christian chroniclers complained that, for the first time in the history of the country, there was a surfeit of lawlessness, a profusion of gamblers, of gangs of robbers and slave-stealers. Drunkenness was common and profanity prevalent, they said. Immorality had increased as standards of honesty and veracity declined.[30]

It was considered that religion and morals were at the lowest ebb in the United States.[31] In 1794 there occurred the whiskey rebellion in western Pennsylvania, provoked by a tax on the free-style distillation of spirits by backwoods farmers. President Washington was forced to call out the militia from Pennsylvania, New Jersey, Maryland and Virginia. The affair was only a suppuration provoked by a terrible epidemic of intemperance in the body politic, drunkenness being indulged in to a frightening degree, to incredible excess.[32] The recurrence of epidemics of yellow fever and small pox between 1793 and 1802 was regarded by many in Philadelphia as divine judgment.

It was obvious that American Christianity had declined, for morals were bankrupt and infidel clubs abounded, with the usual deterioration in matters of sex permissiveness. About twenty men and seven women composed an 'infidel club' which claimed the right to indulge in lasciviousness. Most of them came to a bad end.[33] Some were shot, for murder or for robbery; some were hanged, for horse theft, murder, and the like; some drank themselves to death and were eaten by hogs or dogs; and of the women it was said that 'not one of them could or would pretend to know who was the father of their offspring.' The reporter knew well the names of the 'infidels'—Miller, Kelly, Smith, Vervillon, Clark—some having been schoolmates.

The concern of statesmen became the alarm of churchmen, for the churches were emptying fast. Dark days clouded the end of the eighteenth century. Its middle fifty years had been a jubilee of the expansion of the Church throughout American territory, but the final twenty-five years were as distressing as the first twenty-five.

The moral decline was reflected in the life of the students in colleges. Collegians were intoxicated with the idea of independence, the responsibilities of which made little appeal while the laxities produced a surge of debauchery.

So far as religion was concerned, the colleges were the seed-beds of infidelity.[34] The University of Pennsylvania, Transylvania College, Columbia College in South Carolina, and others had influential 'free-thinkers' on their faculties. An anti-Church play was featured at Dartmouth. At Yale and Princeton, as at William and Mary, the student bodies were overwhelmingly sceptical, if not infidel. At Bowdoin, as at Yale, the number of believers was counted on one hand.

Timothy Dwight, newly appointed president of Yale, observed that the undergraduates welcomed the newer revolutionary doctrines, not so much on account of their promise of social justice as their invitation to unrestrained gratification. The collegians acted as if the light of human wisdom had just begun to dawn; anything more than thirty years old was suspect; morality was fitted only for children; revelation was without authority or evidence; the world was probably eternal, and materialism the only reality; if, however, there was a God, man was created only to be happy, and, as animal pleasure is the greatest happiness, they resolved to enjoy it to the full.[35]

Lyman Beecher described a typical campus in 1795:

> College was in a most ungodly state. The college church was almost extinct. Most of the students were skeptical and rowdies were plenty. Wine and liquors were kept in many rooms; intemperance, profanity, gambling and licentiousness were common . . . most of the class before me were infidels and called each other Voltaire, Rousseau, D'Alembert, etc.[36]

What was true at Yale in New Haven was true at Princeton in New Jersey, there being in one year no more than two students who professed religion, only five or six who scrupled the use of profane language in common conversation—and in this 'filthy speech' movement the profanity sometimes was of a very shocking kind.[37]

From France, Germany and Britain, affirmed Timothy Dwight, 'the dregs of infidelity were vomited upon us. . . the whole mass of pollution was emptied upon this country.' It was said that anti-Christian Frenchmen subscribed three million francs to print and distribute books to influence the minds of young Americans.[38]

During the last decade of the eighteenth century, the typical Harvard student was atheist.[39] Students at Williams College[40] conducted a mock celebration of Holy Communion. When the Dean at Princeton opened the chapel Bible to read, a pack of playing cards fell out, some radical having cut a rectangle out of each page to fit the pack.[41] Christians were so unpopular that they met in secret and kept their minutes in code.[42] The radical leader of deist students led a mob in burning the Bible[43] of a Raritan valley Presbyterian church. Students disrupted worship services with both profanity and sputum. They burned down buildings; and they forced the resignation of college presidents.

Seven years of war, while they gained independence for the United States, devastated the country. All the Churches suffered, ministers being driven from their homes, their congregations scattered, the church buildings destroyed or desecrated. Anglican and Methodist ministers generally had leaned towards the system of monarchy; Friends and Moravians and Mennonites had refused military service of any kind and suffered persecution from both sides; Baptists, Congregationalists, Lutherans and Presbyterians generally had supported the revolutionaries. Perhaps the Anglicans had suffered the most, a bishop observing in retrospect: [44]

> The congregations of our communion throughout the United States were approaching annihilation. Although within (Philadelphia) three Episcopal clergymen were resident and officiating, the churches over the rest of the State had become deprived of their clergy during the war, either by death or departure for England.
>
> In the Eastern States, with two or three exceptions, there was a cessation of the exercises of the pulpit, owing to the necessary disuse of the prayers for the former civil rulers. In Maryland and Virginia, where the Church had enjoyed civil establishments, on the ceasing of these, the incumbents of the parishes, almost without exception, ceased to officiate. Farther south, the condition of the Church was not better, to say the least.

The last decade before the turn of the century began in discouragement. Bishop James Madison in the diocese of Virginia agreed with the conviction of Chief Justice John Marshall, a devout layman, who wrote that the Church was too far gone ever to be revived; while Bishop Samuel Provoost of New York felt that the situation was hopeless, and simply ceased functioning.

Henry Eyster Jacobs, standard historian of Lutheranism in North America, entitled the post-Revolution period as 'Deterioration,' and the cause was languishing so much that some proposals were made to amalgamate with the likewise languishing Anglicans.[45]

In 1798, the Presbyterian General Assembly condemned the 'profaneness, pride, luxury, injustice, intemperance, lewdness,' greatly abounding in the nation, 'every species of debauchery and loose indulgence' so prevalent. So also the Presbyterian leaders officially deplored the dereliction of religious principles, the prevailing impiety and the corruption of public morals.[46]

In New England, where reaction occurred against certain features of the Great Awakening, the people inclined toward formalism and against evangelism as they grew wealthier. Deism soon became a powerful ally of anti-Evangelicalism. Unitarianism and Universalism,[47] aided by the decline of orthodox Christianity, began to make great progress in the struggle for the control of the churches in New England. In a few decades, Unitarians gained control of many strategic and influential Congregational parishes, splitting the historic denomination irreparably, and drifting into humanism.

Even the Baptists admitted a very wintry season in which the love of many had grown cold; while the Methodists were losing members at the rate of about four thousand a year. These were the two most evangelistic denominations.[48]

Churchmen of all denominations continued to be deeply concerned about the spiritual state of the country throughout the 1780s and into the 1790s. Circumstances were already distressing when the news of the French Revolution swept the country and raised a host of infidel clubs. Statesmen also were disturbed, for in the new-born nation they could not look to law to restore order — for there was little of it; nor could they look to education for improvement—for it too was sadly lacking. The renewal of the churches and renewal of the nation could come from only one quarter— from a revival of the magnitude of the Great Awakening.

Of all the states of the Union and their territories to the west, the conditions on the western frontiers were easily the worst.[49] A committee of Congress reported upon the shockingly desperate state of affairs in the western territories where only one court had been held in five years. It seemed that conditions could not become much worse in matters of social morals or religion.

Even in the Maritime Provinces of British America—where there had been spiritual awakening during the days of the revolutionary war when loyalists were seeking a new life there among the immigrants from Britain—there was a decline that followed the death of Henry Alline.[50] In Ontario, or Upper Canada, the settlers shared the ungodliness of the western sections of the United States from which they fled, their need as great as in western Pennsylvania or western New York, even if local conditions were not as bad as those in lawless Kentucky or Tennessee. All of North America from the Atlantic to the Mississippi needed a revival.

The problem was too big for human ingenuity or human energy. Neither denominational organization nor inter-denominational cooperation could cope with the emergency. Demonic forces with carnal collaboration had forced the Churches into a corner. How did they retaliate and turn the defeat into victory? The only weapon left was prayer, and pray they did. In both Britain and the United States, an unusual spirit of prayer was poured out upon believers—the Union of Prayer in Britain and the Concert of Prayer in North America. Intercessors simply supplicated the God of the Universe to intervene on their behalf, in a revival of religion and an extension of the kingdom of Christ on earth. 'Not by organization, nor by chain of command, but by My Spirit,' saith the Lord of hosts.

2

REVIVAL IN ENGLAND, 1790–

The spiritual tide began to turn in England in the 1780s, although it was not until the 1790s that it reached its first flood. The last decade but one of the century seemed to be a period of preparation in which men were raised up for the opportunities in service which came with revival's high tide.

In the North of England, a local awakening began in 1781. John Valton and George Snowden moved to Manchester that year, and a general revival of religion began in the city and surroundings, producing a great ingathering of souls. This was not achieved without opposition, for, at Gladwick a mob pelted the preacher and people with stones and coal. Seven years of plenty followed, membership doubling.[1]

In the South of England, Methodists reported awakenings. In 1782, there was a remarkable awakening at Winchester during wartime,[2] principally among the British troops in camp, evangelists of the movement being Captain Webb and Robert Brackenbury. Meetings were held in barracks and in the Methodist meeting house in town.

In the West of England, a movement of the Spirit began. There was an intense local revival at St. Just in Cornwall in 1781. On Christmas Day, many intercessors met at three in the morning to sing and pray. The power of God fell upon them, it was reported, and they adjourned to the meeting-house at seven and continued in prayer until nine. Again in the evening they gathered.[3]

Throughout January and February, the movement went on. On 9th March 1782, a Methodist minister preached to the company, and the people continued in prayer until past midnight. It was deemed 'peculiarly remarkable' that in this uncommon revival, and in places in the midlands and the north, the itinerant preachers had very little share.

John Wesley, journeying about the country in the spring of 1784,[4] reported an extensive awakening in the country places round about Newcastle-under-Lyme, saying: 'This country is all on fire, and the flame is still spreading from village to village.' The gallant old veteran was eighty-three.

George Whitefield had died on American soil in 1770, but the Chapel he had built on Tottenham Court Road continued his London ministry, being enlarged to seat five thousand, the largest Free Church auditorium in the world of those days.[5] Whitefield's following was becoming Congregational and more and more churches were being erected in London and the provinces.

Rowland Hill was an ardent young Anglican at Cambridge whose evangelical zeal had earned him discouragement from the Bishops.[6] He was, however, ordained deacon in 1773, becoming a fervent evangelist in the Countess of Huntington's Connexion. He succeeded Whitefield in London ministry, and also preached to great crowds elsewhere in England.

Already, 9th March 1783, the ministers of the Countess of Huntington's chapels had been forced, through episcopal default, to ordain their own candidates for the preaching of the Word.[7] The Countess of Huntington's Connexion, as it was called, also became Congregational in form. In the 1780s, its preachers were ministering to large crowds.

There were less than a hundred and twenty-five Baptist churches in England at the time of the Act of Toleration. During the first half of the eighteenth century, another sixty or so were added; but, in the third and fourth quarters, a hundred and sixty-five were established, a hundred of them in the 1780s and 1790s, following formation of the Baptist Home Mission Society.[8]

In the 1780s, the General Baptists doubled their numbers and multiplied their churches. Their outstanding leader was a Yorkshireman, converted in the Wesleyan revival of the 'sixties, Dan Taylor, who itinerated with the Good News from Land's End to Berwick-on-Tweed.[9] In 1782, Andrew Fuller was appointed pastor of a Particular Baptist church in Kettering, exercising a wide-ranging ministry also. In this renewal of the 1780s, the Particular Baptists also were growing, and, on 5th October 1783, Dr. John Ryland baptized 'a poor journeyman shoemaker,' William Carey.[10]

Forty years earlier, John Erskine of Edinburgh had published a memorial to enlist praying people in Scotland and elsewhere in regular intercession for an effusion of the Holy Spirit on all the Churches. On this, Jonathan Edwards based his treatise, 'A Humble Attempt to Promote Explicit Agreement and Visible Union of God's People in Extraordinary Prayer for the Revival of Religion and the Advancement of Christ's Kingdom.'[11]

John Erskine maintained a voluminous correspondence all his life with like-minded Evangelicals in Europe and America. In 1784, he sent John Ryland and Andrew Fuller, the Northamptonshire Baptists, reprints of his memorial, reinforced by the plea from the pen of Jonathan Edwards on the need of prayer for a general revival.[12] The Baptists shared this challenge with a colleague, John Sutcliffe of Olney. Sutcliffe made the burden his own, and as a result the Association of Baptist Churches in Northampton and Leicester Counties resolved to devote the first Monday evening of each month to 'prayer for the general revival and spread of religion.' Andrew Fuller published a sermon on the subject, 'A Few Persuasives to a General Union in Prayer for the Revival of Religion.'[13] He journeyed far and near in promoting the project.

In 1786, the Baptist Association of the Midlands adopted the challenge for a concert of prayer.[14] Other Free Church congregations in the Midlands participated in the general union of prayer for an Awakening. Methodists recognized the importance of prayer meetings in reviving their work for an article entitled 'Thoughts on the Revival of Religion in the Prayer Meetings in the Present Revival' insisted that the movement following was remarkable for the very 'affectionate attachment' of the preachers to these prayer meetings.[15] Evangelical Anglicans, few in number at the time, showed their sympathy. By the year 1789, the general union in prayer was operating over a very wide network of prayer meetings for revival.

Matthew Henry, the famous commentator, had written: 'When God intends great mercy for His people, He first of all sets them a-praying.' The Concert of Prayer proved to be most significant, not only preparing the way for a general awakening but preparing the way for the extraordinary outburst of missionary zeal in the last decade of the eighteenth century. It is significant that the union in prayer for a general revival preceded the French Revolution by a full seven years. The prevenient work of the Holy Spirit has often anticipated the onslaught of Evil long before believers had become aware of the dangers that lay ahead. It was otherwise in the Concert of Prayer of 1794 in America.

Throughout England, Baptists flourished in the 1790s, a few churches decreasing in numbers for varied reasons. Revivals had been enjoyed in many congregations, and in some of these, membership had tripled within five years.

A glimpse into the prosperity of the Baptist cause in the days of revival is gained in the statistics and reports made during the two years before and two years after the turn of the century. In every instance, prayer meetings abounded; the services for the preaching of the Word were packed out, and the response of the people was encouraging.[16]

The historic First Baptist Church, Bedford, of which the renowned John Bunyan had been pastor, attracted crowds of eight hundred afternoon and evening, and the congregation united once a month in a joint prayer meeting with Second Baptist Church and the Independent congregation.[17] It was 'in a pleasing and prosperous condition' with additions being made to its numbers almost every month. Nor was this an unusual report for Bedfordshire, where all the churches were likewise flourishing.

At Oxford, where Baptists had been refused permission to build in previous years, a new meeting house was erected to seat 530, well filled for every meeting, overflowing to seven hundred for evening worship. Despite unemployment, the church was in a thriving condition, holding a fervent prayer meeting twice a week.[18]

George Hall had done so well in Ipswich that the meeting house had been enlarged to accommodate the increase of a hundred converts received in two years.[19] Reports like this were commonplace.

Particularly in the 1790s, the Congregational churches caught the flame.[20] Their ministers began to preach with new zeal, and with greater success. A passion for evangelistic work took hold of church after church, and by the end of the century, the old meeting houses were crowded; many had to be enlarged and new ones erected in town after town.

One of the converts of the Awakening at the turn of the century was John Angell James, who received a scholarship from Robert Haldane and became a Congregational pastor-evangelist in the growing city of Birmingham, where large crowds rallied to his preaching.[21] There were many such converts in Congregational ministry at home and abroad.

While the Baptists and Congregationalists benefitted so much from the Methodist movement, it must be said that both their theology and methods differed definitely from the Wesleyan enthusiasts. Until the 1790s, their concentration was upon the cultivation of the spiritual life in the meeting houses.[22] They encouraged public declaration of faith, but it was generally without the accompaniments of the intense conviction of sin and the emotional response so recurrent among the Methodists. They found it hard to believe that a drunkard or swearer might attend a Methodist meeting, and be 'born again' and rejoice in full assurance before leaving. In this respect, they lacked the experience of their colleagues in North America, who were familiar with such effects.

The shock waves of the French Revolution were building up in England when, in the year 1791, John Wesley died. Nevertheless, the Methodists appeared to be the likeliest agency through which phenomenal evangelical revival would occur. Among them, unlike the Established Church, there was no inherent opposition to evangelistic enthusiasm, and, unlike some Dissenters, no disdain for the common people.

The answer to prayer was not long delayed in coming. Between 1792 and 1793, a general awakening occurred in the industrial cities of Yorkshire. William Bramwell, for whom William Booth named his son, had been appointed to Dewsbury, where his ministry was appreciated but where he felt concerned about the need of a revival. Bramwell commenced five o'clock in the morning prayer meetings. Then came what the Methodists called 'a glorious revival' in which a hundred converts were added to circuit rolls.[23]

The influence of Dewsbury's revival provoked a similar wide awakening in Halifax. The whole circuit was brought under the Spirit's melting, and six hundred converts were added to membership, chiefly in prayer meetings rather than in the regular services. William Bramwell moved from his revived circuit in Dewsbury to Birstal in 1793, and found a number of the people expecting revival. On Christmas Day, fifty penitents found forgiveness, and on Easter Day fifty more were converted to God, five hundred in all.[24]

In 1793, Leeds also enjoyed an awakening. Moses Roberts and John Allen shared in the preaching, but the work was mainly accomplished through an extraordinary visitation of God, in which all sorts of means and no means at all were used. Some were alarmed by dreams and visions. Others who came to mock the cries of penitents were themselves broken down. Some scoffers mimicked the pentitents, but were thrown into convulsions. The circuit ministers first claimed that nearly a thousand had been added to the rolls, but the statistics showed their estimate to be over-modest. It was admitted that the meetings were attended by much noise and apparent confusion in some places, but in others there was stillness and solemnity.[25]

The Methodists at Hull heard of the extraordinary work
in Leeds, and doubled their prayers for an outpouring of
the Holy Spirit.[26] The people expressed an aversion to outcries in public meetings, but became reconciled to distress
thus expressed by reason of the peace and joy that followed.

Sheffield congregations also experienced revival. During
the greater part of a year, seven or eight persons 'found
salvation' in nightly meetings, culminating in 'a still more
glorious effusion of grace' in which a hundred were won.[27]

A careful Methodist historian noticed that the increase
in these circuits where extraordinary awakenings ensued
was approximately three thousand, whereas in the rest of
the country, more than five thousand were won to the faith.
It was not pointed out, however, that five thousand or so
Methodist members in the extraordinarily revived circuits
gained three thousand, a 60% increase, whereas elsewhere
seventy thousand added five thousand, a 7% increase—
which rather blunted the force of his argument:[28]

> These extraordinary visitations are (not) regarded by
> Wesleyan Methodists as the chief means of maintaining
> and extending the work of God.   The constant and
> ordinary ministration of the Gospel is, in their judg-
> ment, the grand means of true evangelization.

This could have been amended from 'chief' and 'grand'
to 'regular' means; but his conclusion was well taken:

> But, when the preaching of the word is clothed with
> extraordinary power, and crowned with deep and wide-
> spread success, such seasons are hailed as pentecostal
> visitations, and gratefully acknowledged as special
> interpositions of mercy.

In the 1780s, the totals of membership in the Methodist
societies had grown modestly: 1780, 43,830; 1781, 44,417,
1782, 46,331; 1783, 45,955; and so on.   In the 1790s, total
increases doubled and trebled and quadrupled.[29]

Such effects of the general awakening of 1791 onwards
are best seen in the local statistics: for example, Halifax,
1790, 1111; 1791, 1115; 1792, 1124; 1793, 1103; then, after
the outbreak of revival, rising from 1500 in 1794 to 1600 in
1796. This represented a 50% rise in three years.[30]

Leeds Methodists registered a 60% gain during the local
revival of 1794, averaging 2100 between 1790 and 1793, but
rising to and passing 3400 in 1794 and 1795.   Hull Methodists
numbered 600 and more between 1790 and 1793, but doubled
to 1200 and more in 1794 and 1795.[31]

Across the Pennines, in industrial towns in Lancashire, there was a moving of the Spirit, an extraordinary revival in Bolton, where Robert Miller preaching for nine days in 1794 saw a hundred and twenty converts added to the church, the beginning of spreading prosperity.[32]

In 1794, an awakening began in Cornwall. A rather controversial Methodist, Joseph Benson, engaged in a very successful preaching tour of the Celtic county. Fully five thousand came to hear him at first, and the numbers increased to fifteen thousand, filling the street, alleys and houses of Redruth. In a quarry near Gwennap, Benson preached to twenty thousand. Many were the converts of the meetings. In the spring of 1799, the revival was renewed, touching many communities in Cornwall.[33]

The awakening in Cornwall showed itself in the statistics of the Methodists. Membership in the circuit farthest west, St. Ives and Penzance, rose from 1391 in 1790 to 1537 and 1540 in 1791 and 1792; then it declined in 1793, but jumped to 1412 in 1794, and to 1605 in 1796, 1888 in 1797. In the Redruth circuit, the society declined from 1840 in 1790 to 1537 in 1793, but rose to 1855 in 1795, 2328 in 1796, and 2430 in 1797.[34] In St. Austell, only the revival of 1791 had an effect upon membership, being under a thousand in other years of that decade.

There was steady growth in other parts of the country in the 1790s. The preachers were energetic, and the people eager to hear them. Yet the greatest growth was manifest in districts experiencing an outpouring of the Spirit on the congregations.

Thomas Taylor, addressing the Methodist Conference in revival times in 1797 at Leeds, declared perceptively:[35]

> The Almighty stoops still lower and is pleased to make use of simple prayer meetings which have been attended with an extraordinary degree of divine power, even where poor illiterate persons have been the instruments of doing much good.

The local revivals in England seemed to share a number of common and recurrent features. One was the appearance of evangelists who worked through established societies or who founded self-supporting branches in nearby towns. But in other instances, the primary factor seemed to be the spontaneous gatherings for prayer, often at a sacrificial hour. And, in every case, the response of the people was manifest in great crowds, an evidence of mass hunger.

After the Toleration Act of 1689, the number of places of regular worship by Dissenting congregations had been 251, with 900 or so temporary meeting places; in fifty years, the 251 had dropped to 27, with only 500 or so auxiliary rooms of one sort or other.[36] By the end of the eighteenth century, the places of regular worship had increased from 27 to more than 900, with nearly 3500 temporary gathering places in occupation.

At that time, every dissenter in England was excluded from all civil and ecclesiastical employment of 'honour and profit' in the kingdom. No dissenter could be admitted to command in the army or navy, even were his country to be invaded, nor could he be permitted to collect any part of the public revenue, nor to act as a magistrate nor to graduate in either Oxford or Cambridge.[37]

At the beginning of the eighteenth century, according to parliamentary returns, there was only one dissenter in every twenty-five people in England; at the beginning of the nineteenth century, the proportion had risen to one in four.[38] A little over five thousand meeting places reported in the decade, 1801-1810, became more than ten thousand in the decade of Waterloo. During that period, a lecturer of note insisted that 'houses of prayer are erected in every town and filled with congregations.'

An Anglican observer called attention to some things which lent themselves to the increase of Dissenters in the general population:[39]

> Too many among us, I fear, imagine that when they have preached their weekly sermon and read prayers, they have done all that is requisite. Now here the Dissenters beat us completely. I know several instances among them where the same individual preaches three sermons on Sunday and as many in the course of the week.

These same Dissenters employed a style which, in many cases, proved offensive to people of taste, but which was well-suited to attract the attention of the lower orders. In the parish churches, too often the incumbent addressed his homilies to people of distinction and indifference.

Just how strong was Evangelicalism within the Church of England at the end of the eighteenth century? William Ewart Gladstone estimated the number of Evangelical clergy to be one in twenty. Five per cent! And yet, the historian Canon Overton—a High Churchman—claimed that[40]

It would be no exaggeration to say that, morally and spiritually, the dominant religious power, both inside and outside the Church of England, at the close of the eighteenth century, was that which had been evoked by the Evangelical Revival.

The effect of the Methodist movement upon the Church of England is everywhere recognized, but it is a mistake to think that more than a tiny minority of Anglican churchmen welcomed gospel preaching before the decade of 1791. It was not until the nineteenth century that the Evangelical Party of the Church of England began burgeoning. This was accomplished without much outside help.

When John Newton, eminent hymn-writer and Anglican divine, moved to London about 1780, he reinforced a lonely evangelical stalwart, William Romaine, whose evangelistic preaching had provoked opposition and persecution from the church authorities.[41] Romaine encountered such ill-will from his churchwardens —who deliberately refused to light or heat the church in order to keep the multitudes away— that he was compelled to preach with a lighted taper in his hand, the great congregation sitting in silent darkness.

John Newton preached Good News at St. Mary Woolnoth, attracting eager auditors.[42] The Anglican Evangelicals were beginning to congregate in London, and in 1783 they founded the Eclectic Society, a clerical counterpart of the so-called Clapham Sect of influential Anglican laymen.[43] From that time onward, the number of Evangelical clergy and churches multiplied in the capital and its spreading suburbs.

Among the Evangelical Anglican clergy doing significant work during the post-1790 awakening were Richard Hart at Kingswood, near Bristol; Thomas Robinson at Leicester; Thomas Clarke at Chesham Bois; and John Venn, rector at Clapham, ministering to one of the most notable congregations in all of England, serving the 'Clapham Sect.'[44] And in 1786, William Wilberforce, an Anglican layman, made a resolution to live for God's glory and his fellow-creatures' good.[45] That same year was designated the 'wonderful year' in the development of missionary passion.

The great change in the Church of England was noticed by the Baptists, who commented in 1801:[46]

It has pleased God, within these four to six years, to open the eyes of many of the Established Church . . . they are not too proud to go anywhere to preach or to hear the Gospel preached.

The population of Great Britain at the beginning of the nineteenth century was approximately ten and a half million and there were half a million in military service. Another five million people inhabited Ireland.[47]

The cities and great towns of England were burgeoning at the turn of the nineteenth century. London, with a total of 864,845, was ten times as populous as the next largest:[48]

Manchester	84,020	Norwich	36,963
Liverpool	77,653	Bath	32,200
Birmingham	73,670	Portsmouth	32,166
Bristol	63,645	Sheffield	31,314
Leeds	53,162	Hull	29,516
Plymouth	43,194	Exeter	17,398
Newcastle on Tyne	36,963	York	16,145

The progress of the Awakening was noteworthy in 1801. The Baptists officially commented that 'the Westleians' appeared to have reaped the greatest numerical gain, great numbers having joined them in the year previous.[49]

In the year 1805, the work of God among the Methodists in Bradford was reported in a prosperous state, but as the autumn season approached, an outpouring of the Spirit was manifest.[50] The doors of the octagon church were scarcely ever closed for more than ten weeks, by day or night, often a full congregation retiring to find an equally large company awaiting entrance. Regular preaching gave way to earnest intercession. Fully a third of the nine hundred received into fellowship before 1806 were young people.

In the early part of 1806, an awakening occurred in the Keighley district of Yorkshire.[51] At Yeadon, prayer groups multiplied in private homes, overflowed and filled the local chapel with three or four hundred intercessors. In prayer meetings and in regular meetings, believers were revived and outsiders converted, five hundred joining the society at Yeadon alone.

In 1813, an extensive awakening took place in Bath, the watering-place in Somerset.[52] Henry Moore and colleagues preached so powerfully that the life of the believers was profoundly deepened and many outsiders were hopefully converted to God.

By the second decade of the nineteenth century, not only the Methodists but the Baptists and Congregationalists were enjoying times of refreshing as a matter of course, and the meeting houses were the scenes of stirring revivals and of steady pastoral evangelism.

Lorenzo Dow, a most eccentric American evangelist who was unrecognized by any Methodist authority, returned to the British Isles after having participated in camp-meetings on the American frontier, the excitement of which had made a powerful appeal to his volatile temperament.[53]

In 1806, after various forays into the Irish countryside, Dow preached in England, retailing the story of the camp-meetings, new in the American states and even newer to English Christians. In 1807, he met a group of younger men who seemed eager to experiment with the method. Lorenzo Dow returned to the United States in early May.

Dow was not the only vehicle of information. A British Methodist minister, Joshua Marsden, who had ministered in Nova Scotia for many years, reported from the States:[54]

> I cannot contemplate without astonishment the great work that God has performed in the United States. It is here we see Methodism in its grandest form. . . In England, Methodism is like a river calmly gliding on; here it is a torrent, rushing along and sweeping all away.

Descriptions of the great camp-meetings were circulated among British Methodists. They made a deep impression on the mind of Hugh Bourne, a zealous young Methodist who had been converted at the turn of the century and who had participated in an unusual 'outpouring of the Spirit' in 1804.[55]

Bourne and his friends decided to meet on the slopes of a local hill, Mow Cop, for a day's praying, announcing the meeting for six o'clock in the morning of 31st May—with a typically British proviso that there would be no gathering if the weather were inclement.

Zealous Methodists gathered, and prayer meetings went on all day, but as the numbers attending increased to many thousands, a considerable contingent of unconverted people drawn by curiosity appeared and came under conviction of sin. From six o'clock in the evening, people began to depart, leaving many inquirers to the counsel of leaders.

In July 1807, the Methodist Conference held in Liverpool announced that it was their judgment that, even supposing that camp-meetings were allowable in America, they were highly improper in England and likely to be productive of considerable mischief. Conference disclaimed connection.[56]

Within the year, young Bourne was expelled from the local Methodist society. He and his associates continued feeding converts into Methodist societies until they were refused, whereupon they formed their own societies.

The new body operated without a name until 1812, when they adopted a phrase of Wesley's to call themselves a Society of Primitive Methodists. They increased rapidly in numbers and even more so in activity.

The Primitive Methodists promoted field-preaching in summertime in Britain, and attracted vast crowds every-where, at Mow Cop, Nottingham Forest, and other suitable rallying points throughout the country, with many converts enrolled in the new societies. They seemed to win the rapt attention of the working masses in a way that the more respectable Wesleyan Methodists failed to do.[57]

It is difficult to discover who first nicknamed them 'the Ranters,' a term of opprobrium from early generations of agitation. They were subjected to hooliganism, as Wesley had been a century earlier, but this attracted crowds.[58]

The fact must not be overlooked that, during these times of revival in the churches, Great Britain was engaged in a life and death struggle with Napoleon. The morale of the nation was high, despite an outdated, oppressive military system. The morale was spiritually generated.

With a high proportion of the population under arms in the army and in the navy, there was a considerable dis-location of social and personal life. On the debit side were the temptations of lonely men away from home; on the credit side were the spiritual concerns caused by uncertainty of life. There were many instances reported of faithful worship and spontaneous evangelism on the part of citizen soldiers, even on the decisive battlefields.

A local awakening was reported among British troops at the Rock of Gibraltar, affecting the 46th, 51st and 61st Regiments. Immediately, persecution broke out, which in military life proved very demeaning. General O'Hara intervened on behalf of the converts, saying: 'Let them alone! I wish there were twenty for one of them, and we would have fewer court-martials in the garrison.' So the persecution faded, and the movement was effective for years, with two hundred or so attending the prayer and fellowship meetings.[59]

By the eve of Waterloo, the progress of the Awakening had taken on such proportions in England that observers reported 'great multitudes of Evangelical ministers in the Established churches' and 'vast accessions recently made to the number of chapels and meeting houses among various classes of Dissenters.'[60]

In 1814, the year before Waterloo, the county of Cornwall became the scene of what a qualified historian called 'one of the most remarkable and extensive revivals of religion ever known' in any country of the world.[61]

The movement began in Redruth and was effective in all of the peninsula beyond Truro.[62] Meetings for worship had been well attended during the latter months of 1813, and in the early weeks of 1814 there was a great solemnity. Between the 13th and 20th February, an increasing number of people under conviction professed faith and found peace. A Sunday afternoon sermon was followed by many 'crying for mercy,' and, in the evening, the message provoked an outburst of congregational praying that went on till one in the morning. The community was greatly stirred.

The usual evening meeting on Monday, commencing at seven, again provoked an extraordinary concert of prayer, and the congregation remained until two in the morning. By noon Tuesday, the auditorium was spontaneously crowded by seekers, and the ministry and response went on all day and all night, until four in the morning. On Wednesday, a noon meeting for the examination of candidates for membership brought a host of penitents as well as converts, and the building was not cleared until nine the following morning. Before noon Thursday, the church was again crowded and continued so, all afternoon and evening and night and all next day, Friday. The assembly was marked by intense conviction of sin, crying for mercy and amendment of ways, the ministers and workers giving themselves continually to praying with the penitents and ministering the Word to the seekers for assurance of salvation. Saturday morning was devoted to admitting converts to trial membership and to appointing them to classes for fellowship and instruction.

All this created a profound impression in west Cornwall. The manager of a mine in Camborne besought a responsible miner to explain, and was assured that a general opinion in the community held that it was a great work of God which signified the coming end of the world. The movement soon spread to other places. In Tuckingmill, the family prayers of a godly house went on for hours as people round about flocked in, necessitating a move to the church where the penitents became so preoccupied with entreaty of God that the preacher in the evening service could not be heard at all but spent the rest of the night in comforting the distressed in spirit. Such outbreaks were spontaneous.

Soon the work became general. The people thronged the chapels, seeking peace with God. Every parish was visited and the chapels were occupied night and day for a week in some places, for two or three or four weeks in others. It was more intense in rural districts than in towns, though it certainly impressed the townsfolk as the greatest religious movement they had known.

The results of the awakening were incontrovertible: the Methodist circuits of Redruth, Truro, St. Austell, Bodmin, Penzance and Helston, those most affected by the movement, counted 9,405 in their membership in 1813; a year later, the returns gave 14,616, a net increase of 5211 in only five months, or 55%. However, the number of members in these circuits declined in 1815, but by only two per cent of the total.[63]

There were not many critics of the movement, but two rushed into print. An Anglo-Catholic clergyman in Penzance preached a sermon in the parish church there, and printed it in London immediately afterwards. He asserted that the revival was a wicked contrivance and a delusion, calculated to damage the cause of true religion. And a young surgeon in Falmouth wrote a letter, feebly witty and clever, to a medical review, diagnosing the movement as an epidemic disease which affected only the minds of the lowest order. Responsible ministers refuted both the critics.

It can be seen from the records that this second period of evangelical revival was very different to the earlier one of the 1740-1770 generation. Those were the days when Whitefield and Wesley ranged the country, encountering the fiercest opposition, which expressed itself in rioting by the mobs. Few indeed were the clergy of the Established Church who supported the Evangelists, or themselves preached a message of repentance and conversion. Few were the old-line Dissenting ministers who imitated the Evangelists and preached for decision in the meeting houses or fields. The earlier movement, apart from the experience of the leaders themselves, was scarcely a revival: it was direct evangelism encountering a kind of folk movement of the lower classes.

After the death of Whitefield and Wesley and the Countess of Huntington, the movement continued the strategy of open-air evangelism, but now there was a supporting body of new converts, who became subject to the enduement of the Holy Spirit, hence phenomenal revivals. And the same Breath of God blew upon the dry bones of Church and Chapel.

Despite the growing number of Evangelicals in the State Church, no Evangelical bishop was appointed till 1815 when Henry Ryder was consecrated Bishop of Gloucester.[64] But, all the while, the evangelical leaven was at work.

In the Church of England, revival flowed in different channels than in the Free Churches. Evangelical clergy began to have second thoughts about the implications of field-preaching and ministry in unconsecrated places, feeling that such a policy when applied to a national parish system would in fact result in schism. They therefore began to devote their energies to the indoctrination of a body of clergy who would carry evangelical ideas into their parish pulpits.

In this second generation of Evangelicals, none exerted wider influence in the Church than Simeon of Cambridge. Charles Simeon was born on 24th September 1758. At the age of eighteen, a day of fasting made a deep impression on his life and, before he reached the age of twenty-one, he found his peace with God.[65] On 26th May 1782, Simeon was ordained in Trinity Church, Cambridge.

As a young and enthusiastic clergyman, Simeon had been influenced by the nearby Evangelical rector of Yelling, Henry Venn. Early in his career, Simeon preached at a farmhouse to a responsive crowd of people, but satisfaction turned to dismay when Venn sent a kindly letter deploring the lapse.

Simeon, therefore, maintained an attitude of charitable aloofness toward his brethren among the Dissenters and Methodists. Trans-fertilization of ideas came in another way. Significant for him, and blessed for many Scots, was a visit to Scotland in 1796. As a loyal Anglican clergyman, he faced the problem of preaching in Presbyterian pulpits in Scotland; and he met the objections of conscience and of critics by deciding that 'where the King must attend'—as an upholder of the Church of Scotland by law established—an Anglican clergyman might preach.[66]

Simeon moved to Cambridge, became a Fellow of King's College and Vicar of Holy Trinity. He not only preached an evangelistic message in Cambridge and round about, but devoted his life to combining a zeal for evangelism with the regular discipline of the Church. In this he made a profound impression upon the younger clergy in training at the Cambridge colleges, and soon the Simeonite clergy became a dominant force in English life. Had it not been for Simeon, Evangelicals might have abandoned the Church of England for the easier course of itinerant ministry.

3

AWAKENINGS IN WALES, 1790–

The little principality of Wales, with Monmouth, about a sixth as large as England, supported only a twentieth of its population. The mountainous nature of the terrain and the wet climate had served in previous centuries to keep the people in dire poverty, while their language isolated them from the populations around them. But the industrialization of England brought about a demand for fossil fuel, of which Wales had plenty in quantity and quality.

The Evangelical Revival of the eighteenth century had made its appearance in Wales a generation before Whitefield and the Wesleys had begun to preach their message with power. This Welsh Revival produced the figure of Daniel Rowland, a Welsh Anglican, whose ministry was transformed by a spiritual visitation in his congregation, and under whom there were successive stirrings in the parish of Llangeitho. It also produced Griffith Jones, described as the greatest Welshman of the century, and one of the greatest benefactors of the Welsh people.[1] Griffith Jones not only itinerated in and around Llanddowror parish, but established the Welsh circulating schools which within a generation were teaching 158,237 pupils, children and adults.[2]

Whitefield and the Wesleys were much impressed with Griffith Jones, and Whitefield in particular enlisted quite a following in Wales, among whom were Daniel Rowland and William Williams. From this movement came the Welsh denomination named the Calvinistic Methodists.

Thus it was that a spirit of revival was manifested here and there in Wales in the 1780s.[3] Another extraordinary outpouring of the Spirit occurred at Llangeitho in 1781; and a great revival began in Carmarthenshire under the fervent preaching of Isaac Price, a Congregationalist minister at Crug-y-bar. From Carnarvonshire in the north of Wales to Carmarthenshire in the south, reports of local revivals were given in 1784-85, all ages and sorts of people in the village of Brynengan experiencing spiritual transformation, while at Twrgwyn the movement lasted a considerable time.

At Trecastle in 1786, another awakening occurred, but in 1787 there was a startling revival in Llanbryn-mawr in Montgomery, where Richard Tibbott was the Congregational minister, the influence of the movement proving to be quite irresistible, adding ninety to a little village church.[4]

The Baptists and Congregationalists of the Midlands of England interested their Welsh confreres in the Concert of Prayer for revival of God's work at home and its extension abroad, so in various parts of Wales intercessors multiplied who devoted the first Monday evening of each month to such prayer, including Calvinistic and Wesleyan Methodists.

A month after the death of Daniel Rowland at the end of 1790, in the wake of the French Revolution that caused such fear throughout Great Britain, a powerful awakening began in Llangeitho, significantly affecting family worship.[5]

A 'great revival of true religion' in North Wales began in 1791 under the ministry of Thomas Charles of Bala.[6] In September 1791, thousands attended the meetings in the town of Pwllheli, enjoying 'a very great, powerful and glorious outpouring of the Spirit on the people in general.' Some of the wildest and most inconsiderate young people of both sexes were awakened. In October of 1791, there was an extraordinary awakening at Bala, which began during the preaching of Thomas Charles one Sunday evening. At nine or ten o'clock that night, 'there was nothing to be heard from one end of town to the other but the cries and groans of the people in distress of soul.'[7] That same night, according to Thomas Charles of Bala, a spirit of deep conviction and of serious concern fell upon whole congregations in the area, followed by protracted prayer meetings throughout the week, with great effect.

Outstanding men of God traced their spiritual birth to such awakenings, including Robert Roberts of Clynnog, and John Elias of Anglesey, and Ebenezer Morris of Twrgwyn, converted at Brynengan, Bala, and Trecastle before 1792.[8]

Before the turn of the century,[9] awakenings occurred in Cardigan, Carmarthen, Pembroke, Carnarvon and Anglesey —Thomas Charles, John Elias, and Christmas Evans, and others of note being the evangelists of these awakenings. The movements were so wholesome, so full of grace and power, and so lasting in effect that the morals of the people were raised to new heights, the means of grace in word and ordinances were more esteemed, while powerful preachers arose from the dedicated lives of some of the converts.[10]

Christmas Evans, the son of a shoemaker, was soundly converted during one of the local revivals, and became a fervent evangelist in Anglesey, the island called 'the Mother of Wales.' Baptist churches throughout the principality owed much to the ministry of Christmas Evans, one of the ablest preachers in the Welsh tongue. He was much in demand for the building up of churches as well as an evangelist sharing in the various local revivals.

Likewise, William Williams adorned the Congregational ministry as an evangelist and preacher, itinerating in Wales to address eager audiences both large and small. Daniel Evans, a contemporary, contributed much to growth as a pastoral evangelist. Revivals accelerated the multiplication of Independent churches until Congregationalists became the most numerous Free Church body in Wales.

The Wesleyans had only three circuits and five hundred members in Wales in 1790, but these began to multiply, the first chapel being built in Denbigh, in North Wales— spreading from there over the northern and southern shires. At the British Wesleyan Conference of 1800, Dr. Thomas Coke, Methodism's leading evangelist and scholar, set out a plan for evangelizing the Welsh in their own language. Himself a native of Wales, he had little difficulty in finding a couple of Welshmen, John Hughes and Owen Davies, who followed Edward Jones to North Wales and found the people open to the message.[11] At the first love-feast of Wesleyans in Denbigh in 1802, eighty of the three hundred new converts testified of what the Lord had done for their souls.

Although a great majority of the leading Evangelicals in Wales in the eighteenth century were clergymen or laymen of the Established Church of Wales, they received but little encouragement from the bishops. In 1803, Thomas Burgess, a friend of Evangelicals, was appointed Bishop of St. David's. He found his clergy poorly educated, neglectful of duty, and sometimes drunken or immoral.[12] In the next two decades of his episcopate, he raised the standards of education and discipline and promoted Sunday Schools and distribution of the Scriptures in Welsh. Other bishops followed his good example, but while the Church recovered its spirituality, it never caught up with the Free Churches. In 1811, forced by episcopal denial of communion to converts of the societies still within the Church and a dearth of ministers to serve, Thomas Charles and his friends ordained a score of lay-preachers, a breach being made and never mended.[13]

There was a phenomenal awakening at Aberystwyth in 1805.[14] It began in a Sunday School established by two young laymen. One of the founders was leaving Aberystwyth, and was engaged in fervent prayer for his young charges, when the Holy Spirit fell upon him and the children so powerfully 'the whole gathering became lost in tears and demonstrations.' Thomas Charles went to Aberystwyth for an associational meeting of the Calvinistic Methodists, and reported:[15]

> At Aberystwyth, and in the adjacent parts, there are general and powerful awakenings among the young people and children. Some hundreds have joined the religious societies in those parts. . . . The concourse of people assembled on the occasion was computed to amount to at least twenty thousand . . . Hundreds of children, from eight years old and upwards, might be seen in the congregation, hearing the word with all the attention of the most devout Christian, and bathed in tears.

In the 1810s, there were other revivals which made an impact upon children, and some which moved only the older people, as at Ty-mawr in Lleyn.[16] Yet another awakening began at Llangeitho at this time, described as 'the quiet revival' on account of an absence of the Welsh phenomenon of moliannu (or praising).[17]

In Merioneth, 'a very favourable season to work for the Lord' was reported. In June of 1814, the attendance at the Calvinistic Methodist meetings rose to fifteen and twenty thousand, a considerable number for a rural country.

The growth of the Free Churches in Wales assisted the development of Welsh nationalism. Cordial relations were maintained with English-speaking associates, but language tended to keep the Welsh apart. There was considerable competition between the various denominations, but their cooperation in the great spiritual movements far transcended that of their friends in England. Because of the poverty of the country, emigration from Wales to Pennsylvania and to the Colonies was steady. These Welsh emigrants, often miners, played a significant part in the affairs of the local churches in the far-off English-speaking commonwealths.

Without a doubt, this period of the eighteenth century awakenings was the formative period of Welsh character. The revivals of the period of the French Revolution, until the Battle of Waterloo in 1815, decided the characteristics of Welsh Christianity and contributed much to the mission fields, as Welsh names in all sectors certify.

4

SCOTTISH REVIVALS, 1790–

The awakenings in Scotland in the days of Whitefield had considerable effect upon the churches, but the movement left the greater mass of the people untouched. True, the line of evangelical preachers never died out in either the Highlands or the Lowlands, among the Gaelic or the Scots-speaking. The evils which beset the Scottish Church in the early eighteenth century intensified during later decades, chiefly in a sorry effect of lay patronage in parish life.

As in other Reformed countries, such as Switzerland and the Netherlands, much of the energy of Scottish religious life was channeled into theological debates resulting in secessions from the Establishment.[1] There were dissident Cameronians, Covenanters who objected to uncovenanted monarchs; there were dissident Seceders, who objected to lay patronage and formed an Associate Synod which split into Burghers and Anti-Burghers; there were ministers who formed the Relief Presbytery, also objecting to lay patronage; there were Sandemanians— in all, about one hundred and twenty congregations of Presbyterian dissenters counted a hundred thousand members. There were also the Baptists and Congregationalists, who shared a Reformed theology. and the Episcopalians and Roman Catholics, who did not.[2] All participated in the theological free-for-all. Yet there were continuing signs of spiritual life, for the Scottish Society for the Propagation of Christian Knowledge engaged in worthy efforts to evangelize the country.

The dominant philosophy in Scotland was that of the party of the Moderates, who professed to be broad-minded and void of enthusiasm. There were many brilliant men among them. However, their philosophy did little for the common people of Scotland. Drunkenness was widespread and too many cases of sexual laxity were reported. Yet the form of religion was maintained, even though ministers got drunk at ordinations, and elders drove reluctant communicants to the Table with sticks, and the young people frolicked in dancing after communion.[3]

As in England and Wales, though there were movements of revival in Scotland in the 1780s, the greater awakenings began after the impact of the French Revolution was felt. The outstanding leaders of the Awakening in Scotland about the end of the eighteenth and the beginning of the nineteenth centuries were two brothers who preached in English, and a Highlander who preached in Gaelic.   There were many others, but the Haldanes of Edinburgh and MacDonald of Ferintosh stood head-and-shoulders above them.

Robert Haldane of Airthrey was born in 1764, and his brother James Alexander Haldane four years later, of a noble Scottish family of Norwegian ancestry which held the lands of Gleneagles.[4]   Their uncle, Adam Duncan, became an admiral on the outbreak of war with France in 1793;   he commanded the North Sea fleet against the Dutch, whose ships he defeated in 1797 off Camperdown, for which service he was created a viscount. Lord Duncan, modest and genial, was universally popular, and though he died in 1804, his fame and popularity helped his nephews, who themselves had served with distinction in the Royal Navy, one quitting naval service in 1783 and the other in 1795.

Robert Haldane and his brother James both welcomed the news of the French Revolution as a promise of a new day of freedom and justice, but were soon disillusioned, deciding that the perfectibility of human nature by secular means alone was fallacious.[5]

James Haldane began his career as a lay evangelist in the village of Gilmerton on 6th May 1797.[6]   At that time, lay preaching in Scotland was not only a novelty but an affront to the ministers of the Church, whether Moderate or Evangelical. Opposition was forthcoming.

The greatest revival preacher that the Highlands ever produced was John MacDonald of Ferintosh, a parish in the Synod of Moray and Ross.[7]   Scholarly, proficient in English and fluent in Gaelic, he possessed a golden heart and a silver tongue.   Ordained a minister of the Church of Scotland, he ministered within its bounds, though readily preaching in the open air.   It was said that almost all the revival movements in the Synod arose from his ministry.

There were several notable Evangelicals ministering in the Highlands and Islands before the general revival of the early nineteenth century.   But, on the whole, the Highlands and Islands were in comparative darkness so far as gospel preaching was concerned.

Movements in the western Highlands began in the late 1790s. In 1797, the Relief Synod sent two of its ministers on an evangelistic tour of the peninsula of Kintyre. Douglas and McNaught preached to great congregations, up to 2000 in some places, a great hunger for the gospel being evident.[8]

James Haldane, accompanied by his friend Campbell, set off in 1800 to tour the whole of the seventy miles length of the peninsula jutting south towards Ireland.[9] They held four meetings a day in the villages, with varied receptions. They were arrested, but, cheerfully offering to take an oath of allegiance, they were released by the magistrate, and so addressed greater crowds than ever on the way back. In Campbelltown, the largest inhabited place, they addressed a thousand people in the morning and fifteen hundred in the evening, in the open air. Thus began an awakening.

In 1800, James Haldane visited the island of Arran, then populated by about five thousand people.[10] 'Darkness covered the land and gross darkness the people,' it was said. But in 1804, many were awakened through the ministry of Angus Macmillan, converted in the movements of 1800, graduated from the University of Glasgow in 1803.[11] The power of the preaching of Neil MacBride was also felt. But in 1810, sinners had become bolder in sin and more abandoned to wickedness.[12] Prayer meetings were begun, and in March of 1812 there came another awakening, marked by outcrying and by agitations of body and mind, many so converted! MacBride died in 1814, and was succeeded by a minister unfriendly to revival, denying the doctrine of regeneration.

In 1805, a catechist, John Farquharson, visited Skye; he stirred up much interest, but, so far as is known, the only fruit of his ministry was the conversion of Donald Munro, a blind fiddler.[13] Prayer meetings were begun, and a parish minister, Donald Martin, was converted. Martin employed Munro as catechist and evangelist, but after two years, Martin removed to Inverness, and his successor dismissed the blind evangelist and, in fact, persecuted him.

However, John Shaw, a native of Moulin, settled in Skye. Shaw, as minister of Bracadale, encouraged evangelism, and in 1812 a great awakening began in Skye, in which the gifts of Donald Munro were greatly in demand. Hundreds professed conversion and lives were transformed.[14] Shaw died in 1823 and was succeeded by Roderik McLeod, also a thoroughly converted man whose support of the cause was enthusiastic, the revival in Skye having lasting effect.

The northern Highlands and contiguous Lowlands were just as needy in spiritual matters as elsewhere. James Haldane embarked on a tour of the north in 1797, Robert Aikman being his companion-in-arms. They preached at a number of towns between Perth and Aberdeen, and sallied into Moray, assemblies of a thousand or so gathering in the open air. An associate, Joseph Rate, amazed at the response but concerned about their spiritual ignorance, spoke to crowds of up to four thousand in Inverness.[15] Meanwhile, Haldane and Aikman crossed over to the Orkney Islands, then returned to the county farthest north, Caithness.

James Haldane preached in Thurso to 300 people 'who seemed rather unconcerned.' The crowds doubled and then trebled, and reached three thousand by Sunday night, and very attentive crowds of this size continued attending.[16] In Wick, the crowds increased to four thousand. Haldane and Aikman did not hesitate to criticize the ministry of local parish incumbents found wanting in theology.

> Of the effects of the word on this occasion . . . some
> have compared its operation to that of an electric
> shock ... there was an astonishing authority and a sort
> of indescribable evidence attending . . .

James Haldane's influence on the Gaelic Highlands was limited, because of the language. He sent Gaelic-speaking agents into the glens; but it was the ministry of the Apostle of the North, John MacDonald, which carried on the work of revival among the Highlanders, within the State Church.[17]

There were the same two influences at work in the central Highlands, the influence of the Haldanes and their Society for the Propagation of the Gospel at Home working through agents outside the bounds of the presbyteries, and the influence of loyal Evangelical ministers, working within the boundaries of their own parishes and those of friends.

English Evangelicalism, since the days of Whitefield, had a stimulating effect upon Scottish Presbyterians. Thus, when Charles Simeon of Cambridge visited Scotland in 1796, he received a warm welcome from many ministers. He toured the shires of Argyll, Perth and Stirling in the company of James Haldane, and left a lasting impulse.[18]

The minister at Moulin, in Perthshire, was Alexander Stewart, of vague theology but well-meaning objectives. Ten years after his ordination, during the early summer of 1796, Charles Simeon arrived there, accompanied by David Black and James Haldane.[19] The size of the congregation may be gauged by the number of communicants—a thousand. Stewart testified later of the blessings which came to him through Simeon's preaching, prayers and conversation:[20]

> He was a man sent from God to me, was my guest for two days in June 1796, preached in my church, and left a savour of the things of God which has remained with with us ever since.

As a result of his own conversion, Alexander Stewart preached, from August 1797 to January 1798, a series of sermons on the fundamental doctrines of the Christian faith. A 'quiet revival' resulted, the movement becoming general by March 1799. David Black, revisiting the place, affirmed that he had never witnessed such a revival before. And yet there was no excitement, there were no unseemly outcries and no convulsions. Stewart declared that his congregation before the revival were not addicted to open vice other than lying and swearing. Rather they were sober, industrious, and peaceable. The revival ran on until 1802, converts as late as 1839 giving testimony of permanence.[21]

Among the converts of the Moulin Revival of 1799 were James Duff and Jean Rattray, both under seventeen. They were later married, and their union brought into the world a child destined for worldwide fame, Alexander Duff, who visited Charles Simeon in Cambridge in 1836.[22]

In 1798, Haldane and Aikman undertook a tour of Perth-shire, and extended their work by means of the usual open air evangelism, prayer meetings and Sunday Schools. That same year, Robert and James Haldane and their friends founded the Society for the Propagation of the Gospel at Home, to employ itinerant preachers, circulate tracts, and establish Sunday Schools.[23] Before the end of 1799, there were forty missionaries itinerating in the Highlands.

In 1800, John Farquharson, lay catechist and evangelist, spent some time at Breadalbane, raising opposition from the gentry and the ministers of the Established Church, so that every inn within thirty miles of Loch Tay was shut tight against him, and only three families would give him shelter. In spite of opposition, he moved from village to village and read the Bible and simply expounded its message to any who would listen. In the spring of 1801, there was some response, but a year later there was an extraordinary revival which won a hundred converts to vital faith. Dissension arose in 1804, and Farquharson emigrated, but four little Baptist congregations emerged from the movement.[24]

In 1810, Robert Findlater was appointed to the parish of Breadalbane and saw some stirrings in 1812. The expectation of blessing increased, and in September of 1816, 'the Apostle of the North,' John MacDonald of Ferintosh, preached to crowds of up to ten thousand. The awakening ran on for two or three years until the end of the decade.[25]

In 1798, Robert Haldane sold his estate at Airthrey in order to devote himself more fully to the work of the Lord. That summer, the Haldanes invited the famous Evangelical preacher, Rowland Hill, to come up from England and open the Circus in Edinburgh for evangelism.[26] The place seated 2500, and was crowded out. Rowland Hill also preached in Leith, Stirling, Crieff, Dunkeld, Perth, and Kinross, then returned to Edinburgh to preach in the Circus and in the open air to fifteen thousand.[27] He then tackled the east coast towns up to Dundee, everywhere attracting great crowds. In Edinburgh, his auditors increased in number to twenty thousand; then, accompanied by James Haldane, he set off south, preaching in the great cities and towns of England.

In 1799, the Haldanes and their associates, unconvinced as to any prospect of renewal in the Church of Scotland, and convinced of congregational principles, seceded from the national church and committed themselves to Independency. General Assembly retaliated by denouncing the movement as a radical conspiracy related to the French Revolution. But it cannot be denied that the Haldane movement served to accelerate the spread of Evangelicalism in the Church.

The Haldanes preached in churches wherever invited, in hired halls, or in the open air. This ministry attracted an extraordinary attention and the results were lasting, inside and outside the Churches. An outraged Assembly of the Kirk of Scotland passed acts against 'vagrant teachers and Sunday Schools, irreligion and anarchy,' and the lesser Presbyterian bodies also condemned free-lance work.[28] None of this at all deterred the brothers Haldane from continuing with their itinerant ministry the length and breadth of Scotland.

The effect of the preaching of the Haldanes, no longer even laymen in the Church of Scotland, throughout the towns in the Highlands and Lowlands, was somewhat like that of Whitefield and Wesley in England. It strengthened the Evangelical sentiment in the State Establishment, even though the powers that disapproved offered opposition. It separated from the Church at an earlier stage than did the Methodists, Wesleyan, Whitefield or Huntington.

James Haldane devoted the summer months of 1800 to evangelism in the Lowlands of Scotland.[29] In the ancient town of Ayr, he preached in the open air to crowds of up to five thousand. He ministered the Word to gatherings from Stranraer in the southwest to Berwick in the southeast. He did not hesitate to tackle the university city of St. Andrew's, a stronghold of Moderatism, gathering the common people and soldiers in their multitudes, displeasing the professors but stirring the people's hearts.[30]

In May of 1801, the congregation which had been filling the Circus in Edinburgh moved to its own building, named the Tabernacle.[31] James Haldane, ordained there as its minister, occupied that position for nearly fifty years. The Tabernacle became a venue for evangelistic preaching in the Scottish capital, feeding all denominations.

The movement of the Spirit in Scotland was not confined to extraordinary outbreaks of revival in the Highlands and Lowlands, in the Church of Scotland and outside its bounds. Everywhere, there was a renewal, a quiet work in both individuals and congregations, leading to the conversion or the commitment of men and women to Jesus Christ.

One such was Thomas Chalmers, a thoughtful scholar, who entered into an experience of faith during the winter of 1810-11.[32] In 1815, Chalmers became minister of the Tron, a strategic congregation in the heart of Glasgow. There the church building was packed out, and the able minister engaged in a work which was evangelistic, educational, and socially progressive in its effects.

Andrew Thomson held a similar position in Edinburgh. There were others of like conviction emerging in all the cities and great towns of Scotland.[33] These Evangelicals, formerly held in contempt, supported each other in synod and presbytery, and formed an ever-growing party in the General Assembly. It was not long before the Evangelicals challenged the domination of the Moderate party.

Meantime, it was from the Evangelical organizations that a stream of dynamic Scots went forth to the circumference of the earth. The Moderates seemed to have had nothing to export, leaving the field to men of more scriptural conviction. A Scottish Missionary Society and a Glasgow Missionary Society were formed in 1796, the same year that General Assembly of the Church of Scotland voted down the proposal of two of its synods suggesting the formation of a missionary enterprise to evangelize the heathen world.[34]

The importance of the Awakening in Scotland cannot be overestimated. Due to various factors, the evangelical development of the Scots seemed to be one stage ahead of that of the Scandinavian countries, and of the Netherlands and Switzerland, in which the Reformed faith was strong. The tremendous expansion of the English-speaking world in both the United States and Britain's Second Empire gave the Scots a running advantage in influencing the progress of Evangelical Christianity in the English-speaking countries, and the same was true of the mission-fields during the Pax Britannica, with few exceptions.

But the greater importance of the Awakening of the turn of the nineteenth century rested in its effect upon internal developments in Scotland. Its converts captured the leadership of the most dynamic sector of the Church of Scotland, which became the Free Church of Scotland; and, in due course, it captured the leadership of the Establishment also, making reunion inevitable.

5

REVIVAL AND TURMOIL IN IRELAND

As in Scotland and England, the tide of spiritual blessing rose in Ireland in 1791, though in the face of political tension and economic distress. All the denominations were affected by it, but it was among Methodists that the most immediate response arose.

In 1791, a work of God began at Newry, in County Down. The congregations in the Methodist meeting-house packed the place, and a divine dynamic drove the message of the Word home to hearers; and such was the impact and the response that a solemn awe appeared on almost every face. In this 'glorious outpouring of the Spirit' in a small town, there were more than a hundred conversions. It resembled an extraordinary awakening occurring in County Fermanagh in December 1783 and January 1784, when the 'power of the Lord descended upon young men and maidens, old men and children. Enniskillen and Ballinamallard became strongholds of Methodism in the absence of Presbyterian people.[1]

In the years following the French Revolution, affairs in Ireland were going from bad to worse. French principles spread among the disaffected Presbyterians of the North, so much so that the British authorities more greatly feared rebellion in Ulster than an uprising in the Roman Catholic South. The United Irishmen prepared for revolt, and it was hoped that, with the help of the French, an Irish Republic would be set up. In 1797, General Gerard Lake 'disarmed the North' by ruthless methods, and the 1798 Rebellion was foredoomed to failure. Militant Presbyterians rose in both Antrim and Down—'Remember Orr!' was their rallying cry in memory of one of their number, William Orr, hanged for sedition—and the Roman Catholics rose in Wexford. Both were crushed, and never again did Protestants and Roman Catholics take up arms, for in Wexford the rebels began to slaughter the Protestant Irish among them.[2]

Some idea of the distress prevailing in Ireland may be gained from the address of the Irish Methodists to their brethren in London:[3]

> The scenes of carnage . . . are truly affecting . . . loss
> of trade, breach of confidence, fear of assassination,
> towns burned, country laid waste, houses for miles
> without an inhabitant, and the air tainted with the stench
> of thousands of carcasses . . . Some of us were im-
> prisoned for weeks by the rebels, exposed to fire and
> sword, and plundered of almost every valuable, yet we
> have not suffered the least injury to our persons. We
> bless God that in other parts of the kingdom there has
> been an ingathering of souls as well as a deepening of
> His work in the hearts of His people.

In the days of distress, there were significant movements.
Thus the Evangelical Society of Ulster was founded in 1798,
and was patterned after a society founded in Dublin in 1792.
One of its founders was the Rev. Thomas Campbell, Anti-
Burgher minister in Ahorey, near Portadown, afterwards
famed as a founder of the Disciples of Christ in the United
States.[4] The Evangelical Society of Ulster was chartered
to extend preaching throughout the towns and villages of the
province. Its activities influenced ministers in the Synod
of Ulster and in the Secession presbyteries, and built up a
sentiment for revival in the churches and evangelism among
the masses.

The Presbyterian Synod of Ulster was mainly deistic in
the latter half of the eighteenth century. Much of the local
preaching was moralistic homily.[5] In Ulster, there were
ministers who refused to subscribe to the confession of
faith because of their heretical tendencies; and there were
ministers who refused to associate with the majority on
account of their concern for doctrine. These evangelical
Seceders erected forty-six churches and ordained forty-six
ministers in the forty-six years prior to 1792.[6] Methodists
exercised a goodly influence on both bodies, in spite of a
doctrinal difference.

The deadly indifference of the last quarter of the eighteenth century affected the Church of Ireland, but perhaps
not as much as its sister Church of England. There were
still many clergymen who distrusted deism and welcomed
evangelicalism in parish life. But few were the leaders.
Before the end of the century, the Primate of the Church of
Ireland (the Archbishop of Armagh) and the Archbishop of
Dublin had withdrawn support from the British and Foreign
Bible Society and from the other religious societies sprung
up in the awakening of the 1790s.[7]

Benjamin Williams Matthias,[8] reared in Dublin as an orphan, was ordained to the ministry of the Church of Ireland in 1797, and preached for many years in Bethesda Chapel in Dublin, though without episcopal license until 1828. A score of young men passed under his ministry into the university, and from Trinity College into the ministry of the Church, for Matthias was an Irish Simeon, and his men rose high in the hierarchy, as (for example) Dr. J. H. Singer, who became Regius Professor of Divinity in Dublin and later Bishop of Meath.

The evangelical awakening among the younger clergy of the Church of Ireland commenced about the time of the 1798 Rebellion. Within seven years time, there arose many evidences of a resurgence of spiritual life in the Anglican community in Ireland. The baptism of grace was experienced by the other denominations also, a general improvement in the state of Irish Protestantism.[9]

The young Evangelicals found themselves engaged in an uphill fight for their faith in the Church of Ireland. Their methods were spiritual, as those of Peter Roe and Robert Shaw, two young clergymen who promoted meetings for the deepening of the spiritual life of the clergy. Shaw proved so indefatigable in his spiritual service that his colleagues complained that he was mad. 'Sir,' observed his Bishop, 'if Mr. Shaw is mad, I wish he may bite all the clergy in my diocese.' In Carlow, there resulted an extensive revival of religion.[10] Otherwise, the young Evangelicals supported the introduction of the evangelical societies of those years, and and other agencies of the Awakening.

This resurgence of evangelicalism within the Church of Ireland produced many converts from the Church of Rome, sometimes by the hundreds a month. Persecution arose, and some sought relief in emigration. The Bible Society circulated the Scriptures in Irish Gaelic, and the movement continued; by mid-century, the Bishop of Tuam in the west was able to tell the visiting Lord Roden that upwards of ten thousand had left the Roman Church in his diocese.[11]

Meanwhile, the Methodists in Ireland were operating within the framework of the Church of Ireland, and many of their converts went into the episcopal ministry. It was usual for Methodists to attend the episcopal service in the forenoon on Sundays, and their own meeting in the evening. There was a cordial relationship between the Methodists and the evangelical Churchmen and evangelical Presbyterians.

The Methodist statistics for Ireland before and after 1800 reflected not only the revivals but also the political turmoil and the consequent emigration of so many overseas. Up to the year 1797, the membership of the Irish churches hovered between 16,000 and 17,000, but in the years that followed the 1798 Rebellion, they jumped to 19,000 and then in a single year (1801) to 24,000, a more than 25% increase, remaining at that approximate figure for five years.[12]

The Methodist evangelists possessed a great advantage in being thoroughly bilingual in a country where half the population spoke the native Erse. In 1799, the Methodists launched an evangelistic campaign aimed at the majority of the Irish population. Wearing black skullcaps, they tackled the market places, exposed to abuse, and filth, and mud, and barking dogs, and squealing pigs, and man-handling.[13]

The evangelists were James McQuigg, Charles Graham, and Gideon Ouseley, all fearless and dedicated ministers. Graham and Ouseley formed a team, based on Ulster but itinerating farther south, preaching on horseback to huge crowds in the open air. Sometimes they enjoyed respectful attention, and in other instances their lives were threatened. Everywhere, in the North and West and South, numbers of converts, many from Catholicism, were added to the local societies.[14] There were elements of revival in the pioneer evangelism. Daniel O'Connell, the Irish patriot, wrote to James Warren Doyle, Roman Catholic Bishop of Kildare, and commented that 'the Methodists were never in so fair a way of making converts.' [15]

Upon occasion, the Roman clergy were grateful for the ministry of the Methodists, even a Bishop commending them, while in some places the Roman clergy contributed to the building of Methodist chapels, one saying that it would keep the evangelists off the streets.[16]

The Methodists likewise exercised a lively ministry in towns where they had erected meeting houses for worship. In 1799, a revival-awakening occurred in Bandon, a town in the County Cork, and in less than two weeks two hundred and fifty people professed conversion, while many in the district round about were influenced for good.[17]

At the turn of the century, there were prostrations of convicted folk in places as far apart as Bandon in Munster and Drum in Ulster.[18] The Methodists, sharing doubtlessly John Wesley's judicious judgments regarding manifestations, neither overrated nor underrated them.

At the troublous turn of the century, Ireland received a visit from the American evangelist considered eccentric by his friends, crazy by his critics. Lorenzo Dow, Methodist freelance, set forth from American shores without the customary letters of commendation because, he admitted, he could not obtain them.

Dow encountered both hostility and friendship in Ireland, and some of the friends offered him money for a speedy return to the land of his birth.[19] The Methodists in Dublin were wary of him, but in the provincial towns the curiosity of the people gained him a hearing. He fell ill, and finally accepted passage home. But he returned to the British Isles and made a mark on Methodism.

Of Baptists, there were but few in Ireland. Since the days of Cromwell, there was a church here and there. But in the evangelical ferment of the early nineteenth century, an outstanding recruit was enlisted. Alexander Carson, graduate of highest class at Glasgow, became pastor of a Presbyterian church at Tobermore.[20] His evangelical convictions were reinforced by evangelical experience which moved him to embrace the doctrine of believers' baptism, and he built up a church of five hundred members in a very small town.

In the last decade of the eighteenth century, the Baptists in Ireland reported that, 'barren as this country has been for many years, there is now a little revival'; two new churches had been formed in Belfast.[21]

In October 1801, the Scottish evangelist, James Haldane, visited the North of Ireland and preached to great crowds in various towns, including Belfast.[22] It was remarkable that he was immediately invited to minister in the Church of Ireland parish church in Portadown— not in holy orders; not even an Anglican.

The few Congregational churches in Ireland shared in the times of spiritual prosperity but made only a slight contribution to the national religious life, being a minority in a minority. Much the same was true of the Moravian and the Quaker assemblies, chiefly in the North.

The Baptists, like the Congregationalists, the Moravians and the Quakers in Ireland, were limited in influence by the smallness of their numbers. But, in the struggle for the truth of New Testament Christianity against sacerdotalism and rationalism, they were the allies of the Evangelicals in the larger denominations, and they enjoyed more than their share of blessing when revival came.

Of course, the Roman Catholic population outnumbered all the others put together.[23] They suffered grievous hardships, being barred from the trades and professions, from teaching or holding office, from voting or jury duty, from owning arms or a horse. These injustices were whittled down as the years went by, but the struggle for emancipation intensified. The Roman hierarchy often supported the Crown, but the clergy and people wherever possible persecuted the Protestants who sought to evangelize their masses. None of the evangelical societies succeeded in penetrating a monolithic resistance of the Roman Catholic Church. But in every awakening, local or widespread, there were many individuals who professed faith in the Good News of free salvation. Some of them moved to other places, sharing in colony life, and others emigrated to escape persecution, which fell heavily on converts from Rome.

An Evangelical Anglican organ in London, commenting upon the state of the Irish kingdom in 1807, called the Bible 'a scarce book,' available in one-in-three of the Protestant families, one-in-five-hundred Roman Catholic familes. It reported gloomily: [24]

> The present uncivilized state of this country must be a subject of painful reflection to every serious mind. Such is the deplorable ignorance of the southern parts in particular that it may be truly said that 'darkness covereth the land and gross darkness the people.'

The comparative dearth of Scripture in the language of the Roman Catholic majority hindered any penetration of the masses by evangelical truth. The Irish majority had suffered so much at the hands of nominally Protestant rulers that it became a matter of loyalty to adhere to a most intransigent form of medieval religion.

6

SCANDINAVIAN MOVEMENTS, 1790–

German Pietism had entered the Scandinavian countries at the beginning of the eighteenth century, but the movement did not profoundly affect their national lives in the way that Whitefield and the Wesleys influenced the English-speaking countries.

In Norway, Denmark, Sweden and Finland, there were outstanding men who embraced the Pietist way of life and there were many more who showed a friendly spirit—including King Frederick IV of Denmark, who, though not himself a convert, did not hesitate to help the evangelists and missionaries of the movement.[1] A majority of these Scandinavian Pietists preferred to support the Lutheran State Churches of the North, but this did not save them from persecution, for the ecclesiastical authorities sought not only to restrain the Pietists but to destroy the movement. This they attempted through Conventicle Acts, aimed at preventing groups of believers meeting together for worship and prayer and reading—hence called Readers.

During the eighteenth century, Denmark's monarchy controlled the destinies of Norway, and the Swedish Crown dominated the country of Finland. Before the middle of the century, King Christian VI issued an edict in Copenhagen designed to ensure the strictest uniformity throughout his dominions by eradicating all Pietist gatherings.[2] In Sweden, Pietists and Moravians won a following, but royal decrees sought to liquidate their conventicles, and the restrictions also bore heavily upon their Swedish and Finnish-speaking disciples across the Gulf of Bothnia.

During the latter half of the eighteenth century, all of Scandinavia was influenced by the philosophy of the German Enlightenment, with its contempt for revealed religion, leaning towards deism and encouraging scepticism. The influence of the philosophers of the French Revolution also had its effect, while the counter-action of the Evangelical Revival in Britain and the American Colonies seemed too remote to affect Scandinavia in the eighteenth century.

After the outbreak of the French Revolution, the same Spirit that provoked a revival for the redemption of British society from 1790 onwards began to move in the kingdoms of Scandinavia.

On 3rd April 1771, Hans Nielsen Hauge was born into a peasant family in the Tune parish of Østfold in Norway. He was confirmed in the Lutheran Church fifteen years later, the product of a healthy life among free farmers who studied Luther's catechism and Pontopiddan's moderately pietistic writings. Young Hauge was still searching for the reality of Christian experience, when, two days after his twenty-fifth birthday, he entered into a new enjoyment of assurance of salvation, ecstatic in spirit. 'My soul,' he said, 'was in that instant so uplifted to God that I was no longer conscious of myself.'[3] Hauge was experiencing the same emotion that stirred the soul of Wesley a lifetime earlier.

Hauge felt impelled to preach. He was a layman, one of the farming class that cherished an independent spirit and showed no fear of the upper class of society.[4] The common people heard him gladly. For eight years, he itinerated up and down the country. At first, he reached the eastern parts of Norway, addressing crowds in Frederikstad, Moss, and Drammen, and in the capital, Christiania, now Oslo.[5] Then he journeyed southwest along the coast and north to Bergen, always enjoying a great response. He tramped the trails of Gudbrandsdalen in east-central Norway. In 1803, he sailed from Bergen along the coast northeast to Tromsø, within the Arctic circle, preaching in the little towns and hamlets scattered on the shores of the fjords.[6] Like Whitefield and Wesley, he reached beyond the formalist congregations to the hungry masses, not in industrial slums but in lonely places. Bishop Johan Nordal Brun of Bergen protected him, but other bishops and clergy were actively hostile.[7] He was arrested ten times between 1797 and 1804, but he always urged his followers to remain within the Church of their fathers. He was arrested again in 1804, indicted in 1809, and remained ten years in prison until 1814.[8] His disciples became the evangelical force in Norway, and his movement far surpassed any other in all of Scandinavia.

Within a Lutheran context, Hauge preached a simple New Testament message, stressing the need of repentance and conversion, of holiness and commitment. His preaching was quick and powerful, laced with emotional understanding. He relied on lay preachers to carry on his work; he succeeded.

The nationwide revival which stemmed from Hauge's ministry was unique in the history of Norway, and was felt throughout the nineteenth century and into the twentieth. More than any other Norseman, he helped unite the common folk in a national and spiritual consciousness that prepared them for national responsibility and worldwide influence as soon as the nation emerged from a centuries-long eclipse.

This Norwegian awakening seemed to lack any lines of communication with other concurrent evangelical revivals. That it occurred at the time of the Awakening of the 1790s in England and Scotland may be attributed to the action of the Holy Spirit, so often spontaneous and simultaneous as well as communicated by human instruments.

In Denmark, just before the French Revolution, the peasants were emancipated from servitude and given the opportunity of owning their plots and farms. One result of this was the disintegration of village life revolving around the parish church; and consequently there was a falling off in church attendance, for even the village pastors were then appointed by the local gentry or the Crown.

The Enlightenment had brought about a concern for better schools and land reform; but, lacking any transforming message, it brought about a decline in morality. However, the Bishop of Sjæland, Nicholas Balle, primate of Denmark, strongly opposed rationalism and attracted large attendances in Copenhagen at the turn of the century.[9] An evangelistic impulse of Haugean origin was felt, coming from southeast Norway, still under the Danish Crown.[10] In 1801, a Danish Evangelical Society was founded on the island of Funen, circulating the Danish New Testament as part of its regular operations.[11] In 1805, two of Robert Haldane's missionaries bound for India were detained in the Danish capital, and immediately set about advancing the Gospel cause in all of Scandinavia, winning the support of even the King in the formation of the Danish Bible Society. In 1807, the British bombardment of Copenhagen in a pre-emptive strike against Napoleon caused many Danes to think more serious thoughts and turn to God.[12] There were movements here and there, but nothing of the magnitude of the Haugean awakening in Norway emerged; nevertheless, the forces of Pietism were reviving, and an evangelistic Lutheranism gained strength, opposed in part by the rationalism of the day, and partly by Lutheran formalism of an orthodox origin. Certainly, the spiritual climate of Denmark improved.

Throughout Sweden, there was a decline in spirituality in all church circles, whether influenced by Pietism or by the Enlightenment. Among the former, the Moravians had enjoyed some prosperity, but the fact that the unfortunate King Gustaf IV Adolf—who succeeded to the throne in 1792 at the age of 13, and who was removed for incompetence in 1809—had shown kindness to the Moravians worked against their interests.[13] The Enlightenment had a following in the upper classes and higher clergy, presenting a mild form of rationalism without much effect on the nation. Drunkenness was epidemic, and many clergy were thoroughly addicted.

A series of disasters afflicted Sweden during the first decade of the nineteenth century, and Swedish armies were forced to evacuate Finland and possessions in Germany. This caused much heart-searching among the people, and a stirring of religious interest was noted. In 1808, a tract society—Evangeliska Sällskapet, modeled on the Religious Tract Society of London—began its ministry of literature distribution.[14] Also with encouragement from London, from the British and Foreign Bible Society, the Swedish Bible Society was organized with royal support.[15] In the Church of Sweden, there were several developments that suggested a return to a more evangelical religion. This was encouraged by replacement of a collective rural system of farming by individual ownership of land, fostering independence.

Henrik Schartau, of German ancestry but Swedish birth, was thirty-two years of age when the French Revolution burst upon Europe.[16] He contended against the rationalism of the day, and later reacted against the devotional sentimentality of Moravianism, moving towards a Lutheranism both churchly and evangelistic. In Lund, the university city in the south, many students were attracted to his preaching, carrying its preparatory message to many parts of Sweden; and artisans and farmers as well as scholars and clergy flocked to his meetings.

In 1808, Pastor Jakob Otto Hoof awakened from a stupor of drunkenness and was soundly converted, becoming an ardent evangelist.[17] Within a few years, an awakening began in southwest Sweden, in Göteborg and Svenljunga, spreading northward. It attracted the common people, and its theology reflected Schartau's middle way. In southeast Sweden, an evangelical revival began in Växjö and Hälleberga districts under the preaching of Peter Lorens Sellergren.[18] Revivals occurred in middle Sweden, touching life in Stockholm.

At the same time, at the northern end of the Gulf of Bothnia, there occurred a resurgence of evangelical zeal in a new movement of Readers, lay evangelists who met in groups for prayer and praise, reading and exhortation.[19] In the North, away from Stockholm, these groups tended to separation from the Church, though Lars Levi Læstadius, a pastor in Haparanda who denounced sin and encouraged public confession, formed a 'church within the Church' that continued throughout the century.[20]

Across the Gulf of Bothnia lay Finland, one-tenth of whose population were Swedes, the remainder being of a mixed Finno-Ugrian stock, related to the Estonians and the Hungarians and peoples farther east, such as Komians and Mordvinians. Long a dependency of the Swedish Crown, which gave the Finns equal rights with Swedes, Finland had shared in Swedish Lutheran life. In 1809, Finland became a grand duchy of the Russian Empire. The country had been wasted by war, and the churches were weakened by the influence of the Enlightenment which reached its peak there in the 1790s, the Pietist movement being enfeebled.

In 1777, Paavo Ruotsalainen was born, and, after a long spiritual struggle, was converted in 1796.[21] There existed a striking similarity between the Awakening which began with Ruotsalainen and the movement under Hauge in Norway, yet without lines of communication.[22] In southwest Finland, the part most influenced by Sweden, local revivals were felt in the first decade of the nineteenth century; they made much of prayer and praise services, often producing ecstasy. In the north, there were similar movements. Ruotsalainen acted as a sobering influence upon the enthusiasts, and won a following among some of the Lutheran clergy, though the awakening as a whole seemed to be a lay movement. Paavo Ruotsalainen continued preaching powerfully, and attracted crowds from every walk in life.

Across the Gulf of Finland, the German Enlightenment blanketed Estonia and Latvia, where much of the leadership of the churches was in the hands of the German landed folk, as was much of social life. In 1811, serfdom in Estonia was abolished, the same year that the British and Foreign Bible Society founded an Estonian auxiliary.[23] These actions were repeated in Latvia, preparing the way in both of these countries for a resurgence of nationalism and a revival of evangelicalism.[24] The tide was turning on the Baltic shores, even in the tiny bays of Protestants in Poland and Lithuania.

7

IN THE EASTERN STATES, 1790–

In the night of dismay and despair felt by churchmen of all American denominations regarding spiritual conditions in the new nation after 1783, there were rays of hope and a dawn of expectation in the east. As in Great Britain, occasional awakenings occurred locally in United States in the 1780s, although the full measure of revival did not sweep the churches until late in the following decade, somewhat later than was the case in Britain. These localized revivals had a useful function in raising up leaders for the generalized awakening soon to follow. They were so wholesome and so free of extravagance of any kind that they reassured more careful Christians and encouraged intercessors everywhere to pray for a Divine visitation. The valleys were being made full of ditches in preparation for a flood of divine blessing. Some of the outstanding preachers of the Second Awakening were converted or called during these local revivals.

Thus, in Boscawen in New Hampshire in 1782, a pastor of a small, inland congregation—Dr. Wood—had modestly hoped that his work might be crowned with the salvation of at least one soul. Instead, a movement began which lasted twenty years, and out of that tiny community came no less than a hundred students for college, of whom more than forty entered the Christian ministry.[1] There were other instances of preparatory movements in New England.

Likewise, in the middle 1780s, a series of awakenings occurred in western Pennsylvania,[2] in which there were hundreds of converts, from whose number were enlisted leaders for a much wider work of grace in the following decade in that same frontier area. Preparatory work was in evidence in other Middle Atlantic States, such as New York and New Jersey.

As in England, local awakenings began in New England towns in 1791, like showers before a deluge not to come until the Concert of Prayer opened the windows of heaven and poured out a blessing which could not be contained in the churches, rural or urban.

Moses Hallock, a veteran of the revolutionary war, in 1791 engaged in evangelism at Plainfield, Massachusetts, and rejoiced to see a revival follow soon after.[3]

About the same time, a weekly union meeting for prayer was being held in the vestry of the First Baptist Church of Boston, led by the ministers of First and Second Churches, influenced by the Union of Prayer among Baptists in England. The vestry became uncomfortably crowded, and soon the main auditorium overflowed. Throughout the winter, despite the blizzards, the place remained crowded. First Baptist Church of Boston added 138 to its membership, and a larger number joined Second Baptist Church.[4] At this time, all the Congregationalist churches in Boston had succumbed to the Unitarian persuasion—except Old South Church. Baptists truly felt that the awakening among them helped preserve orthodox Congregationalism in Boston.

There was a similar movement up country soon after. Edward Dorr Griffin, graduated at Yale in 1790, had studied under the younger President Edwards. Licensed in 1792, he returned to his father's home and found himself the only professing Christian in a family of ten. One of his sisters was his first convert. He began preaching in New Salem, provoking 'a revival of great power' and founding a new church. That was the beginning of blessing for him.[5] He reflected: 'The year 1792, it has often been said, ushered a new era into the world. In that year commenced a series of revivals in America, which has never been interrupted . . .'

The growing concern for prayer soon reached its climax. In 1794, following the British example, Isaac Backus and Stephen Gano, outstanding Baptists, and a score of other New England ministers, issued a circular letter inviting pastors and churches to engage in a Concert of Prayer for spiritual awakening. Addressed to ministers and churches of every Christian denomination in all the United States, it suggested devoting the first Tuesday in January 1795 and once a quarter thereafter to public prayer until the Almighty deigned to answer their pleas for a general awakening.

Response was immediate, general, cordial, and earnest. The Presbyterian Synods of New York and New Jersey soon recommended the call to all their churches. Throughout the country, the Methodist Episcopal Church dedicated its time to prayer and fasting. Likewise, Congregationalist and Baptist associations joined in the intercession, and the Moravian and Reformed communities cooperated.

It was not until the Concert of Prayer in 1795 that the general awakening became noteworthy. It waxed strongest in communities most removed in influence or distance from Harvard and its Unitarianism.

Jeremiah Hallock had been converted at the age of 21, and soon after was called in 1780 to military service, in which he won a following for Christ among the soldiers. In 1783, he became a student-minister assisting the pastor at West Simsbury, Connecticut, and a local awakening began, resulting in the conversion of a hundred people. In 1785, he was installed as minister there. Despite his zeal for God, the congregation began to decline, hurt by the prevailing climate of anti-religious feeling for twelve tedious years.

In October 1798, the visits of other ministers won a few younger folk to Christ, after which numbers of young men sought the pastor out at his home. Soon the congregation was visibly affected. The meetings produced an intense conviction of sin, yet the work was 'by no means noisy, but rational, deep and still.' Some of the most convinced of the local infidels became the brightest of converts.[6]

Late in October 1798, Christian people in New Hartford, Connecticut, heard of the moving of the Spirit in West Simsbury. At the same time, a great work had begun in Torringford, hence church people in New Hartford began to search their hearts again. On a Sunday in November, the Spirit of God manifested Himself in the public service, and a general work of revival began in earnest. Meetings were commenced in various parts of the town, attended by deeply affected crowds, though without convulsions or outcries. It was not long before fifty families were affected.[7]

In Farmington, Connecticut, people of both sexes and of every age flocked to the meetings, walking for a couple of hours through storms and other hazards. The movement began in February 1799 and by August of 1800 threescore of the converts had been admitted to membership, besides a great number already in fellowship thoroughly revived.[8]

'After twelve tedious years,' the awakening began at the town of Canton in Connecticut in the winter of 1798-1799. It began about the same time in Harwinton,[9] as it did in the village of Goshen.[10] In Plymouth, in February 1799, 'like a mighty wind' the Spirit came upon the people.[11] In not one instance was there any report of extravagance of sight or of sound. Neither critical deist nor suspicious churchman was able to find fault with the meetings.

The awakening in Connecticut proved most effective in the community of young people. In 1797, the revival in the town of Somers began with the young people and then affected the middle aged folk. In not a single instance was the local stirring accompanied by noise or outcry.[12] The awakening in 1798 reached Torringford where the Rev. Samuel J. Mills was minister, and it also began with young people.[13] The pastor's son, also named Samuel J. Mills, came under deep conviction of sin at that time, the joy of forgiveness being delayed for three years. Samuel J. Mills, Junior, became the ardent missionary advocate, one of the outstanding men of the first quarter of the nineteenth century.

A third reviving began at Norfolk, Connecticut, in January 1799. The more spiritual people there had heard of the work of God in nearby towns, and began to pray for a visitation. Interest became so general that meetings were conducted in four or five different parts of town. By summer 'displays of divine power and grace' had become conspicuous beyond anything of the kind hitherto witnessed.[14] A universal awe spread over the town. The people convicted were 'by no means noisy or boisterous.' More than a hundred and fifty townsfolk professed conversion. Ammi Robbins conserved the fruits of this third harvest.

In the months before the awakening at Granville, a town in Massachusetts, 'great stupidity' prevailed and youth had become addicted to sinful diversions, according to their minister, Dr. Timothy Cooley.[15] In 1798, praying people began to intercede for blessing, and before long the work was manifest among the young people, overtaking them with conviction even during their revels. Some of the most gay and thoughtless became promising converts, while whole families repented. There were no 'outcries under conviction . . . nor rants of joy after receiving comfort.' The 'glorious work' spread rapidly through the parish.

In Lenox, Massachusetts, the Rev. Samuel Shephard had found his congregation composed of the aged and infirm, without anyone in early age.[16] Not a single young person had been received into membership for sixteen years. Prospects were altogether melancholy when the showers of blessing began to fall in the spring of 1799. By October, the fruits of the harvest were being garnered. The movement was free of any extravagance of gesture or outcry. Five times the largest number in any previous year were received. In many other Massachusetts towns, results were similar.

The spiritual influences at work in Massachusetts and Connecticut began to be felt in Vermont and New Hampshire before and after the year 1800. Nominal Christians awoke from stupor in Halifax, Vermont, and a visible shaking of dry bones was reported, followed by outright conversions of sinners. Although there was an intense conviction of sin, there were no disorders.[17] In Rutland, after eighteen years of deadness, surprising manifestations accompanied a work of grace. Similar reports came from Rupert and other towns, telling of days of prayer and fasting followed by a general conviction of sin without extravagant outcry.[18]

The town of New London, New Hampshire, consisted of about fifty families when a work of grace began. Conviction of sin became so powerful that the busiest men and women set aside their business affairs and sought for spiritual counsel. Within a year the church of eighteen members had welcomed another hundred, converts of all ages from eight to seventy years old having been admitted, including thirty-seven couples.[19] In Newport, the pastor of the local Baptist church baptized twenty-nine in four weeks.

Maine was sparsely populated at the end of the century, but the Second Awakening reached its towns and hamlets in due course.[20] A Congregationalist church in Portland added an average of forty new members year by year for many years.[21] Fasting and prayer were greatly used for spiritual benefit, and there were no extravagances.

In the awakening of before and after 1800, the ministers of New England churches called in no evangelists without settled charge to assist them. They did all the preaching themselves, and helped one another as the occasion required. Sometimes, pastors paired their activities, and visited other parishes by request. No protracted meetings were held, use being made of Sunday services and regular week-day lectures. This had the effect of strengthening these set services and made it easier to integrate new converts.

Much the same was true of the Middle Atlantic States, except in their western territories where frontier conditions prevailed. There seemed to be no records of emotional extravagance in meetings in New York and Philadelphia, or in lesser towns in the States of Maryland, Delaware, New Jersey, Pennsylvania and New York.[22] Unlike New England, these states possessed considerable numbers of Baptists and Methodists, particularly prone to demonstrative conduct in the west and the south.

Of course, the Awakening affected New York City, where churchly conditions were very different to those of Boston. New York's churches were largely Presbyterian or Dutch Reformed, with numerous Methodist and Baptist societies, also Episcopal and Lutheran parishes. The problem faced by Congregationalism in Boston— Unitarianism—was minor in New York, but there was always militant deism in society.

Many New York ministers and their congregations joined in the Concert of Prayer from 1795 onwards in expectant faith.   Dr. John M. Mason, installed in New York in 1793, saw an answer to his prayers after the nineteenth century dawned, when such an ingathering was experienced that his two hundred members multiplied fourfold.[23] The Rev. Philip Milledoler, later president of Rutgers College, served as minister of Rutgers Street Dutch Reformed Church in New York between 1807 and 1812, and witnessed an awakening that lasted three years and increased his congregation from eighty to more than seven hundred.   The movement came through ministration of the Word and regular communion. And from February 1809, when eighteen members were constituted a Baptist church in New York, until December 1822, a continuous movement of the Spirit was recorded, so great being the increase that a new place of worship was built, and within a few years it became necessary to build again.[24]

The awakening swept Long Island in 1799.   A church in Bridgehampton was crowded throughout October in what was described as 'a remarkable revival of religion' which produced a deep solemnity. The movement continued in force throughout January, February and March.[25] Instructed were one hundred converts who ranged in age between ten and sixty-five, of whom seventy joined the local congregation. Scepticism and infidelity, of which there was plenty in post-revolution days, were swept away; taverns were deserted by their erstwhile patrons; differences and prejudices were healed and brotherly love was restored, while family feuds were settled and family religion restored.

In 1798, there occurred 'a wonderful display of divine power' in Palmyra and Canandaigua,[26] the beginning of the great revival of 1799-1800 in western New York, affecting Baptists, Congregationalists, Methodists, Presbyterians and other denominations, overcrowding their churches and swelling their memberships.[27] During the winter of 1807-08, the movement was renewed with even greater effect; and it continued till the War of 1812 disturbed that frontier.

Newark, New Jersey, was the scene of a widespread and long-lasting awakening that began with a day of humiliation, fasting and prayer for an outpouring of the Spirit. Aaron and Hur Societies were formed to uphold the hands of their ministers, and before long whole congregations were being moved by a pervasive influence. Ministers in pairs began itinerating among prepared congregations, in some of which a hundred converts were added to membership by 1803.[28] In 1807, another great awakening began in Newark, described by Edward D. Griffin, later president of Williams College as 'a deluge' of blessing.[29] It was marked by an intensity of intercessory prayer, whole congregations affected, even the little children, a hundred in tears 'as affecting as it was unexpected.' Among the two hundred and forty converts in his congregation were drunkards, infidels, apostates, with children under ten, oldsters over seventy, and many poor Negroes. The revival was provoked by news from nearby Elizabethtown.

In New Jersey, there were two godly brothers serving as Presbyterian ministers, William McDowell of Morristown and John McDowell of Elizabethtown, both of them happily involved in revival movements.[30] In 1807, the Presbyterian congregation in Elizabethtown was swept by a revival which went on for eighteen months, Christians being challenged to greater dedication and a hundred and twenty outsiders added to the church. Five years later, a similar movement added another hundred and ten.[31] The conviction of sin was accompanied by sobbing in some cases, and by a trembling and faintness in other occasional instances.

As in New Jersey, so also in eastern Pennsylvania where Baptists, Congregationalists, Methodists and Presbyterians and others shared in the general awakening of the churches. Philip Milledoler, a capable minister and future educator, had served in the Pine Street Dutch Reformed Church in the city of Philadelphia at the turn of the century, and there enjoyed an outpouring of the Holy Spirit in a revival which lasted eighteen months and was effective until 1805.[32]

From 1795 till 1799, a series of divine visitations was enjoyed by churches generally throughout Pennsylvania's western counties, around Pittsburgh. Many pastors were receiving upwards of a hundred new members. This great work prepared the way for a greater movement in 1802, overflowing from the extraordinary movements in Kentucky and Tennessee.[33]

In 1803, a committee of the General Assembly of the Presbyterian Church announced that there was scarcely a presbytery from which some pleasing intelligence had not been received. It was noted that in eastern and northern presbyteries, the awakenings were of a general nature, whereas in the western and southern, the movements were more extensive and extraordinary.[34] The more numerous Methodists and Baptists were experiencing the same spiritual upheavals and rejoicing in them. Congregationalists in New England, with the exception of those becoming Unitarian, supported the movement and grew rapidly with it; Reformed churches cooperated in it; some Episcopal churches, despite the sorry state of their denomination, were warmed by it; and, in spite of linguistic and cultural barriers, the German-speaking groups were touched by it. Communications between the United States and the United Kingdom were very well maintained, correspondence between religious editors being constant, Americans rejoicing that 'Great Britain was the scene of an equal onward movement' in the churches.[35]

It is not necessary to detail reports of the awakenings in every state to confirm the claim that the Second Awakening was effective from Maine to Maryland. The recording of local movements here and there has served to show that the Awakening in the Eastern States before and after 1800 was without emotional excesses, without the bitter recriminations of earlier movements, that it was fruitful and long-lasting. It has seemed the better part of honesty to point out that many historians have passed directly from the Great Awakening of Whitefield's day, to the Revolution, to the nationalization of the denominations and the great decline, and then to the western frontier revivals with their physical eccentricities. Even those who mention seaboard awakenings have done so in a paragraph or two, devoting pages of detail to the excess of emotion among the illiterate people of the frontier. The population of the Eastern States was ten times that of the frontier territories, and the number of churches and people revived and converted in the east vastly exceeded the number in the west. How can the disparity of attention be explained? The sensational has apparently been as attractive to church historians as to newspapermen; and ideologists have been eager to denigrate the word 'revival' by stressing excesses of human response in a minority of cases, rather than credit far greater achievements in Evangelical Christianity to the recurring outpourings of the Spirit of God.

8

ON THE WESTERN FRONTIER, 1790–

The turn of the century witnessed enormous movements of population from the eastern states into the great valleys on the western side of the Allegheny mountains. In 1801, the population was thus distributed:[1]

Maine	151,719	Maryland	349,692
New Hampshire	183,858	Virginia	886,149
Vermont	154,465	North Carolina	478,103
Massachusetts	422,845	South Carolina	345,591
Rhode Island	69,122	Georgia	162,634
Connecticut	251,002	Kentucky	220,960
New York	586,203	Tennessee	105,602
New Jersey	211,149	Ohio Territory	45,365
Pennsylvania	602,365	Indiana Territory	5,641
Delaware	64,273	Mississippi Terr.	8,850

The total in 1791, 3,929,326, had become 5,305,638 in 1801.

Because of the great need on the western frontier, there were covenants to spend the third Saturday of each month in prayer and fasting, and it was agreed to pray half an hour after sunset on Saturdays and a like time before dawn on Sundays for an outpouring of the Holy Spirit.[2]

As many as fifty thousand people in some areas were without a preacher of any denomination. Infidelity was so strong and moral breakdown so great that Peter Cartwright, the Methodist circuit-rider, declared:[3]

> Logan County, when my father moved into it, was called 'Rogues' Harbor.' Here many refugees from all parts of the Union fled to escape punishment or justice; for although there was law, yet it could not be executed, and it was a desperate state of society. Murderers, horse-thieves, highway robbers, and counterfeiters fled there, until they combined and actually formed a majority. Those who favored a better state of morals were called 'Regulators.' But they encountered fierce opposition from the 'Rogues,' and a battle was fought with guns, pistols, dirks, knives, and clubs, in which the 'Regulators' were defeated.

To such a place came the Rev. James McGready, who had been well converted during the sporadic revivals of the 1780s and who had been impressed by the movement that originated in Hampden-Sydney College in 1787. McGready had been ordained a Presbyterian minister, but served as a pastoral evangelist in North Carolina. James McGready's appearance was unprepossessing, his voice tremulous and coarse, his gestures uncouth, and his manner inelegant. It was said that he was so ugly that he attracted attention on the street. But he possessed such a zeal and earnestness that his handicaps were soon forgotten in his preaching.

In North Carolina, McGready's ministry had provoked reviving or resentment. In 1796, McGready accepted the pastorate of three small Kentucky churches.[4] As he was intensely committed to the Concert of Prayer, he signed up many intercessors for a covenant devoting half an hour at sunset Saturdays and half an hour at sunrise Sundays to intreaty for an outpouring of the Spirit. This local concert of prayer continued for three years, until its intercessors were overtaken by night and day counsel of sinners.

At Red River, in July of 1798, the Lord's Supper was celebrated, and the accumulation of prayer together with the powerful preaching produced a great solemnity.[5] The boldest and most daring sinners were reduced to tearful conviction. On the last Sunday in August, McGready was assisting John Rankin at Gasper River, and many hearers were prostrated, groaning in their conviction. This spirit of conviction ebbed and flowed for a couple of years, at the same time that the widespread awakening in New England was raising up intercessors for the west.[6]

'The winter of 1799,' said McGready, 'was for the most part a time of weeping and mourning with the children of God.' During the summer of 1800, all previous revivals in the area seemed nothing more than a few scattering drops before a mighty rain.'[7] The great awakening in the west had begun, changing the frontier and the nation.

In July 1800, families of settlers arrived from their farms and tethered their teams while they camped for a few days to listen to the preaching of the Word and to share in the celebration of the Lord's Supper. Soon these camp-meetings multiplied, and a whole new way of worship and evangelism was re-discovered.[8]

Barton Stone, a Presbyterian minister, journeyed across the state of Kentucky to observe for himself:[9]

> The scene was new to me and passing strange. It baffled
> description. Many, very many, fell down as men slain in
> battle and continued for hours together in an apparently
> breathless and motionless state, sometimes for a few
> minutes reviving and exhibiting symptoms of life by a
> deep groan or a piercing shriek, or by a prayer for
> mercy, fervently uttered. After lying there for hours,
> they obtained deliverance. The gloomy cloud that had
> covered their faces seemed gradually and visibly to
> disappear, and hope in smiles brightened into joy. They
> would rise shouting deliverance, and then would address
> the surrounding multitudes in language truly eloquent
> and impressive. With astonishment did I hear men,
> women and children declaring the wonderful works of
> God and the glorious mysteries of the Gospel.

Barton Stone studied carefully the cycle of conviction, confession, forgiveness and testimony, all so spontaneous. He concluded that, whatever the accompaniment, it was the result of the operation of the Spirit of God. Later that year, in August 1801, a memorable meeting was held at Cane Ridge, Kentucky. The roads were crowded with wagons, carriages, horses and men on foot, proceeding to a camp-meeting. Military observers estimated that twenty-five thousand people, more or less, were assembled. As many as five preachers addressed the crowds simultaneously in different parts of the encampment. Methodists and Baptists and Presbyterians cooperated in the ministry, all of one mind, the salvation of sinners. Multitudes were converted. The reports of the work, to quote a standard historian, Leonard Woolsey Bacon, were sober and cautious, not hotly enthusiastic or weakly credulous.[10]

Quite a number of people suffered prostration, that is, physical collapse, generally remaining conscious but helpless.[11] Much more frightening, subjects of conviction began to tremble, the trembling giving way to spasmodic jerking. This reaction appeared in people who resisted the message or ridiculed it, as well as in willing hearers. Scoffers came armed with pricks and prods and bottles of whiskey to keep themselves from falling under the influence, to no avail— then their fright became alarming. People helpless under this influence wailed or groaned or cursed or struggled. It was as if a terrier were shaking a rat. Of course, there were second-hand raconteurs who exaggerated grunts into barks, people clinging for support to 'treeing the devil.'[12]

Lorenzo Dow, generally described as 'eccentric' by his friends and 'crazy' by his critics, insisted that he had passed a meeting-house where the undergrowth had been cut for a camp-meeting, between fifty and a hundred saplings left breast-high 'for the people who jerked to hold on by' and the earth stamped as by horses. Lorenzo Dow did not say that he had seen such sights, and evidence offered George Howe seemed to contradict him.[13] More than one observer insisted that the saplings so cut down were hitching-posts for tying horses. Critics who distrusted Lorenzo Dow and all his words were very ready to believe him in this case.

Peter Cartwright, a whimsical man often given to extreme expression, derived a retrospective amusement from the sight of young ladies jerking their heads so that their pony-tails or 'long loose hair would crack almost as loud as a wagoner's whip.' Another observer added: 'but not very loud.'[14] It is obvious that a woman's hair could be jerked to look like a whip, but not to sound like one. Grunts elicited by jerks were exaggerated into barks.

A recent study by Dr. John B. Boles wisely concluded:[15]

> These grossly exaggerated revival exercises, which have been cited widely to discredit the revival, were probably restricted to a comparative few. . . . Except at the very start, they were never a significant factor in the camp meetings.

It is of interest that the Baptists of Kentucky insisted that their meetings were comparatively quiet, the excesses apparently occurring among less enlightened people.[16] The Methodists soon learned, as in Wesley's day in England, that the physical accompaniment did not necessarily ensure spiritual accomplishment. William Warren Sweet[17] insisted that entirely too much stress had been placed upon the emotional excesses of camp-meetings and all too little on the routine work of the frontier churches and preachers. The Presbyterians regarded the phenomena as accidental, and, at the opening of the Kentucky Synod at Lexington in 1803, the Rev. David Rice expressed a majority opinion:[18]

> Is it worse to be repenting, forsaking sin, flying from the wrath to come, crying for mercy, hearing sermons, praying and singing praises to God, and even to spend whole days and nights at these exercises, than in debauchery, cursing and swearing, drinking and revelling, gaming and cheating, quarrelling and fighting, or even fiddling and dancing?

In the weeks and months following the Gasper River outbreak and the Cane Ridge climax, revivals broke out in
church after church, camp-meeting after camp-meeting. A
chain reaction had begun, touching off implosions in county
after county in Kentucky and Tennessee. The common folk
were engulfed by the flood, leaving little islands of critical
opposition or amused indifference among the upper classes
who professed but rarely practised an Episcopalian religion.
Baptists, Methodists and Presbyterians shared in the movement cordially, for everyone was so busy aiding converts
that there was no competition.

By January 1801, the Awakening had reached Nashville
and Knoxville as well as Louisville and Lexington. Some
indication of the impact upon the Baptists is noted in the
records of the Elkhorn Association, the oldest organization;
in 1799, its twenty-nine churches reported twenty-nine
conversions, but in 1801 the churches of the association
reported 3011 received by baptism and testimony, organizing
nine more churches; a year later, twelve more churches
were organized. Church histories indicated that the converts
proved their worth as outstanding members for a generation
to come.[19] Bishop Asbury reported a pleasing intelligence
from every circuit, with converts aplenty and new churches
everywhere.[20] The Presbyterians gained likewise from the
revival, but were hindered by Genevan ecclesiology from
gathering congregations the way that Baptists and Methodists
did. The Baptists went, as farmer-preachers, to start new
congregations; the Methodists sent, as circuit-riders, to do
the same; the Presbyterians waited for a call, and even
those who itinerated seemed more interested in contacting
lapsed or unrelated Presbyterian families.

The crucial test of the genuineness of the 1800 Awakening
was not the size of the crowds or the degree of excitement,
but the spiritual fruits. Dr. George A. Baxter affirmed:[21]

> On my way, I was informed by settlers on the road that
> the character of Kentucky was entirely changed, and
> that they were as remarkable for sobriety as they had
> formerly been for dissoluteness and immorality. And
> indeed I found Kentucky to appearances the most moral
> place I had ever seen. A profane expression was hardly
> ever heard. A religious awe seemed to pervade the
> country. Upon the whole, I think that the revival in
> Kentucky the most extraordinary that has ever visited
> the Church of Christ.

The Methodist historian, William Warren Sweet, cagily observed that 'the influence of the revival upon western society was both good and evil, with good predominating.' He then cited a number of witnesses certifying the moral reformation, including David Rice, who noted that drunkards, profane swearers, liars, quarrelsome persons and the like were remarkably reformed.[22] The only deleterious effects catalogued by Sweet were the frontier schisms, which truly followed the Awakening but were scarcely caused by it.

The Cumberland Presbytery sought to meet the need of the multitudes by licensing local preachers unqualified by Presbyterian regulations for ordination. These exhorters itinerated, Methodist-style, among the vacant congregations, but drew the fire of stricter Presbyterian ministers. The conservative party initiated actions against active ministers and disavowed untrained pastors, forcing the dissolution of the Cumberland Presbytery, which was re-constituted as the Cumberland Presbyterian Church.[23] That this schism was due to an inherent defect in the Genevan system was manifested by the fact that the Methodists suffered no such secession, thanks to their provision for local preachers. It is therefore unwarranted to blame the Awakening.

The Methodists suffered a secession on other counts. The able Bishop Asbury ruled the conferences with an iron hand, more arbitrarily than any Anglican bishop would have dared. Francis Asbury was 'a born conservative and a born autocrat' who brooked no opposition and took no advice.[24] This provoked a schism in Virginia, Kentucky and Tennessee, the dissidents taking the name of Republican Methodists. But this separation took place in 1792, before the general Awakening of 1801 onwards, and was due to an inherent defect in the Methodist Episcopal system that while they preached a 'republican gospel,' they operated under a monarchial system of government.[25] The Baptists suffered no such 'republican' secession, being fully democratic.

Barton Stone, an outstanding leader of the revival in Kentucky, with several other ministers, was charged by the Presbyterian Synod with preaching erroneous doctrine. He and his presbytery seceded to form the Christian Church, one of the components of the Restoration Movement known as the Disciples of Christ, Churches of Christ, or Christian Churches. But Stone had voiced his doubts about strictest Calvinism at his ordination, long before the Awakening.[26] A similar secession occurred under Thomas Campbell.

9

IN THE SOUTHERN STATES, 1790–

The Concert of Prayer enlisted many intercessors in the Southern States, in which less than two-fifths of the country's population dwelt.[1] In Virginia, North Carolina, South Carolina, Georgia, and the Mississippi Territory, there were Anglicans, Baptists, Methodists, Presbyterians, and a sprinkling of other denominations. As in other parts of the Union, the Episcopal Church was the victim of the revolutionary change. Presbyterianism followed the Ulster-American settlers down the broad valley of Virginia into the piedmont area of the Carolinas, little churches being built everywhere the Scotch-Irish settled. Methodism did not reach the South until the decade of the Revolution when Devereux Jarratt, an evangelical Anglican,[2] encouraged local preachers to evangelize the people, the Methodists still being members of the Church of England. The Baptists were of three strains: Particular or Calvinistic, General or Arminian, and Separate or Edwardsean—the latter group having come from New England—and all three were by nature evangelistic, all suffering persecution until the coming of Independence.

Conditions were far from encouraging on the southern frontier, where a back-country itinerant of Episcopalian affiliation bemoaned the fact that so many thousands had never seen or read or heard a chapter of the Bible; that so many tens of thousands had never been baptized or heard a sermon; and that many more had never heard the name of Christ except in cursing and execration.[3]

There were preparatory revival movements in the South also in the middle 1780s, the awakening at Hampden-Sydney College in Virginia being an outstanding example. Baptists and Methodists as well as Presbyterians shared in the post-1787 movement, their demonstrations of religious feeling being more exuberant. The revival reached the frontiers of Georgia in 1788 and 1789, Abraham Marshall being an outstanding Baptist leader, Hope Hull a Methodist, and Moses Waddel a Presbyterian, all active in revival.[4]

In the Southern States, a preparatory work of revival quickened intercession and raised up leaders as an answer. After the Revolution, the Baptists, the Methodists, and the Presbyterians had begun to grow in states to the South, even to the far reaches of Georgia, where local revivals were reported in the various denominations. All three of these denominations in the south were committed to evangelism.

In Virginia, a sorry state of affairs existed at Hampden-Sydney College, a Presbyterian school. On campus in 1787, there was drunkenness, cheating, lying and profanity, the students being utterly careless in conduct and character. A group of three students, all unconverted—so far as one can ascertain—but concerned about conditions on campus and about their own spiritual destiny, decided to hold a prayer meeting to entreat the Almighty. They locked themselves in a room to avoid ridicule or uproar.[5] All were novices about intercession. 'We tried to pray,' said one, 'but such prayer I never heard the like of. We tried to sing, but it was in a most suppressed manner, for we feared the other students.' They were discovered, and a tormenting mob tried to break down the door and rough them up.

The president of Hampden-Sydney College was Dr. John Blair Smith, born 1756, converted 1770.[6] Called upon to investigate the uproar, he rebuked the rowdies and told the praying youths that they could meet in his private room. This they did, and thus began a remarkable college revival. Many vicious and profane students were converted, and the movement was extended over three or four counties by the preaching of Blair Smith, who won more than two hundred young people to Christian faith within a year and a half— several of whom became outstanding leaders in the greater awakening soon to come.

Some historians have dated the Second Awakening in the South from 1787, when college revivals were experienced at Hampden-Sydney and Washington Colleges and spread by John Blair Smith to nearby counties.[7] That these localized awakenings prepared the way for the Second Awakening is undoubted. But they were not general, and there came a pause in the movement before the hurricane of the revival of 1800 swept the Southern States after first having struck Kentucky and Tennessee. The chronology suggested sporadic revivals in New England, the Middle Atlantic States, and the South in the 1780s, the Second Awakening cresting in New England in 1797, the West in 1800, and the South 1801.

The awakenings of the late 1780s did little to change the condition of society at large in the South. A French Duke, De La Rochefoucault, who toured the United States between 1795 and 1797, observed that 'religion is one of the objects which occupies the least of the attention of the American people,' and he added that the Virginians were the least addicted.[8] Even William Ellery Channing of Harvard, who spent some time in Richmond, was sure that 'Christianity is here breathing its last.'[9] By 1796, Devereux Jarratt was finding the situation gloomy and discouraging among not only Episcopalians but Baptists, Methodists, Presbyterians and the rest.[10] A tourist from Britain wrote sadly of church buildings falling into decay, with windows broken, doors off hinges, lying open to pigs and cattle.[11]

These were the conditions prevailing when the Concert of Prayer, officially or unofficially, gathered intercessors for a covenant with sacrifice. Fasting and prayer became frequent among the remnant of believers, not only local congregations, but circuits, presbyteries, associations of churches, synods turning to God to intreat His intervention.

Even before the answer to prayer came from Kentucky, an extraordinary movement occurred at the Rocky River Presbyterian Church in North Carolina in 1798, so lasting in its effects that ten years later a day of thanksgiving for the work was celebrated with enthusiasm.[12] When news of the outpouring of the Spirit in Kentucky and Tennessee began to reach the western parts of North Carolina, revival swept a gathering for communion at Cross Roads in 1801; and under the ministry of William Paisley, a great awakening moved the whole community in 1802.[13] In the month of March of that year, 262 wagonloads of people descended upon Cross Roads, bringing the attendance at divine services between Friday and Tuesday up to 10,000 people, ministered to by fourteen Presbyterians, three Methodists, two Baptists, two Lutherans, one Dutch Reformed and one Episcopalian.[14]

The awakening spread rapidly throughout the State, for the prayers of the saints and the needs of sinners were met. In Mecklenburg County, a dozen Presbyterians with help from Baptist and Methodist ministers preached to fully six thousand people amid unusual manifestations of repentance. In Guildford, Orange and other counties, awakenings were experienced throughout 1801-02. Fruits of the awakenings in North Carolina were gathered for many years, including many zealous ministers and dedicated laymen.

The awakening in North Carolina attracted huge crowds across the State throughout 1802 and 1803 and continued into 1804 and 1805.[15] The vast crowds gathered in the open fields, and ministers of all denominations served their needs.

A hundred and seventy miles inland from Charleston in South Carolina, in Lancaster County, there stood a pioneer Presbyterian Church known as Old Waxhaw.[16] In May 1802, when the Rev. John Brown was minister, there occurred a memorable revival of religion. A score of ministers of the various denominations attended, among them four Baptists, three Methodists and eleven Presbyterians. The lay people came in twenty carts and a hundred and twenty wagons, to a total of 3500, a great crowd for a sparsely settled area.

The announced objective was a service of communion, and the preaching was designed to prepare the hearts of the participants. Great was the response among the frontier Carolinians.[17] Believers were challenged to commitment of life, backsliders were restored, nominal Christians were brought to real faith, and frankly unconverted people were converted to God.

As the gathering met in the open field, and not in a local church, a host of scoffers assembled with them to mock at the proceedings. It was chiefly among these antagonists that physical prostrations occurred. Loud-mouthed and defiant critics collapsed in a heap. Some, seeing what was happening, came fortified by strong drink, even waving their bottles, but went down like ninepins, wailing in fear. One such scoffer was smitten to the ground. When at last some concerned minister got round to him, he urged the helpless man lying prostrate on the ground to pray. 'I'll be damned if I do,' the sinner panted. He lay helpless all night, and was last seen creeping away on all fours.[18] Some sinners fell instantaneously, as if struck by lightning, and lay helpless but conscious, full of apprehension and conviction. In most instances, these subjects of seizure were very grateful for the counsel offered them by ministers or laymen, and soon repented of their ways and professed faith in Christ, afterwards rejoicing with abandon proportionate to their earlier concern. Such converts were enrolled as inquirers, and were given instruction in the church of their choice.

Francis Asbury had been itinerating among Methodist circuits early in 1801, inspiring his preachers with stories of what had been happening elsewhere. The Baptists and the Presbyterians shared equally in the movement.

The communities around the town of Spartanburg shared in equally stirring awakenings, a dozen Presbyterians and their Baptist and Methodist colleagues preaching to five thousand seekers. Ebenezer Cummins asserted:[19]

> I have seen and heard things which no tongue can tell, no pen can paint, no language describe, or of which no man can have a just conception, until he has seen and heard and felt.

Some idea of the gains to the churches may be garnered from annual statistics of the Southern Methodists in South Carolina in forty years, starting with the year 1787 when the membership stood at 2,075 white and 141 black; 1797, 3,715 white and 1,038 black; 1807, 14,419 white and 5,111 black; 1818, 21,059 white and 11,587 black; 1828, 35,173 white and 18,475 black. From a total of 4,753 in 1797 to 53,648 aggregate in 1828 represented nearly forty per cent increase per annum, an incredible increment.[20]

The Baptists gained hugely from the South Carolina back country awakening. In the revivals of 1802-1803, the little frontier church of Padgett's Creek gained 420 members, Bethel 247, Fairforest 216, Bush River 149, Big Creek 124, and thirty-five new churches came into existence with ten thousand whites and blacks as members; in all, a gain of 80% in three years. The Baptist churches of South Carolina entered the new century with a tremendous burst of spiritual life and an equally astonishing increase of numbers.[21]

In 1802, the great awakening appeared in Georgia and continued effective until 1805.[22] There were, as in other states, showers of blessings before the torrential downpour. In July 1801, a quarterly meeting of Methodist preachers dissolved into lamentations and streaming eyes. Revivals began to be reported from local congregations.[23] In July 1802, Moses Waddel attended a four-day meeting at a little Presbyterian church named Nazareth, and was startled by 'persons falling to the ground as suddenly as if they had been pierced through the heart by a bullet or a sword' during very ordinary preaching. The numbers attending were estimated variously from five to eight thousand people.[24]

Throughout 1802, the camp-meetings progressed, in one instance attracting ten thousand people, ministered to by twenty-five pastors, including an Episcopal clergyman. The movement was felt most strongly from 1802 until 1805, but remained effective for many years to come.[25] Relays of ministers addressed the huge interdenominational meetings.

The believers in Virginia were in touch with the leaders of the Concert of Prayer in New England, and in many towns there were intercessors. By 1800, localized revivals were occurring in the Old Dominion, increasing the expectation of a more widespread movement. The Roanoke Baptists in 1797 had appointed four evangelists to visit the churches of the Association, seeking especially the revival of the local ministers.[26] By 1802, the Roanoke churches had baptized more than thirteen hundred converts.

At Christmastime 1801, an interdenominational group of ministers met in Bedford County to promote a mobilization of spiritual resources in anticipation of the coming Revival. Soon the Baptists, Methodists and Presbyterians were taking part in united gatherings in several counties. In April 1802 Francis Asbury reported a general revival on the peninsula forming Virginia's eastern shore.[27] Great outdoor meetings were gathered in all parts of Virginia, the people attending and the preachers ministering to their needs being of various denominational loyalties. The response was the same, the simple exhortations to repentance, the intense spirit of conviction, the prostration of a number of people, the counsels of ministers and godly laymen, the startling testimonies of the penitents, and the thorough reformation of character.

In what is now West Virginia, a communion service in late September 1802 went on all night, accompanied by all the manifestations of the camp-meetings.[28] Two weeks later, because of this interest, another communion service was celebrated, attended by ten thousand people camping for four days. Ten ministers preached and offered counsel.

Camp meetings continued in Virginia, the Methodists in particular being addicted to the method for several exciting years, and the eccentric Lorenzo Dow itinerated throughout the area in early 1804.[29] Bishop Asbury reminded his circuit ministers: 'We must attend to camp-meetings, they make our harvest time.'[30] Asbury's Journals were filled with his references to camp-meetings, but the itinerating bishop made sure that the converts and inquirers were taken care of by the local class meeting, which made them into active church members.[31] The Baptists, although their ministers were largely farmer-preachers, administered discipline in monthly congregational meetings.[32] They excluded without fear those unrepentant of drunkenness, adultery, gambling, stealing, dishonesty, abusing wives, and mistreating slaves. the Presbyterians also administered strict discipline.[33]

10

REVIVAL IN BRITISH AMERICA, 1790–

In the last decade of the eighteenth century, what was known as British America consisted of the colonies of Newfoundland, Prince Edward Island, Cape Breton Island, Nova Scotia, New Brunswick, Labrador, Lower Canada— later Quebec, and Upper Canada— later Ontario. Forty thousand loyalists fled the United States after the Revolution, losing their property entirely, but they were given generous grants of land in the Maritime Provinces and Upper Canada.

The effects of the Newlight Awakening in the Maritime Provinces, begun in revolutionary times, were still being felt throughout the 1780s.[1] Congregationalism as established by New England immigrants suffered eclipse, party due to the secular disruptions of war and party to the religious disruptions of secession.[2] Henry Alline died in 1784, but the Newlight movement continued, some of its congregations becoming Baptist. Immigrants from the Scottish Highlands augmented the Presbyterian cause, and Methodists from England established Wesleyan societies; all the while, the colonial authorities were striving to establish the Church of England as the Church of the Empire.

As elsewhere, in 1791 a 'great moving in the minds of the people' was reported, the beginning of a new series of revivals in the Maritime churches.[3] By the turn of the century, revivals of religion were breaking out periodically, sometimes described as 'waves of mass hysteria' by the critics of a hundred and fifty years later, who admitted:[4]

> When religious feelings grew strong, meetings went on for days and weeks; the whole church—indeed, almost the whole community—gave itself up to the cause of religious salvation.

All work was suspended during these extraordinary outbreaks of spiritual rejuvenation. Hundreds of converts were added, principally to the Baptist, the Methodist and evangelistic churches. David George, a Negro preacher who had followed black refugees to Halifax, preached very effectively to Negro settlers in the area.[5]

Harris Harding, a successor to Henry Alline, ministered at Liverpool, on the coast of Nova Scotia, in July of 1791. The older Christians stood by, weeping or wondering at the response of the young people to the message.[6] In September, he worked in Barrington, with much the same result. In the New Year of 1792, people were flocking in great numbers to hear the Good News, and doors were open everywhere for meetings.

The movement towards God produced an outstanding leader among the Baptists, Joseph Dimock, who wrote from Granville in mid-1791:[7]

> I can tell you that all I have ever seen before is small in comparison with what I have seen here . . . Many meetings continue until almost midnight, sinners crying aloud for mercy . . . some meetings have continued all night . . . The work prospered. The people thronged to meeting sometimes from fifteen to twenty miles distant. Often I have known young females to come twelve miles on foot on Lord's day morning before we had breakfast.

The movement continued in strength. Joseph Dimock toured all of Nova Scotia in 1798 and noted reviving seasons, with unusual attention, frequent lectures, Christians hungering and thirsting after righteousness, a hundred candidates baptized at Cornwallis, 'the greatest change' at Nictaux.[8]

Thus it continued into the 1800s. There were unusual revivals of religion during the winters of 1806-07, 1807-08, and in 1809 fifteen churches of the Baptist Association were enjoying spiritual prosperity.

Awakenings were recorded by other folk. In the 1790s, Yorkshire Methodists migrated to Nova Scotia,[9] and in 1801 the Rev. Joshua Marsden was appointed missionary there by the British Wesleyan Conference.[10] Already, the Methodists of American origin were introducing the camp-meetings to their Maritime circuits. Marsden proved a very capable evangelist, moving whole communities, enlisting especially the young people. He reported from St. John in 1806:[11]

> The magistrates and principal inhabitants cannot deny that there is a great change in the place for the better, as many of the young people who are subjects of this work were once loose in their principles and irregular in their practices, but they are now new creatures; and one can hardly go through the street of this little city without hearing the voice of praise, or seeing the young men assembling together for prayer.

> Our little chapel is crowded, that you can scarcely see
> any thing but human heads; and the meetings are solemn
> beyond any thing seen in this place for a long time. Often
> towards the conclusion a cry for mercy begins which
> spreads from one to another till the union of the voices
> of those who are either praying, crying, or rejoicing,
> forms what worldly people call confusion. Our meetings
> are become the common topic of conversation. Some
> wonder, some mock, some acknowledge the power of
> God, and several not in society defend the cause to the
> utmost of their power. But, as yet, none of the rulers
> have believed on Him. The good that is done is chiefly
> among the poor and middling classes of people.

Newfoundland, where much spiritual destitution existed
at the end of the eighteenth century, received a Methodist
missionary, and many humbler people responded to the
Wesleyan message.[12] The Society for the Propagation of the
Gospel subsidized missionaries to the island population, and
slowly extended the Church of England operation.

The Church of England cause in the Maritime Provinces
received both spiritual and material support from the High
Church S. P. G., and both political and material support
from the colonial governments. The general Awakening of
1790 onward seemed not to have conferred any benefit upon
the Anglican communion, which regarded the evangelical
preachers— in those times before Anglican Evangelicalism
waxed strong— with relentless hostility.[13]

Scottish and American Presbyterian missionaries were
working among immigrants to the Maritimes, some coming
from the south and many more from the Scottish Highlands.
The Scottish Awakening at the turn of the century had not yet
begun to influence the sending of immigrants or the sending
of missionaries to cater to their needs. Presbyterianism
was also augmented by the affiliation of Congregationalists
who professed a distaste for the Newlight evangelists and the
exuberance of their meetings.

It is of interest that the awakenings in British America—
unlike those of the 1790s in New England—manifested an
exuberance of feeling, whether of sorrow for sin or of joy
in forgiveness. These British Americans, like the trans-
Appalachian settlers in Kentucky and Tennessee, were up-
rooted people, frontiersmen, in a society perhaps more
law-abiding than the trans-Appalachian West, but not as
settled as New England.

In 1791, when the larger province was divided into Upper and Lower Canada, Upper Canada—now Ontario—had been settled by twenty thousand people of European stock, of whom ten thousand were loyalists from the United States. At that time, the land was covered by primeval forest, and the settlers suffered incredible hardships in the wilderness. As late as the winter of 1793-94, many struggling people at times subsisted on nuts, leeks, greens and the bark of trees. Starvation was close at hand. Predators, such as wolves and bears, raided the farms. Loneliness afflicted little families occupying the generously granted but severely isolated lands.[14]

A Carolinian loyalist, Major George Neal, found it wise to move to the opening territory of the Canadian Niagara, where in 1786 he took possession of a grant of land but also visited the scattered settlers, preaching the Good News.[15] A similar start, also Methodist, was made around Kingston, east of the lake.[16] But it was not until 1790 that the first regular Methodist preacher, William Losee, began to work in Upper Canada, appointed thereto by the Methodist Episcopal Conference directed by Francis Asbury in New York. Losee was a fearless horseman and a tireless evangelist, but his coming to Canada preceded the outbreak of the great awakening in western New York State by about seven years. Those seven years were devoted to church planting.[17]

About the same time that Methodists began to pioneer, a Presbyterian evangelist also crossed into Upper Canada. The Reverend Jabez Collver began to itinerate faithfully in the Niagara district in 1793, using an evangelistic method of preaching that anticipated the Cumberland Presbyterians, thus winning many displaced or lapsed Presbyterian families and occasional outsiders to a vital evangelical Calvinism.[18]

Anglicans were also settling in Upper Canada, coming as loyalists from the United States or as immigrants from the Mother Country. They were very ill-served for ministers, for the Church of England had yet to receive the missionary impulse from the Revival at home, and the Episcopalians in the United States were still in a state of shock following the Revolution. The Bishop of Quebec disdained the services of the itinerant Methodists as 'a set of ignorant enthusiasts whose preaching is calculated only to perplex the understanding and corrupt the morals; to relax the nerves of industry and dissolve the bonds of society.'[19] Neglect was the enemy of Anglican progress, prejudice of vital evangelism.

Upper Canada, principally the lower peninsula of Ontario, was settled largely by loyalists from the south and disbanded soldiers from the British forces, including some Hessians. The loyalists were much more subject to influences at work in the American West than in either New England or England. In the late 1790s, the American western frontier was being swept by extraordinary revivals of religion, and these soon communicated themselves through the Methodists, but also through the Presbyterians and later the Baptists.

In 1796, Darius Dunham served as presiding elder of the Methodists' quarterly meetings. Calvin Wooster, a more ardent evangelist, remained behind in one meeting to pray with penitents, when the power of God fell upon them, some being filled with joy unspeakable while others were prostrated.[20] Dunham returned to try and stop 'the raging of the wildfire,' but was himself overcome. This, reported the historian of Methodism in Canada, was the commencement of a revival which spread throughout the whole province.

It was well said that 'the growth of Methodist influence in the country after 1795 . . . was phenomenal.' In 1797, the membership stood at 800; in 1798, 900; in 1800, 1200. In 1802, Nathan Bangs commenced his ministry in Canada and a general revival in Niagara peninsular circuits ensued, adding 300 to the membership there.[21]

Jabez Collver was joined by another Presbyterian, the Reverend Daniel Eastman, who arrived in 1801, and seven years later a Welshman, Lewis Williams, assisted them. Rather than waiting, Presbyterian-style, for calls from congregations, these ardent evangelists held services wherever people could be brought together. Local revivals were much in evidence during their ministry.[22]

By 1805, there were 1800 Methodists in the membership of the Canada Conference.[23] Two more evangelists arrived from the United States, William Case and Henry Ryan, and that summer a camp-meeting was held for the first time in Canada, drawing people from miles around, provoking the usual demonstrations of spiritual impact, prolonged prayer meetings, intense conviction of sin, cries of penitence, shouts of deliverance, and joyful testimonies.[24] There were many conversions and many additions to the churches.

In 1810, an extensive awakening occurred in western Ontario, under the preaching of William Case. The moral standards of the people had been disintegrating, and violent opposition was offered anyone trying to remedy matters.[25]

> The first sermon I preached in this place was attended
> with almost a general weeping; the sermon produced
> among some of the wildest of them a visible alteration.
> They began to hang around, as if loath to leave the place,
> and, accounting me no longer their enemy, appeared
> to wish for an opportunity to speak with me, which I
> embraced, and spoke to them one by one.

Case, in his letter to Asbury, observed that these settlers responded to the message in the very same manner and spirit as in the awakenings in the States, without having had previous instruction or experience or suggestion. The 1810 Revival spread throughout the settlements on the Thames River and into nearby districts.

A majority of the Baptists in the Thirteen Colonies had supported the American Revolution, hence few Baptists were found among the first settlers in Ontario. In 1798, Reuben Crandall, a Baptist evangelist, built the first Baptist church in Upper Canada.[26] Within five years, a colony of Scottish Baptists from Breadalbane—where such stirring revivals had taken place—arrived in the Ottawa Valley. Baptist evangelism was accelerated by the arrival of John Edwards, of the company of the Haldanes in Scotland, an excellent evangelist who itinerated through the settlements.[27]

In Lower Canada, or Quebec proper, a settlement of loyalists was made, not far from the Vermont border. In 1794, missionaries of the Woodstock Baptist Association in Vermont visited them, and an awakening occurred which lasted several years.[28] The French-speaking districts of Quebec remained untouched by Baptists, Methodists or any other evangelical denomination, although, of course, there were churches formed in Montreal for English-speaking citizens of that river port.

Immigrants continued to cross the Atlantic to settle in Upper Canada. Many of them left the Old Country as members of the Church of England or the Church of Scotland, but lapsed into indifference because of the lack of provision for ministry by either established Church. The Methodists in particular were successful in winning these unchurched people back to Christian faith and practice. As the British Awakening of 1790 onwards began to have effect upon the Established Churches in England and Scotland, missionaries and ministers of Evangelical Anglican and Presbyterian convictions began to follow the immigrants. They too were part of the general Evangelical Awakening of those years.

Napoleon's continental system of boycott against Great Britain led to British counter-measures which provoked the United States into the War of 1812. The war was very unpopular in New England, which even threatened to secede from the Union. But the war hawks saw an opportunity of annexing Canada to the Republic, and armed invasion was begun at three points. Most of the action was fought in the Niagara peninsula, where the invading Americans sorely misjudged the temper of the Canadian settlers who, instead of revolting, rose in arms and defeated them. Bitterness was caused by the American burning of Toronto, or York, whose inhabitants were turned out into a bitter winter— the reason for the retaliatory burning of Washington.

As so much of the evangelistic enterprise in Ontario was sponsored by Americans from south of the border, the War of 1812 greatly hampered the Methodist, Presbyterian and Baptist ministries in British territory.[29] The pro-British sentiment was strong enough to repudiate American-related religion, and the colonial clergy of the Church of England were able to reap an advantage. The revival awakenings came to an end temporarily in Canada, as they did also in the parts of the United States most affected by the war.

The coming of peace brought about a resurgence of the movements of revival, and again extraordinary outpourings of the Spirit were reported in Canada as well as the United States. The earliest revivals were no passing experience. The foundations of Canadian evangelicalism were being laid in these phenomenal, if circumscribed awakenings.

After 1812, the Methodist evangelism was augmented by Baptist preaching in Upper Canada.[30] Tensions between the British-aligned and American-aligned partisans grew. A further complication arose as the Baptists, Methodists, and Presbyterians combatted efforts of a conservative official-dom to establish vested interests.[31] This the evangelicals resisted strongly, making sure that there would be no church establishment in Canada. In the 1830s, there was incipient rebellion in both Quebec and Ontario, breaking out into open insurrection in 1837 under Louis Papineau in Lower Canada and William Lyon Mackenzie in Upper Canada, both revolts put down by force. The turmoil in Canada in the 1830s inhibited the spread of the American Awakening of the time across the border, although there were many local revivals reported by evangelical churches in the Maritimes as well as Ontario. Anglican evangelicals remained weak.

11

AMERICAN COLLEGE REVIVALS, 1800–

The records have made clear that the twenty years between 1792 and 1812 were years of evangelical awakening in North America, preceded by sporadic revivals which had raised up leaders for the main movement that began after 1791 but did not become general until 1798 in the Eastern States, 1801 in the West and the South. The Concert of Prayer begun in 1795 appeared to be the catalyst of action, the general intercession of God's people preceding an outpouring of the Spirit of God and its attendant conviction of sin. The response of the people to this conviction was varied, from quiet and solemn meetings in the Eastern States to noisy and explosive gatherings in the West and South.

It is a noteworthy circumstance that the awakenings in the academic community of the Atlantic seaboard took place during the second decade of the twenty years of movement. Apart from the Hampden-Sydney revival of 1787, it was not until the new century that the collegiate community responded.

Of course, during the last decade of the eighteenth century, intercession began on campus with a handful of students participating, supported by godly parents in home churches. In college after college, these students took the initiative in beginning Christian fellowships. It would be impossible to divorce the student movement from the awakenings that had commenced in the nearby communities. At Harvard, Bowdoin, Brown, Dartmouth, Middlebury, Williams and Andover, new societies were formed.[1] To resist the ungodly influences which prevailed, they committed themselves to mutual watchfulness, ardent prayers, frequent fellowship, mutual counsel and friendly reproof.[2] In most cases, they were tiny societies. For example, three students at Brown University formed a 'college praying society,' which met weekly in a private room, 'for fear of disturbance from the unpenitent.'[3] About the same time—11th December 1802— three juniors and four sophomores formed themselves into the Harvard Saturday Evening Religious Society. It also was a secret society in its early years.[4]

When the brilliant Timothy Dwight, grandson of Jonathan Edwards, came to the presidency of Yale College in 1795, he invited his students to attack freely the truth of the Scriptures, and he answered them in a series of pungent sermons in chapel. Among his topics were 'The Nature and Danger of Infidel Philosophy,' and 'Is the Bible the Word of God?' Then he proceeded to grapple with the problems of materialism and deism in his direct exposition of theology.[5] Dwight had no difficulty in holding attention.

One of Dwight's main contentions was that the philosophy which opposed Christianity in every succeeding generation had uniformly worn the same character, rested on the same foundations, proceeded from the same disposition, aimed at the same ends, and produced the same means. He claimed that Hume's concessions to adultery and suicide were pale reflections of Greek philosophers who taught the same. He met the prevailing ridicule with quiet argument. He pointed out that infidel philosophy possessed no means of restraining vice or promoting virtue.[6] He lectured brilliantly.

After Timothy Dwight's notable baccalaureate sermon of 1796, in which he exhorted his beloved students to 'embrace Christianity,' the tide began to turn at Yale, and came in full flood in 1802. One third of the student body made profession of faith that year.   Many were to follow suit year after year in season and out of season.

Thus began a movement in American schools of higher learning. There followed revivals of religion in Andover, Princeton, Washington and Amherst and other university colleges, inaugurating half a century of student awakenings. In not one of these eastern college awakenings was there any extravagance reported. Revivals began quietly and continued without fanaticism of any kind; there was undoubtedly an appeal to the hearts of the students, but first their minds and consciences were moved.[7] No one could gainsay a great change of character or a lifetime of service to humanity.

Anti-Evangelical sociologists seem to delight in stressing the emotional extravagances of the Awakenings on the far frontiers of Kentucky and Tennessee, ignoring the fact that the frontiersmen were generally illiterate and that at the same time in the college towns there were occurring deep and thorough religious revivals without any extravagance whatsoever.[8]   To this day, the emotional response of people is affected by temperament and education, by tradition and discipline, by experience and control.

At Hampden-Sydney College, Blair Smith had determined to use all means to prevent physical manifestations of feeling from expressing themselves among the students. There was a marked lack of dubious emotion in every subsequent movement on campus.[9]   Freedom from abnormal excitement became a marked characteristic of the collegiate awakenings.

Full half a century later, Bishop Charles P. McIlvaine of Ohio, an Anglican, in commending the sane and serious 1858 Awakening throughout the United States, compared it with the collegiate revivals of his youth, when, at his alma mater, he witnessed a revival of religion which was 'quiet, unexcited, and entirely free from all devices or means' peculiar to what he considered 'promoted revivals.' [10]

The college awakenings had a significant effect upon the corporate life of the colleges. The colleges appointed as president and professors the most dynamic Christian men available; campus prayer days were held regularly in term; and the college sermon became a regular feature of worship and religious education. By 1815, for example, the day of prayer had become a regular feature at Yale and Williams, Brown and Middlebury.[11] Among the evangelists who became presidents were Francis Wayland, Brown; William Neill, Dickinson; Philip Milledoler, Rutgers; Heman Humphrey, Amherst; Jeremiah Day, Yale; Ashbel Green, Princeton; Moses Waddel, Franklin; Henry Davis, Hamilton; Edward Griffin, Williams; many others became professors.[12]

The evangelistic impact of the days of prayer on campus was noteworthy. Amherst, Dartmouth, Princeton, Williams and Yale, to name a few, reported the conversion to God of a third to a half of their total student bodies, which in those days usually numbered between a hundred and two hundred and fifty. In 1802, Yale reported 75 converts; in 1815, 80. The figure for the 'unpopular war' year of 1812 was only 20. In subsequent years, half of those who entered Amherst 'without piety' professed conversion. In 1803, Dartmouth added 25 names to its roster of believers; in 1815, 60. At Princeton, more than 50 professed conversion in 1815. Of these converts, about fifty percent became ministers of the Gospel to serve the revived seaboard and frontier churches of the various denominations.[13]

A student Christian society was formed at Yale and other colleges were quick to follow suit. The Student Moral Society at Yale discouraged profanity, immorality and intemperance. Soon it comprised between a third and a half of all students.[14]

Following the Awakening at Williams College, several new converts formed a confidential society.[15] At Harvard College, the Saturday Evening Religious Society, formed to combat French infidelity, united in 1821 with a Wednesday Evening Society to become the Society of Christian Brethren. Dartmouth's theological society in 1813 dismissed a member for being intoxicated with liquor. It is noteworthy that these collegiate societies carried on a voluminous correspondence between campuses. As a result, voluntary student Christian societies were formed in rapid succession, more than ninety being established between 1810 and 1850.[16]

It may be asked, if the revivals of religion on campus were so thorough, why was it necessary to seek further awakenings? At Yale in 1802, half the students entered the ministry, and after their departure the number of active Christians dwindled to a dozen or so.[17] Then followed the awakening of 1808, which transformed the student body again. At Bowdoin, in 1811, there was not one who professed religious faith, with quite a few men reckless in conduct and openly immoral in character.[18] There followed another revival of religion which changed the campus.

There were other factors at work in influencing students. At Yale in 1802, of 63 converts received into church, 55 were children of pious parents;[19] again, of 70 converts, 60 were the offspring of church members, a generation later.

Between the two very different movements of evangelical revival, the college awakenings and the frontier revivals, there was much interplay. The college awakenings provided a flock of dedicated scholars for the uncouth western settlements, and converts among the roughest pioneers were encouraged to prepare in eastern schools for their western ministry.[20] As a result, a host of new schools and colleges were founded in the newly settled parts of the country. The awakening also equipped American evangelists who extended its influence for a lifetime. There were examples in almost every denomination.

The collegiate awakenings continued through enrollment after enrollment of college classes. They so perpetuated themselves in a long period of vigorous activity of profound social and religious significance. They were a major force in the founding of colleges, in the work of philanthropy, and in the extension of the Church at home and abroad. College awakenings moved the best and produced the best——without the emotional reactions which tickled the sceptics' fancy.

12

UNDER THE SOUTHERN CROSS, 1790–

The Cape Colony was one of the few European settlements outside Europe and the Americas, with thirty thousand Dutch. The spiritual life of the Hollanders at Table Bay had moved on quietly through the eighteenth century, theirs a religion 'severely unemotional and chiefly a matter of form'[1] which exercised 'but little vital influence over the everyday life of the congregation' meeting in Cape Town.

In the last quarter of the eighteenth century, there were signs all over Protestant Christendom of disquiet with the deadly deism of the period, and this showed itself in Cape Colony also. In 1786, a brilliant young Hollander, Helperus Ritzema van Lier, arrived at Table Bay to become minister of the Groote Kerk.[2] He was as evangelistic as he was precociously scholastic,[3] a teenage Doctor of Philosophy who became an ardent evangelist in his twenties.[4] In the 1790s, Van Lier exercised a very effective ministry in Cape Town, winning many burghers to a vital faith in Jesus Christ, some of whom became pioneer missionaries to the heathen near at hand and far away. Van Lier burned out in seven years, but left an abiding memory of purity and power.[5] Certainly, that he was not 'a voice crying in the wilderness' was made clear by the arrival of Michiel Christiaan Vos,[6] a graduate of the University of Utrecht, who returned home to minister in the parish of Tulbagh, with a response to evangelism.

Converts of Van Lier's preaching sought to reach with the Gospel the Hottentots,[7] Jan Jakob van Zulch working in the Wagonmakers' Valley, while others evangelized the people of mixed blood around Cape Town, as did Mrs. Machteld Smith,[8] a truly remarkable self-appointed missionary who helped extend the work far and wide.[9] These pioneers laid the foundation of missions sustained by the Dutch Reformed Churches of South Africa in the nineteenth century, more particularly extended by later Awakenings. Said Latourette: 'The tide of religious life which was so evidently rising in Europe and the United States was also having its effect in the Dutch churches of South Africa . . .'[10]

Meanwhile events were transpiring in Europe which were to change the face of South Africa. France had emerged as a revolutionary power, and, in view of the threat, the Stadholder of the Netherlands arranged in 1788 with the British to occupy the Cape to prevent its falling into the hands of the French.[11] When French armies overran Holland in the winter of 1794-95, the British occupied the Cape for about eight years, returning it to the Netherlands at the Treaty of Amiens. The second British occupation came in 1806, again as a war measure against France.

These vicissitudes of war had no untoward effect upon the preaching of the Gospel in the Cape Colony, whether among the burghers in Cape Town and its satellite communities or on the widening frontier among the Hottentots and other heathen tribespeople.

Garrisoning the Cape was a strong British force, comprising the 72nd and 83rd Regiments, among whom were a few active Methodists who suffered petty persecution for the faith. For four years, John Kendrick (a soldier-Methodist preacher) had failed to find one serious person among a thousand men of the regiment,[12] a judgment that seemingly ignored the likelihood of believers grown indifferent or lukewarm because of the temptations of army life.

But, late in 1809, an earthquake shook the Cape Peninsula and round about, rocking the settlements for eight days and putting fear into the inhabitants.[13] George Middlemiss, in the 72nd Regiment, found that this godly fear had led to a seriousness about the more important things of life and a thirsting after salvation, followed by an outpouring of Divine grace,[14] and John Kendrick noted the same with 'unspeakable satisfaction' concerning the 83rd Regiment at Saldanha Bay, north of Cape Town:[15]

> The spark of grace began to catch from soul to soul.
> Prayer meetings now commenced among them, and
> such a cry for mercy followed as is most wonderful.
> The room frequently has been so crowded that many
> have been unable to approach the door.

As the Spirit was outpoured, the soldiers sought the Lord with cries and tears, notorious sinners pleading for pardon. Soon there were fifty men in the Methodist Society. The number of English-speaking Evangelicals at the Cape grew into the hundreds, but there came an amicable parting of the ways into Arminian and Calvinist gatherings, the two parties soon taking permanent denominational form.

Between 1769 and 1779, Captain James Cook made his epic voyages through the Pacific Ocean, opening up a new continent for settlement and the islands of the South Seas to western civilization.[16] The intrepid discoverer met his death in Hawaii while the War of the American Revolution was still raging.

Transportation, even for petty crime, had become a not unusual sentence in Great Britain in those days. It became impossible for British authorities to send transportees to the United States and undesirable to land them in British North America, so it was proposed to sentence them to the uncolonized continent, Australia, in the far south.

The first contingents of prisoners left Britain before the outbreak of evangelical revival in the 1790s, hence it was impossible for any of them to have been influenced thereby, and, even had time permitted, it was unlikely that many of the converts or workers in the Awakening would have been included among the transportees.

So Captain Arthur Phillip arrived at Botany Bay in 1787, escorting a company of 717 'convicts' assisted by a couple of hundred marine guards. Some 'convicts' had been transported for petty crime, the law being noted for severity. Phillip found his 'convicts' as well behaved as the folk in the towns from which they came.[17] A second fleet arrived with another contingent. Of the full thousand aboard, a quarter had died and a half were sick or dying.

Christian work on the Australian continent took the form of a home mission rather than a foreign mission. The first chaplain sent out with the unwilling settlers to Botany Bay was Richard Johnson, an ardent evangelical who owed his appointment to the interest of Wilberforce and the Clapham Sect. Six years later, in 1793, Samuel Marsden was appointed assistant to Johnson. He too was an ardent evangelical with not only a burden for evangelism but also for the welfare of both convicts and aborigines.[18]

As the Church of England followed the English settlers, so the Church of Scotland followed the Scots. Methodism entered Australia in a typical and spontaneous fashion. Congregationalists and Baptists made small beginnings in Australia, as did the Lutherans.

There were no settlements made in New Zealand, far to the east, in the last quarter of the eighteenth century and for several decades of the nineteenth. Missionary work began before the end of the Napoleonic Wars, however.

A new element was added to the complex of settlement in Australia before the end of the eighteenth century. In 1798 occurred the rebellion of the United Irishmen, which involved some Presbyterians in the north as well as many Roman Catholics in the south. The Irish exiles took with them a hatred of Britain, and, as many of them were men of education and character, their antipathy to authority made them more dangerous than the convicts from England's industrial slums. It was not until 1820 that permanently settled priests were able to cater to the Roman Catholics, and in the meantime many Irishmen became alienated from the practice of religion.[19]

The general revival of religion which occurred in Great Britain in 1791 had little effect upon the settlers being transported against their will to Australia. It did, however, raise up a number of Christians eager and anxious to share their faith with the spiritually destitute in the overseas 'home mission field.'[20] The first of the Anglican chaplains were thoroughly evangelical, and the Methodists enlisted a couple of teachers to serve in Sydney, where they discovered a number of Methodists from England. The Presbyterians in Sydney erected their own house of worship, but waited for years before any ordained minister came to officiate. In due course, John Dunmore Lang emigrated at his own expense, and made a significant contribution to his spiritual kinsmen, though occasionally provoking opposition by his forthrightness. The Baptists were more tardy in opening up a work in Sydney, as were the Congregationalists, though refugee missionaries from Tahiti tried to gather a congregation and were hindered by their friend, Samuel Marsden, whose tolerant charity did not include lay ministry.

A significant factor in the evangelizing of Australia was the comparative absence of any revival tradition. There is a scarcity of records of any early spiritual awakenings in the settlements. One reason undoubtedly was the antipathy which the 'convicts' in some of the penal settlements felt towards the authorities who had sent them there for often trifling misdemeanors. They resented compulsory religion instituted by the authorities, and when they had served their sentences, they demonstrated their liberty of conscience by not attending church services. It was not until the third general awakening in the 1830s that anything resembling revival was reported from Australia. A pattern of minority enthusiasm, majority hostility or indifference, was set up.

13

ORGANIZING FOR ADVANCE

It has been noted the there were sporadic movements of revival in Great Britain and the United States during the decade preceding the French Revolution, but that a general awakening began in the 1790s. The same pattern is seen in the formation of the evangelical societies founded to advance the work of evangelization, for most of them had their roots in the 1780s, but reached their organizational form between the dates of the Bastille and Waterloo, in Great Britain, but after Waterloo in many other countries.

Latourette, in his consideration of the Great Century and the movements within Christianity through which the expansion of the faith had been chiefly accomplished, first noted the 'revivals' which were particularly effective in the United Kingdom and the United States; second, the organizations in large part growing out of them.[1] The European countries also shared fully in the movement.

It was in Great Britain that the first of these organizations had their beginning.[2] Reasons for prior British leadership included the effects of the Evangelical Revival on the thinking of Christians and the effects of the industrial revolution on the income of the people. With their desire to serve, the people were given the wherewithal to serve, an over-ruling of Providence later seen in other countries and in other centuries.

The rekindling of evangelical revival in Britain during the decade before the outbreak of revolution in France had caused a stirring in the hearts of dedicated Christians, and when the awakening became more general, their ideas were taken up and their burdens shared in a remarkable burst of organizing enthusiasm, all the more remarkable in wartime. In nearly every case, the initiative came from men who had been involved in local evangelical revivals, whether of the staider type within the Church of England, or the more dynamic kind occurring in companies of believers outside. Some of these founding fathers have been remembered for their works, the source of their dynamic forgotten.

To meet the demands of a population increasing in wealth and literacy, whose appetite for the printed Word was being whetted by the Awakening, spontaneous efforts were made. George Burder, a Congregationalist minister at Coventry, who had been influenced by George Whitefield and William Romaine, continued active as a pastoral evangelist. In 1799, he urged the formation of the Religious Tract Society to promote the diffusion of evangelical literature.[3] It was supported by both Church of England and Free Church folk, and its example was followed elsewhere, the foundation of the American Tract Society taking place a quarter of a century later, its avowed objective the providing of suitable Christian literature to the religiously destitute.[4]

The awakenings in Wales in the late 1780s had produced a hunger for the reading of Scripture among the common people. In 1787, an appeal was made from Wales for more Bibles in the Cymric tongue. The extraordinary revivals of 1791 onward catapulted Thomas Charles of Bala to the place of leadership in spiritual affairs in the principality. Thomas Charles continued active in these startling movements. When little Mary Jones tramped fifty miles over the Welsh hills with her six years' savings, only to find that the last copy of the Welsh Scriptures had been sold, she returned in tears to her home. Thomas Charles of Bala took up the matter with the Society for Promoting Christian Knowledge and, failing to persuade them, made a suggestion to the Religious Tract Society that a Bible Society be formed.[5] He returned to his work in the Awakening. The outcome was the foundation of the British and Foreign Bible Society in 1804.[6] It was interdenominational in character, dedicated to the dissemination of the Scriptures without note or comment, at home or abroad. Its first officers largely were members of the 'Clapham Sect,' another expression of the awakening of Napoleonic times. It is very clear that this history-making event resulted from the Awakening of 1791 onward in Britain. After the Battle of Waterloo, the American Bible Society was formed to combine the efforts of several state-wide associations begun as a result of the American Awakening, and following the example in Britain. Bible Societies were formed in other European countries, generally after the coming of peace.[7]

The Bible became the chief text-book of the Sunday School movement in Great Britain and the United States and elsewhere in the Protestant countries.

During the eighteenth century, many isolated attempts were made to evangelize children. Griffith Jones in Wales had concentrated upon teaching the young as well as adults to read. Hannah More, a godly Anglican woman committed to supporting the Establishment, circulated cheap tracts, and became concerned about the illiteracy of the rural folk in the Mendip Hills. While sharing a contemporary Anglican notion of full education for only the governing elite, Hannah More set out to provide elementary education for children in the rural countryside.[8] As her concern arose from her evangelical convictions, she too was interested in the Bible as a text-book. Just before the outbreak of the Revolution in France, she settled down in a country home near Bristol, and became wholly absorbed in the work of teaching the children. She was an intimate friend of Wilberforce and the Clapham Sect of Evangelical reformers encouraged her.

Joseph Lancaster, an evangelical Quaker, was likewise concerned about the hordes of illiterate and lawless children roaming the streets of London.[9] He devised a method of teaching a class of boys, then using them to teach a younger set while he taught them a second year, thus developing a school based upon the monitorial principle. In 1805, George III learned of the remarkable experiment whereby a single teacher kept order among hundreds of boys. The King asked how it could be done. 'By the same principle,' replied the Quaker, 'that thy Majesty's Army is kept in order!' So impressed was the King that he lent his support, and these monitorial schools fast multiplied. The Royal Lancasterian Society was formally constituted in 1810, becoming in 1815 the British and Foreign School Society. This monitorial school was a necessary development on the way to the public school system. It had its birth in the Revival.

In 1780, a social reformer named Robert Raikes stood among the unruly children of Gloucester's working class and asked himself: 'Can anything be done?' A Voice answered: 'Try.' And he tried.[10] He gathered the illiterate children on Sundays and taught them to read, using the Bible as the inevitable text-book. In 1803, the interdenominational Sunday School Union was formed, as much a product of evangelical revival as Raikes himself. One of the early promoters in London professed a desire to teach everyone in the world to read the Bible. Before the end of the second decade of the new century, the Sunday School movement in England and Wales had a half a million scholars enrolled.

It was in 1784 that John Sutcliffe called upon the Baptist Association of Northampton and Leicester Counties to set aside the first Monday of each month to pray for a general outpouring of the Holy Spirit and a spread of religion. John Sutcliffe had been challenged indirectly by Jonathan Edwards whose 'humble attempt to promote explicit agreement and visible union of God's people in extraordinary prayer for the revival of religion' included the advancement of Christ's Kingdom on earth pursuant to Scripture promises and the prophecies concerning the last time.[11]

Jonathan Edwards's writings helped Sutcliffe and others of Calvinistic conviction to reconcile their doctrine of Divine sovereignty with their notion of human responsibility. It is noteworthy that Sutcliffe served as pastor to William Carey and was an affectionate colleague of Andrew Fuller, the one becoming a pioneer of missions abroad and the other an advocate of missions at home.

Divine sovereignty and human responsibility were fused in the fire of the revival prayer meetings. It was natural that British intercessors were most concerned about the need of revival in Britain, but, when their prayers were happily answered, it was easy to direct the intercession into missionary enterprise, aimed at winning the whole wide world. Dr. R. Pierce Beaver, writing for an ecumenical readership, recognized the dynamic of prayer, affirming that 'the Concert of Prayer undoubtedly helped produce a climate favorable to the use of the missionary societies in the last decade of the eighteenth century.'[12] Another high authority, Dr. Ernest A. Payne, declared:[13]

> ... It was probably these prayer meetings, as much as any other single influence, which prepared the little group of ministers to venture on the formation of a missionary society.

The noted Anglican mission director, Dr. Eugene Stock, looking back after a century's success, picked the year 1786 as the 'wonderful year' in the development of missionary passion.[14] In that year, William Wilberforce resolved to live for God's glory and for the good of his fellow-men. It was in 1786 that William Carey first suggested to the group of Baptist ministers at Northampton that they must consider their responsibility to the heathen.[15] It was in 1786 that Dr. Thomas Coke initiated a Methodist mission to the people of the West Indies.[16] Many were the intercessors burdened for revival at home and missions abroad that year.

The answer to these prayers did not come until the last decade of the century. On 30th May 1792, William Carey at Nottingham preached a missionary sermon to assembled Baptist associates, urging them to 'expect great things from God: attempt great things for God.' Within six months, at a specially convened meeting of the association, what was soon to be called the Baptist Missionary Society was formed and Carey sailed for India in 1793.[17]

The founding of the Baptist Missionary Society is usually regarded as the inception of modern Protestant missionary enterprise. There had been several efforts to evangelize the non-Christian world before 1792, but they were limited in scope or in objective. The Northamptonshire shoemaker appears in retrospect to have been the first Anglo-Saxon of evangelical faith in either Britain or America to propose that Christians undertake to carry the Gospel to the world's unevangelized millions. A real enthusiast for geography and linguistics, he cobbled shoes, taught school, and preached the Good News.[18] Carey not only promoted but pioneered in missions; and he urged not only Baptists, but all Christians to share in the evangelization of every creature.[19]

Thomas Haweis, an Anglican Evangelical who had served the Countess of Huntington as a chaplain and who had been rebuked for so doing by an Anglican court, found himself superintending ministry in the revival years following 1791, when the Countess died. Still in Anglican orders, Haweis proposed the formation of the London Missionary Society, as an interdenominational organization, in 1795.[20] In 1796, the missionary ship 'Duff' sailed for the South Seas and so began the ministry of this remarkable society, which drew its support at first from Anglican and Free Church people revived in the Awakening, but later more and more from the churches of British Congregationalism.

In 1795, the Eclectic Society of Evangelical clergymen sponsored by Charles Simeon discussed a suggestion that a mission to the non-Christian world be initiated by members of the Church of England. From Simeon's prompting came the Church Missionary Society, founded in 1799 as a society for missions to Africa and the East. Strange to relate, the first missionaries of the Church Missionary Society were Germans trained at a missionary school in Berlin. The sponsoring Eclectic Society, of course, was comprised of ordained leaders of the Awakening among Anglicans in the revival times following 1791.[21]

In the year following the French Revolution, the British Methodist Conference set up a committee of management for the West Indian venture, and in successive steps finally committed its resources to the formation of the Wesleyan Methodist Missionary Society in 1817-18.[22]

In 1796, the Scottish Missionary Society and the Glasgow Missionary Society were formed by the leaders of the 1791 Awakening in the Lowlands of Scotland; but that year the General Assembly of the Church of Scotland rejected a proposal to begin a missionary enterprise. The opposition was spearheaded by the anti-Evangelicals, just as support was forthcoming from leading Evangelicals.[23] It was not until 1824 that General Assembly reversed its decision and sent missionaries out to India—including Alexander Duff, nurtured in the afterglow of the Scottish Revival.

Prior to the American Revolution, missionary-minded British Christians had sent support to missionaries on the American frontier engaged in evangelizing the Indians. It was natural that this interest should flag, and that loyal subjects of the King would be only too ready to turn over that responsibility to his former American subjects so very determined to be independent.

With the loss of the American Colonies, the fortunes of war and the blessings of naval supremacy made possible the building of a Second Empire, retaining Canada in North America but opening up India in Asia and Cape Colony in Africa. To these new fields, the main stream of pioneers made their way, but among the first enterprises was the mission to the South Seas, a no-man's-land of islands in the far Pacific. William Carey himself had thought of going to Tahiti, for he was an avid reader of Captain Cook's travels. There was no lack of opportunity for British folk.

At the end of the Revolution, American missionary work was in a sorry state. Christian Indians, whose missionaries had largely supported the Mother Country, found their tepee villages overrun by American forces, their congregations scattered, with some in flight to Canada.[24] The Scottish S.P.C.K. showed some interest in reviving their work, and the Congregational Establishment in New England decided to revive theirs.[25] In 1787, a Society for Propagating the Gospel among Indians and Others in North America was founded. Thanks to the revival in Virginia in 1787, the Presbyterians there recovered a missionary vision, and there was a measure of interest among the Reformed.[26]

The early nineteenth century awakening had immediate effects upon the Negro inhabitants of the United States. In the North, Negro Baptist churches sprang up in Boston, New York, Philadelphia and other big cities. In 1800, the black members of a New York Methodist Episcopal Church withdrew quite amicably and formed Zion Church, which in 1821 took the lead in founding the African Methodist Episcopal Church, Zion.[27] Several years earlier, the Bethel Methodist Episcopal Church in Philadelphia, founded about 1792, had initiated the formation of the African Methodist Episcopal Church, with support from Bishop Asbury.[28] The two Negro denominations maintained their separate identity. In the South, Negro Baptists and Methodists continued to worship largely in white congregations, occupying humbler space.

Before long, the greatest work in evangelizing the Negro population was being done by black Christians themselves, but often with white encouragement. White Christians gave freely to Negro educational enterprises.[29] The standard of education among black ministers was inevitably low, and their churches were handicapped by the evil effects of slave relationships which often broke up families, leading to a laxity in marriage which persisted till modern times.[30]

*   *   *   *

Heman Humphrey, president of historic Amherst College, reviewing the Second Great Awakening during the progress of the Fourth, delivered himself of an opinion which was formed close to the events themselves:[31]

> The organization of these institutions ... the Religious Tract Society ... the British and Foreign Bible Society, the Baptist Missionary Society, the London Missionary Society, the Church Missionary Society, and kindred evangelical movements in the mother country, far spreading the gospel ... all are fruits of this blessed work of the Spirit graciously poured out about 1792, in a period of darkness when the hearts of Christians were failing them for fear.

Heman Humphrey lived through the Second Awakening, a young Christian; he became a leader in the Third, first in a Massachusetts pastorate, and then in successive revivals, generation after generation, in a collegiate community. His testimony confirmed what so few folk have realised that the great organizations of mission at home and abroad arose in the Second Great Awakening worldwide, not merely from a productive aftermath of the First Great Awakening.

The American Awakening of 1791 onwards had seemingly reached a climax in the New England and Middle Atlantic States within seven years, in the West and South within ten. Almost immediately, a missionary passion began to develop. In 1802, John M. Mason, Reformed divine, declared:[32]

> Let us not overlook as an unimportant matter the very existence of that missionary spirit... which has already awakened Christians... and bids fair to produce in due season a general movement of the Church upon earth.

The Concert of Prayer begun in 1795 had already moved believers to surrender to God for an outpouring of the Holy Spirit upon the whole country. As in Great Britain, it was not difficult to direct the prayers of intercessors towards missionary objectives. It was still a major problem to find new channels for the streams of intercession and sacrifical giving. American Baptists had begun to support the Carey project in India, but they and other Christians were looking for American-based agencies of enterprise.

In the autumn of 1796, a public meeting was held in New York to discuss the news of the foundation and progress of the interdenominational London Missionary Society, and, as a result, the New York Missionary Society was formed on similar interdenominational lines.[33] A missionary was sent to the Chickasaws of Georgia and another to the Tuscaroras in western New York State.[34] John Blair Smith, a revivalist, formerly president of Hampden-Sydney College, had become president of Union College in Schenectady, and in 1797 helped form a missionary society with Reformed backing, tackling the needs of the Oneidas.[35] In 1798, a missionary society was formed in Pennsylvania, and another in Connecticut.[36] In 1799, a society was formed in Massachusetts.[37] Each year brought forth new enterprises, dedicated in the main to a trans-cultural missionary evangelism in North America.

Meanwhile, associations of Baptist churches were taking on responsibilities for Indian missions as well as frontier evangelism, and other denominations were undertaking the same kind of work in their respective ways. Haweis of the London Missionary Society was quoted by his Connecticut Evangelical correspondents as declaring with his confreres that 'It revives our inmost souls to see the spreading of the sacred flame in America,' adding 'I trust that the sound will spread... till it shall reach... from the east to the west.' To Haweis,[38] Indian evangelism was foreign missionary work. It was still domestic to the Americans.

The catalyst needed to convert such apostolic energy from home to foreign missions was supplied by the Awakening also, arising from the widespread revival of student Christianity, more particularly prayer meetings at Williams College.

One summer afternoon in 1806, five students at Williams College were driven from a maple grove where they were accustomed to meet for prayer.[39] They sheltered from the thunderstorm under a haystack, and there prayed about the need of reaching the unevangelized heathen for Christ.

The thunderstorm was of short duration, for the sun soon broke through the clouds as the light of a clear purpose broke upon their souls. Samuel J. Mills, impressed in the revival in Connecticut but fully committed at Williams College, gave the decisive word: 'We can do it, if we will !'

The students organized a society, youthful in spirit and habit, for they met in secret and in cipher recorded their minutes. They found no less than a score of students who sincerely shared their burden.

One among them, Adoniram Judson, was prepared to go out under the auspices of the London Missionary Society, but his friend Mills discouraged him, saying that it was not right that British friends should support their own mission and American volunteers also. In 1810, while completing final studies at Andover Theological Seminary, Mills and his friends went to the home of an interested professor to meet with a number of ministers of their denomination, the state establishment in Massachusetts.

The counsel of their senior brethren was divided. Some thought the proposition a premature one; others felt that it smacked of infatuation; others that it would be too expensive; but after one minister observed that they had better not try to hinder God, a majority supported their younger brethren. Soon the American Board of Commissioners for Foreign Missions was formed; hence out of the Haystack Compact there came the initiation of overseas missionary enterprise, and American foreign missions began their enlistment of the best-educated class in society in the United States.[40]

In 1812, a party of eight A. B. C. F. M. volunteers sailed for India. Before the ship reached Indian ports, war had been declared between the United Kingdom and the United States, and the officials of the East India Company, already prejudiced against British missionaries, were doubly hostile to the American project of evangelizing British subjects, of Hindu faith.

On the voyage to India, Judson and his bride, knowing that they would encounter William Carey, began to re-study the subject of believers' baptism. The Judsons and Luther Rice decided to embrace the Baptist viewpoint, and Rice returned to ask support of American Baptists, who in 1814 founded a general missionary convention of the denomination, later the American Baptist Foreign Mission Society. Forced out of India by an antagonistic British East India Company, the Judsons went on to Burma and wrought there a mighty work for God.[41]

In 1819, the Methodist Episcopal Church of the United States of America formed its missionary society.[42] The overseas missionary project of the Protestant Episcopal Church was begun two years later.[43] Presbyterians, divided by schism, took longer to establish an official missionary society, their Board of Foreign Missions being created in 1837.[44] In that same year, the missionary society of the Evangelical Lutheran Church in the United States took form and commenced operations.[45]

When, at the height of the 1798 Revival in the Eastern States, the New York Missionary Society was formed by the ministers of four denominations, the work was launched by redirecting the Concert of Prayer into missionary prayer sessions every second Wednesday of the month at candlelight, to entreat the outpouring of the Spirit with the proclamation of the Gospel to all nations.[46]

War was raging in January 1815 when the intercessors of the Concert of Prayer were asked to redouble their zeal and pray for a return of peace, a reformation of morals, and a general revival of religion. It was suggested that a return to the first Monday of every month would re-align the prayers of believers throughout Europe, America and the mission stations on other continents and islands. The response was gratifying, a large number of churches fully supporting the union of prayer.[47]

The Concert of Prayer for revival in the 1780s in Great Britain and in the 1790s in United States, and the renewed Concert of Prayer in both countries in 1815 and in several European realms besides, was clearly demonstrated to be the prime factor in motivating and equipping Christians for service in a worldwide movement which totally eclipsed the military might of the nations at the Battle of Waterloo. A century of comparative peace among nations made the great century of pioneer evangelization possible.

14

REVIVAL RENEWED IN BRITAIN, 1815–

The war weary people of many a nation heaved a sigh of relief when Napoleon was exiled to Elba in 1814. Dismay was great when he made his escape and used one hundred days to prepare for a decisive battle. The outcome of the campaign at Waterloo was most uncertain.

In 1815, therefore, the Concert of Prayer was urging its intercessors to pray for a return of peace, a reformation of morals, and a general revival of religion.[1] The Union of Prayer was harnessed immediately to these objectives.

In the historic town of Salisbury, an outpouring of the Spirit began on 16th April 1815, two months before the Battle of Waterloo. A special prayer meeting for penitents followed the regular Methodist preaching. All the classes met for protracted prayer on Monday, the preaching on Tuesday being followed by prayer—'a night of salvation for many.' On Wednesday, there was deep distress in the prayer meeting; on Thursday, great numbers on their knees; and on Friday, the movement was noised abroad in town.[2]

Sunday 23rd April proved to be a 'glorious day,' and all week through the protracted prayer meetings continued in Salisbury. On Sunday 30th, a thousand people were crowded into the chapel, and prayer meetings continued all week. A Church of England clergyman present observed: 'This is the work of God, I see, and very plainly it is.' Attendance kept increasing in May, coming to a climax at Whitsuntide. The movement overflowed to nearby villages, the work at Wilton being 'astonishing,' at Winterbourne 'extraordinary,' and at Amesbury 'singular.'[3]

All this happened during the anxious days before Waterloo, but observers were amazed that the revival went on for a whole year. On 15th April 1816, which was Monday, more than a thousand people assembled at 5 p.m. to hear the converts testify, and remained for preaching and prayer until midnight.[4] Not far away, in Shaftesbury, an awakening in town crowded the prayer meetings till midnight, 1 a.m., or two in the mornings.[5] Revivals were still occurring.

Meanwhile, the Primitive Methodists were gaining much ground. They had become reconciled to the fact that the Wesleyan Methodist leaders disapproved of their open-air preaching, though much in the style of Wesley three quarters of a century before. Hugh Bourne remembered that Wesley had approved the use of women preachers also, so he gave encouragement to Sarah Kirkland to preach in the Primitive circuits. This she did with unusual acceptance.

On Whit Sunday, 1816, Sarah Kirkland shared the leadership of a camp-meeting in Nottingham Forest, attended by fully twelve thousand people.[6] This was the beginning of a widespread awakening in the North Midlands, which vastly increased the Primitive following. In 1820, the first of the connexional Primitive Methodist Conferences was held in Hull, drawing representatives from 7,842 members. Within a year, these zealots had added 8,552 new members to make a total of 16,394; in 1822, the total was 25,218, another increase of 8,824 having been reported.[7] So the Primitive Methodists were thriving on the continuing revival.

Much the same was true of the Bible Christians, another offshoot of Methodism which appeared in 1815 in Devonshire. Its founder was William O'Bryan, or Bryant, who claimed to present a more evangelistic Methodism than that of regular Wesleyans. The movement possessed a great vitality. It spread to other parts of England, but was strongest in the Cornish districts. After O'Bryan's departure for the United States, its leaders included James Thorne and F. W. Bourne, but the best known 'character' produced by Bible Christians was Billy Bray, often called 'the apostle of joy.'[8]

In 1821, revivals were reported in Kent and Lancashire, and there were awakenings in the industrial cities, such as Leeds and Liverpool.[9] In Banbury, the prayer meetings were overcrowded; in Liverpool, the meetings were packed out, without noisy demonstrations, but with between thirty and fifty converts weekly. In Sunderland, in the county of Durham, there occurred an unusual measure of revival, and one chapel welcomed a hundred additional members. Every part of the circuit of Maidstone in Kent was moved, and 227 converts were added. In Derby, 920 believers became 1113 in a single church. A visitation of the Holy Spirit began in rural Tenterden. The midlands towns of Newcastle-under-Lyme and Burslem were moved. There was a movement in the cathedral city of Canterbury, another in Durham—from all sorts of places came intelligence of spiritual renewal.[10]

The Wesleyan Methodists, despite the competition of the seceding groups that claimed to out-Wesley the Wesleyans, were growing steadily in the years following Waterloo; the 181,709 added ten thousand by 1816, between five and six per cent, but until 1819, the increase was only one per cent. In 1820, the first setback in more than half a century was noted in the loss of 4688, which called for a fast-day for special humiliation and prayer for the revival of the work of God.[11] This was followed by the revival of 1821, after which the Wesleyans gained nine thousand and passed the 200,000 mark, gaining eleven thousand the following year and reaching a quarter of a million by the third decade of the century.[12] The loss to Wesleyan Methodism in 1820 was probably a gain for other Methodist organizations, for the Primitive Methodists, the Methodist New Connexion, and the Bible Christians were all growing at the time. It was in 1820 that the Rev. Jabez Bunting was first elected as President of the Wesleyan Methodist Conference, remaining the dominant figure in the denomination until 1858.[13] Jabez Bunting had begun his ministry in revival prayer meetings but later parted company with the more radical preachers.[14]

The spirit of revival was gripping the denominations in general through the evangelical societies. In 1823, the various societies which ecumenically allied the Churches resolved upon another union of prayer for an outpouring of the Holy Spirit.[15] In several large cities and towns, the Evangelical clergy and Free Church ministers conducted courses of lectures in rotation upon such subjects as the Deity of the Holy Spirit, His Personality and His Offices. Revivals were reported in various places.

Reports of local revivals became so commonplace that they were no longer reported as extraordinary events but as 'Prosperity of the Work' at the place reporting. Official Methodist historians wrote of 'Those remarkable seasons of religious prosperity usually termed Revivals.'[16] They conceded the possibility of occasional impropriety, either in the rashness of preachers or the excitement of penitents. They deplored the lack of care provided for the converts, leading to their lapsing into the world again. But they insisted that these strange visitations brought boundless benefits to the churches, and presented them with faithful leaders. The recurrence of revivals in all denominations struck a blow against sectarianism, whether established or nonconformist. They prompted much united action.

Meanwhile, noteworthy changes had been occurring in the Congregational denomination as a result of the Awakening. Doctrinal exactitude was beginning to give way to evangelism. So many converts thronged the churches that the demand for ministers exceeded the available supply. Congregational churches supported the London Missionary Society in its evangelistic outreach overseas, the Home Mission Society in its evangelistic outreach in the towns and the villages of England.[17] John Angell James, converted in the Awakening, an evangelist, was the leading figure in Congregationalism.

The Awakening continued to influence the Baptists in the same way.[18] Although Andrew Fuller died in the year 1815, other Baptist preachers were enabled to reach the people, five thousand gathering at Dewsbury that year to witness the open-air baptism of converts. By 1830, the Baptists had doubled the number of their churches and members at the opening of the century. Robert Hall attracted many of the intelligentsia by his educated eloquence.[19]

By 1830, a majority of Presbyterians in England had become Unitarian, but a number of Presbyterian congregations adhered to orthodoxy, while others became Congregational, affiliating with the Union formed in 1831.

By 1815, Charles Simeon was at the height of his influence at Cambridge and in the Evangelical party of the Church of England.[20] In 1815 also, Henry Ryder was made Bishop of Gloucester, the first Evangelical so elevated, though against the wishes of the Archbishop of Canterbury.[21] The Eclectic Society of Evangelical clergy and the Evangelical Anglican laity of the Clapham Sect continued to expand their influence far beyond their numbers. Charles Richard Sumner became Bishop of Winchester in 1827, and his older brother John became Bishop of Chester in 1828, both ardent Evangelicals. How can growth within the Church of England be measured? In a state church, the number baptized in infancy is of little validity, and the number confirmed at puberty likewise; and the evangelical conversion of those baptized and confirmed is difficult to ascertain from statistics. In the wake of the defeat of Napoleon at Waterloo, the Church of England began to build new churches to accommodate increased attendance. Commended from the Throne and financed by Parliament, five hundred churches were built by 1830; and thrice that number in the 1840s.[22] The Church Building Society was very largely a product of the Evangelical movement, though owing much to Joshua Watson, of higher churchmanship.[23]

There was a renewal of the spirit of revival in Wales following Waterloo. Local movements were reported here and there, but the most significant one was the awakening at Beddgelert in 1817.[24] In 1815, spiritual life was at a low ebb in Carnarvonshire, indifference among the older Christians, worldliness among the younger, and indiscipline among the children, prayer wanting. It was the Sunday School director who begged both old and young to spend their leisure time on Sundays in prayer for revival. Strong conviction soon was felt throughout the area in Carnarvonshire. A notable feature of the awakening that followed was the preaching.

The Beddgelert revival spread throughout North Wales and into the South.[25] An unusual phenomenon reported was a hearing by some of the sound of songs of praise in the air, as if the massed choirs of heaven were overheard. Those who heard it were rooted to the spot. The impact of the general awakening was felt in all the Free Churches and societies, the Baptists gaining eight thousand, Calvinistic Methodists, Wesleyans, and Congregationalists in numbers proportionate to their rolls.

In Denbighshire, an intense revival broke out at a prayer meeting at Bontuchel held in connection with the Concert of Prayer. The year was 1821, and the occasion was the fervent singing of a moving Welsh hymn.[26] 'Moliannu' or praising expressed the ecstasy of many hearts until the congregation was 'lost in wonder, love and praise.' The church was fully revived, and the community was so convicted that the most hardened sinners were soundly converted.

In 1822, a powerful revival swept the island of Anglesey, commencing with the ministry of Moses Jones, who was substituting for an orator from Pwllheli. Moses Jones then spoke in the demonstration of the Spirit with such power that the great congregation was overcome. The whole island felt the impact of the movement.[27]

These awakenings in Wales were both rural and urban in setting. In the country places, they touched the people of the agricultural villages, and in the towns, they stirred the miners as well as the tradespeople. As a result, the lower working classes in Wales were more deeply moved than in England. The chapel became the social focus of both town and village. The revivals produced more than their share of hymn-writers, and singing became a preoccupation of the Welsh, to the benefit of the whole Christian world. Wales became known as 'a land of revivals.'

The year of Waterloo, 1815, was also a turning point in the spiritual history of Scotland. That year, Dr. Thomas Chalmers became minister of the Tron, one of the leading churches of Glasgow. A few years earlier, at the age of thirty, Chalmers had come into a deep evangelical experience. He soon found himself at the head of the growing Evangelical party in the Church of Scotland, still a minority but a challenging one. The Evangelicals in Scotland were busily engaged in maintaining Sunday Schools, preaching against intemperance, protesting the exploitation of the poor, promoting popular education, circulating literature, besides raising opposition against the whole system of lay patronage. Chalmers persuaded the Church to create a new parish with ten thousand of Glasgow's poorest folk, whom he divided into twenty-five sectors of four hundred, served by an elder, a deacon and Sunday School teachers. The experiment soon gained success, for drunkenness and poverty were reduced and education and morals improved. Chalmers preached to huge congregations.[28]

Meanwhile, the Haldanes were exercising a powerful ministry in Edinburgh, but outside the Church of Scotland. James Alexander Haldane, pastor of the Tabernacle, was preaching here and there; his brother, Robert, after a very significant visit to Geneva and French-speaking Protestant districts of Switzerland and France, engaged in the same kind of ministry.[29] Outstanding speakers from south of the border still visited Edinburgh. Also in Edinburgh was the doughty Evangelical, Dr. Andrew Thomson, who shared with Chalmers the leadership of the Evangelicals in the Church of Scotland. His was a pastoral evangelism.[30]

In the north was John MacDonald of Ferintosh, a Gaelic-speaking evangelist of extraordinary power.[31] His influence was felt all over the Highlands. The Rev. Robert Findlater began to attract great congregations to Ardeonaig and Lawers in Perthshire, and invited MacDonald to share in the work in the autumn of 1816.[32] More than four thousand gathered in the open-air. The congregation 'seemed to bend as one man,' and many were the conversions recorded. Nearby was Glenlyon, and here the Rev. James Kennedy, one of the Congregationalist evangelists, reaped a harvest. Day after day, night after night, crowds assembled in barns or in the woods, until entire families professed conversion. The work went on into the winter snows. Scarcely a family was left untouched by the Spirit.[33]

> The moral influence of this revival was manifest to all,
> especially in regard to the Sabbath, in the relish for
> and attendance on the means of grace, both public and
> private, in the perusal of the Scriptures, and in a strong
> attachment to each other. The low and debasing sins
> of drunkenness, rioting, especially at fairs and other
> public meetings, swearing, and irreligious and profane
> talking, were not for a considerable time so much as
> seen or 'named among them.'

It is noteworthy that most of these revivals developed in spite of determined opposition on the part of the Established ministers, generally of the Moderate party. The effect of the revivals was to increase the number of candidates for the ministry, Evangelicals who soon replaced the Moderates and who in turn raised up other Evangelicals, all cooperating to multiply Evangelical parishes in the Church of Scotland.

As in the Central Highlands, so also in the Islands to the west. There were local revivals in the great island of Skye at the time of Waterloo, raising up workers for the Gaelic-speaking churches. One such was John McLeod, from the parish of Kilmuir, who found employment with the Gaelic School Society.[34] He removed to Uig in Lewis, in the Outer Hebrides, and there found 'thick darkness.' The minister was anti-Evangelical, so much so that, when his handyman's son learned to read the Bible to needy fellow-parishioners, the whole family was threatened with eviction. John McLeod began to preach as well as teach and, when complaints were made, he chose to be dismissed rather than give up preaching.

In 1824, the Rev. Alexander McLeod, settling in the parish, instituted prayer meetings, but so little acquainted were his people with intercession, that an elder prayed earnestly that a ship might be wrecked on their shores. Only nine of many hundreds came to communion. The new minister instituted day schools and Sunday Schools, and preached to more and more people. In 1826, MacDonald of Ferintosh preached to seven thousand.[35] In 1828, the whole island was moved by a powerful awakening, as many as nine thousand coming to communion. Among the converts, who ranged from children to elderly, were many future ministers, evangelists, and teachers. This awakening touched other parishes in Lewis and Harris. Sometimes the work was initiated by laymen, sometimes by newly-arrived Evangelical ministers, and often the climactic outbreak occurred during the visit of the 'Apostle of the North,' John MacDonald.

In the northern Highlands, the people were more or less accustomed to hearing the message of salvation, thanks to a succession of worthy parish ministers in various places. In the counties of Moray, Nairn, Inverness and Ross, nearly all the revival movements of the period were associated with the preaching of Dr. John MacDonald of Ferintosh. His own elders had suggested a postponement of his first communion service on account of the death of his wife the week before; but MacDonald insisted, preaching with great power and urging acceptance of Jesus with the words 'Wilt thou go with this man?' with such extraordinary zeal that a motherly woman in the congregation stood up and cried out again and again 'I will!' The great congregation broke down, weeping and praying drowning out the preacher's voice.[36]

A cholera outbreak had struck terror into the hearts of many in Inverness, in 1832, when MacDonald preached on 'Having received from the Father the promise of the Holy Ghost, He hath shed forth this which you now see and hear.' He described in quick sentences the work he had witnessed in eastern Ross, calmly until the end of his discourse when his words seemed to burst into flame, beginning a notable awakening in the capital of the Highlands.[37]

What was happening in Scotland? Moderatism, with its deadening influence, was entrenched in the Kingdom, so much so that its leaders appealed over the heads of ministers and congregations to the royal courts to set aside the choice of ministers in the Presbyterian fashion. The awakenings in the Highlands and Lowlands were building up a mighty pool of evangelical power behind the dam of opposition. Yet one more general awakening would change the face of Scotland.

Latourette has cited the importance of Scotland above that of Ireland and Wales together, above that of Sweden or Denmark or Holland, pointing out that Scottish influence on the world through immigration, missions and theology far exceeded the influence of the other countries of similar size. In accounting for Scottish vitality, Latourette observed that

> The tide of awakenings which had begun to rise before
> 1815 and was countering the torpor of the eighteenth
> century now came to the flood. Revivals swept across
> the country . . .[38]

Meanwhile, the opposition of the Moderates intensified, but it was not a spiritual opposition, appealing rather to the secular power, and exercising political force within the councils of the Church. Their years were numbered.

The defeat of Napoleon in 1815, with its prospect of a lasting peace, brought about a reorientation of political direction in Ireland and a resurgence of evangelical action, benefitting Anglicans, Presbyterians, and Methodists.

Both the Irish Society and the Scripture Readers' Society were founded in 1818 with the express object of teaching the Gaelic-speaking peasantry to read the Bible. Their success and that of the Bible Society aroused the resentment of the Roman clergy. Considerable numbers left the Irish Roman Catholic Church. In Carrick-on-Shannon, Carlow, Cork, Downpatrick, Kilkenny, New Ross, Waterford, and other towns, great Biblical debates were organized, ending in near riots, hence dubbed 'spiritual cockfights' by some.[39]

Conversions from Rome to the Established Church of Ireland became so numerous that the Archbishop of Dublin, William Magee, affirmed that 'In truth, with respect to Ireland, the Reformation may, strictly speaking, be said only now to have begun.' His main opponent, the Roman Catholic Bishop of Kildare, seriously proposed a union of the Irish Roman Catholic Church and the Established Church of Ireland, while the Pope was powerless and conciliatory. While Dr. Magee was Bishop of Raphoe from 1819 to 1822 and Archbishop of Dublin from 1822 to 1831, he encouraged his clergy to become active evangelists.[40]

Meanwhile, the Methodists were still the sponsors of the most evangelistic work in Ireland, not only evangelism but a couple of intensive revivals being reported annually.[41] The Primitive Methodists provided some competition in zeal.

In the 1820s, a decisive controversy erupted between the orthodox Presbyterians and the non-subscribing minority of Arians. The Unitarians of England sent over a propagandist speaker named Smithurst, who visited among other places the town of Killyleagh, where Henry Cooke was minister. Cooke not only debated Smithurst in Killyleagh but followed him everywhere to challenge his arguments.[42] In the Synod, of two hundred ministers, a sixth were Arian. Montgomery and Cooke became the champions of Arianism and Orthodoxy and, when the issue was settled, the non-subscribing Arian minority seceded. From 1830 onward, the Synod of Ulster developed in evangelical conviction an evangelistic message. A union of synods was achieved in 1840, uniting two-thirds of a million people in four hundred congregations, the binding force loyalty to the Westminster Confession. The revival of Evangelicalism had succeeded in Ulster.

The evangelical ecumenism of the nineteenth century produced an interesting development in its second quarter. Dr. Edward Cronin, a Roman Catholic dentist, professed an evangelical conversion in Dublin and received a warm welcome from various Protestant bodies in that city. He was greatly disturbed when told that he must make a choice among them, something he was reluctant to do.[43]

Cronin found a number of like-minded young believers in Dublin — Bellett, Darby, Hutchinson, Parnell (afterwards Lord Congleton), Stokes and Wilson.   His little group had begun 'breaking of bread' on Sundays at a time that did not conflict with the regular worship of the Protestant churches. The meetings begun in 1825 grew in numbers and influence as thoughtful men, dissatisfied with denominationalism, joined the company.   By far, the most brilliant accession was John Nelson Darby, an Anglican curate, whose voice became dominant in the movement.[44]

George Müller was born in Prussia in 1805, and twenty years later was brought into a vital experience at Halle. In England, he came in contact with the Christian Brethren, miscalled the Plymouth Brethren. He married the sister of Anthony Norris Groves, a devoted Brethren missionary. Müller became justly famous in connection with Bristol in which he established the remarkable Orphans' Homes and where he had oversight of a Brethren Assembly.[45] There he came into sharp conflict with Darby.

Darby had (rather unfairly) excommunicated an assembly of Brethren in Plymouth because of the alleged heresy of its leader, B. W. Newton.   Brethren from this excommunicated assembly moved to Bristol and sought fellowship with the Bethesda congregation which, assured that they repudiated the alleged heresy, received them. Darby demanded that Müller and Bethesda should excommunicate these brethren, and, when refused, excommunicated Bethesda and all in its fellowship.   Darby had discovered a principle of ecclesiastical fission which was to fragmentize the Brethren into pieces large and small and to destroy the hope of gathering saints in New Testament fellowship.   His followers were called Exclusive Brethren, of many varieties.

The churches that followed George Müller became known as Open Brethren, maintaining open fellowship more or less with other Christians, though sometimes possessed of an exclusive spirit because of legalism. They engaged in local evangelism, revival, missions, and philanthropy.

About the same time, a brilliant but erratic star arose in Scotland. Edward Irving was born in August 1792.[46] He was appointed assistant to Dr. Thomas Chalmers in 1819, but his preaching scarcely moved the Glasgow congregation. He was more successful as a missionary to the poor.

After an indifferent apprenticeship in the city, Irving was called in 1822 to minister in a Scots church in London. He became obsessed with the interpretation of apocalyptic prophecy, deciding that the year 1830 would be a significant year in which an outpouring of the Spirit could be expected. In Clydeside there occurred a glossolalic manifestation, so a deputation from London went there to investigate. Soon tongues and prophecy were being encouraged in the worship services in Regent Square in London.

Edward Irving was imposing in appearance, sincere in manner, and eloquent in address. He attracted the crowds, and a pleasing Gothic church was erected for them in 1827. For five years, the place became a focus of attraction and of controversy. In 1832, Irving was removed from his pulpit, and in 1833, the Presbytery of Annan to which he belonged deposed him from the ministry and excluded him from the Church of Scotland. In 1834, he died.

The Irvingites formed the Catholic Apostolic Church, which sought to revive the apostolate and prophets as well as the apostolic gifts. It was Irving's monument rather than his actual creation. The apostles itinerated widely, forming congregations in the United Kingdom, the United States and Canada, and in several European countries. An elaborate liturgy was formulated and celebrated with great dignity. The last of their Twelve Apostles died within a year of the end of the century, and the movement became moribund. An offshoot, the New Apostolic Church, appointed additional apostles and spread into a number of countries in Europe and America, claiming a quarter of a million members.[47]

It is significant that both the Christian Brethren and the Catholic Apostolic Church, though vastly different, rose up as ecumenical movements, seeking to unite believers in a restoration of New Testament Christianity. Neither could be cited as intentionally schismatic.

15

SWISS, FRENCH, DUTCH REVEIL, 1815–

After 1815, the power of the Scottish Revival of the early nineteenth century was carried over to the continent so lately freed from the control of Napoleon, but still dominated by the sceptical thinkers of revolutionary times. Geneva thus reflected Voltaire rather than Calvin, and Switzerland had survived the vicissitudes of war, but suffered ideological conquest by the saboteurs of Christianity.

In 1815, the religion of Geneva was 'pure deism.' The professors were ignorant of the Bible. As Frederic Monod recalled it, 'God's Holy Word was to us terra ignota.'[1] All the influences of revival which were sweeping the Anglo-American world were effectively shielded from Switzerland by Napoleon's hostile continental system.

In 1816, Robert Haldane decided to visit France and see if it were possible to witness for the Lord in that desperate country, desolated religiously by the sweep of the Revolution. Finding no openings in Paris, Haldane set out for Geneva, tentatively seeking out the remnant of believers.[2] A small prayer meeting existed, the fruit of the witness of Baroness Barbara von Krudener to a limited circle of inquirers.[3] So before the end of 1816, Robert Haldane took up residence in Geneva. He faced a very discouraging task. Jean-Jacques Rousseau had summed up the situation:[4]

> O Genevans! These gentlemen, your ministers, in truth are very singular people. They do not know what they believe. They do not even know what they would wish to appear to believe. Their only manner of establishing their faith is to attack the faith of others.

In Geneva, Robert Haldane began his lecturing to any students willing to listen to him. He hired a room and used an interpreter.[5] His method was simple: if a student asked him a question, simple or involved, he replied directly: 'What does the Scripture say?' This was so very different from the method of the Reformed professors that students flocked to hear the Scot who 'knew his Bible like Calvin.' A movement was under way.

Haldane had no advantages. He possessed no reputation as a scholar to impress the students; his French was fair, but he needed an interpreter for discussions; his manners were foreign. But he provided twenty or thirty chairs and a long table, with Bibles in French, German and English as well as Testaments in Greek or Hebrew. He himself was a living concordance.

Before long, the wrath of the professors and clergy rose. One of Robert Haldane's chief opponents was the Professor J. C. C. Cheneviere, described by Daniel Wilson, later the Bishop of Calcutta, as 'a harsh, violent, impracticable man. He really frightened me by his fierce attack on evangelical religion.'[6] Prof. Cheneviere used to walk up and down the Promenade St. Antoine, frowning at the students who dared enter Haldane's apartment, angrily taking their names down in his notebook for admonishing later.

Thus, throughout the winter of 1816-17 and the spring that followed, Haldane conducted meetings for the students, counteracting all that was taught them by their professors. The venerable Compagnie des Pasteurs took the issue to court, and mobs attacked the meetings of the Evangelicals.[7]

Haldane nevertheless provoked a revival of evangelical religion in Geneva. Among those whom he influenced were Louis Gaussen, pasteur at Seligny, who republished the Second Helvetic Confession, contended against the heresy in high places, and help organize in 1831 the Evangelical Society of Geneva, and in 1832 the Evangelical Theological Seminary.[8] Another was Cesar Malan, converted in 1816, who began preaching reformation doctrines in 1817, which stirred up a tempest. He tried to remain with the Established Church, was forced out, but gathered a large congregation and built a church.[9] Merle d'Aubigne, later famed as a great historian of the Reformation, exercised very considerable influence in the Church, and was well known as a writer and preacher.[10] Henri Pyt and Charles Rieu were others of note. All these men suffered persecution at first.

Reaction against the Revival drove scholarly revivalists out of the State Church. Free churches were formed in Geneva. The movement spread into the cantons of Vaud and Lausanne,[11] where Alexander Vinet emerged to leadership; and into Neuchatel, where revival began in 1817, Frederic Godet later founding a free faculty of theology. Meanwhile, the preaching of the Good News began again to be heard in various State Church congregations.

In June 1817, Robert Haldane left Geneva for Montauban, just north of Toulouse in southwestern France, where eight years earlier Napoleon had created a Reformed theological faculty to serve French Calvinists. Haldane went there with the conviction that its religion was a lifeless form. Napoleon had placed at the head of the faculty an officer of engineers who disseminated scepticism to the students who had there enrolled to avoid conscription. When conscription ceased, a hundred students withdrew and left the faculty instructing threescore.[12] Yet conditions in Montauban were not as discouraging as they had been in Geneva. Haldane made friends with Daniel Encontre, dean of theology, a brilliant scientist. At Haldane's prompting, Encontre and his friends addressed a letter to all the Consistories of France, suggesting the reprinting of the French Bible, for which twenty-seven thousand francs were needed. Not one replied. Haldane promised twenty-five hundred and secured seventy-five hundred from London, and soon an edition of 6000 was followed by another of 10,000. Haldane rented a home, compiled a commentary, and lectured visiting students, though without the measure of persecution or excitement enjoyed in Geneva.[13]

The evangelical revival in Geneva let loose upon France a group of French-speaking missionaries who helped change the Reformed constituency. At the same time, in London, a Continental Society for the Diffusion of Christian Knowledge was established, and undertook the support of these pioneer missionaries.[14] Pierre Mejanel, a convert of Haldane, took up residence in Paris and worked the departments to the north. Henri Pyt, after visiting Haldane, itinerated widely and accomplished great results in the Pyrenees territory. Felix Neff preached in Grenoble and the valleys of the Alps. Ami Bost also journeyed far and near, and made a deep impression in Alsace and Lorraine. The Continental Society (which was supported by Wilberforce and Rowland Hill) sent the funds needed in this work.[15] In 1820, Frederic Monod, a disciple of Haldane, settled in Paris as a pasteur. The Methodists also sent missionaries from England.[16]

Bible Societies were begun in Strasbourg and Paris, and a Religious Tract Society was organized.[17] And in 1822, a Paris Evangelical Missionary Society was founded to carry the Gospel abroad.[18] The Revival was beginning to permeate French Protestantism. In none of the records occurred any mention of phenomenal manifestations of an outpouring, and none of any carry-over from the Camisards.

The great awakening in the Netherlands, designated by the Dutch as 'Het Reveil,' has been traced by historians in the standard texts in that language to England, Scotland, Switzerland and France.[19] It became effective in Holland in 1817 and lasted more than a quarter of a century.

The Dutch poet, Willem Bilderdijk, gathered around him a number of influential friends, including Isaak da Costa, a convert of Sephardic Jewish background who forsook deism for active evangelical Christianity.[20] Da Costa published a number of provocative books, attacking the spirit of the age as one of slavery, unbelief, superstition and darkness, and the spirit of the ecclesiastical establishment as one with the Sadducees. Another protagonist of revival of Hebrew background was Immanuel Capadose, supported by Willem de Clercq.[21] Guillaume Groen van Prinsterer, a statesman, added his considerable influence by defending Christianity against unbelief and revolution.[22]

The methods of the revivalists involved Bible teaching for adults and Sunday Schools for children, and in the bigger cities missions were organized, their objective the vital conversion of the citizens.

Not all the congregations in the Netherlands were touched by the awakening. Dutchmen have a propensity for debate about theological matters, and preachers took sides. But in the congregations moved by the awakening there was an immediate upsurge of attendance, and many among nominal Christians entered into a vital experience of God.

In Amsterdam, the leaders of the movement were Jacob van Lennep and his friends, and in 's Gravenhage were Willem and Dirk van Hogendorp and Groen van Prinsterer. The latter made a trip to Geneva in 1833 to visit the leaders of the Swiss movement, Malan, D'Aubigne, Gaussen and Vinet.[23] Ten years later, Malan visited the Netherlands and received a great welcome from the revived community.[24]

As in Switzerland and France, the Revival movement gathered its followers particularly from the educated and cultured classes, who developed a keen interest in social improvement without neglecting evangelism. The opposition repudiated evangelism and neglected social action. In the Dutch Lutheran Church, the awakening was much less felt, and Mennonites becoming interested in the revival met with a cold reception in their spiritually-poor associations. The minority groups, such as Baptists and Brethren, imported from the English-speaking world, usually thrived.

The continuing debates among the Dutch Reformed in the Netherlands provoked a split. Da Costa and Prinsterer and many of their friends continued within the Establishment and formed an 'ecclesiola in ecclesia,' taking the modest name of Christian Friends.[25] It was among these Christian Friends, as among the Evangelicals in the State Church of England, that a warm support for the Sunday Schools, Bible Societies, Missionary Societies, and Tract Societies arose. Friends found fulfilment in the various undertakings for the underprivileged. For example, Otto Gerhardt Heldring, a pioneer philanthropist, formed the Inner Mission, and first of all tackled one problem community, Hoenderloo, transforming the village where social and economic handicaps had afflicted the population. He supported temperance work and established homes for women and girls.[26]

George Müller of Bristol found a follower in Johannes van t'Lindenhout, who likewise founded an orphanage. The example of Theodor Fliedner in Germany was followed in the establishment of an order of deaconesses at Utrecht. Ordained clergy and theological students were gathered into active companies to further the Revival, and Lucas Lindeboom became an ardent evangelist in the movement.

Among the supporters of the Awakening were stronger critics of the Established Church. One such was Hendrik de Cock, whose new found zeal was directed into a stricter Calvinism. He was deposed from the ministry, and in 1836 joined with others in organizing the Christian Reformed denomination. The potato famine in the mid-1840s led to a very considerable emigration of its members to Michigan.

Neither in the Netherlands, France or Switzerland was the Revival as intense as in the United Kingdom or United States. In the latter, whole communities—and churches of all denominations therein— seem to have been swept by the movement. In Switzerland and the Netherlands, a majority of the inhabitants professed a nominal Protestant faith, but it had been undermined by rationalism. In France, a tiny minority professed a Protestant faith, also undermined by rationalism, but the majority were lapsed Roman Catholics secularized by revolutionary rationalism. The Awakening in the Reformed countries much more resembled the revival in the early days of Wesley and Whitefield, a minority movement making its way in the teeth of opposition. In Britain and the United States, the Second Great Awakening was built upon the remarkable successes of the First.

16

THE GERMAN AWAKENING, 1815–

Napoleon had overrun nearly all of the German lands at one time or another during his military rampage throughout Europe. Great Britain and Prussia had been the two major Protestant powers confronting France; Britain had resisted successfully, but Prussia, fighting bravely, was overrun. Fear of Napoleon had helped turn the people of Britain toward God; the misfortunes of war in Germany likewise produced a quickening effect. When the British and the Prussian guns at Waterloo destroyed Napoleon's last dreams of conquest, there was much rejoicing throughout the German lands over the providential deliverance from the foreign yoke.

The German Confederation was set up in Frankfurt-on-Main, consisting of thirty-nine sovereigns ruling over the German lands—though Hanover's king was also the British monarch, Holstein's duke was also Denmark's king, duke of Luxemburg the king of the Netherlands. Politically feeble, the Confederation was sponsored by Austria; economically strong was a customs union later sponsored by Prussia.

The earlier phase of preparatory reviving in Britain in the 1780s was paralleled in Germany by the founding of the Deutsche Christentumsgesellschaft, which counteracted the influence of the Enlightenment and promoted evangelism and missionary outreach.[1]

One of the forerunners of the German Awakening was Johann Heinrich Jung, who wrote under the name of Jung-Stilling. His writings reached all levels of German society, and exercised a far greater influence than measurable.[2] In 1800, thanks to inspiration received by the Baron August von Schirnding from Thomas Haweis in London, the Berlin Missionary Seminary was begun under the able direction of Johannes Jänicke.[3] Its first class included seven students, and the Baron paid half the expenses. This school sent out missionaries to the farthest ends of the earth, evangelists to all the German lands. It was not long before the revival so earnestly besought in the German Concert of Prayer had become a reality.

In Bavaria, before the end of the eighteenth century, an evangelical revival movement grew up in certain Roman Catholic circles, which made the University of Dillingen a lively place for fellowship across ecclesiastical borders. Martin Boos was converted about 1789, and his ministry provoked revival after revival as well as persecution and dismissal from his parish. He remained in the fold of the Roman Catholic Church until his death in 1825.[4] Another Roman Catholic evangelical priest was Johann Gossner who also studied under the evangelical professor, J. M. Sailer, afterwards a Roman bishop. Gossner was imprisoned for heresy in 1803, after which he exercised an itinerating ministry before becoming a Protestant in Berlin in 1826. Gossner is remembered as the founder of the worldwide Gossner Missionary Society.[5]

In the first decade of the nineteenth century, a new tide of pietism arose, influenced by the rise of evangelistic and missionary societies in Britain, counteracting rationalism and dead orthodoxy, but limited by political considerations to only a few of the German lands. The leading edge of the tide was Dr. Karl Friedrich Steinkopf, who had pastored the German Savoy Church in London and was a co-founder of the British and Foreign Bible Society.[6]

The Germans supported warmly the work of agents of the British and Foreign Bible Society, whose Robert Pinkerton helped found in succession several German Bible Societies. Steinkopf and Pinkerton were prime factors in the revival soon coming in Germany.[7]

Steinkopf promised the support of thousands of members of the Deutsche Christentumsgesellschaft in 1798 to the new London Missionary Society. In fact, the Germans supplied about a hundred and fifty workers to the burgeoning British missionary societies, including the C. M. S.[8]

In 1806, Baroness Barbara von Krudener was converted in Riga, the Latvian capital.[9] A Moravian shoemaker was the means of her change of heart, but her outreach was to the high and mighty. She discussed salvation with the Czar of all the Russias; the Kaiser attended her Bible classes; she influenced the Prussian, Bavarian, Hanoverian, Dutch and Swedish Queens. She witnessed for Christ in the salons of nobility and in the huts of the poor. She was harried by the police, and finally returned to Russia, where she died in 1824. She was a committed evangelist, a curious interest in extra-sensory perception her known foible.

As early as 1816, an awakening began in the Wuppertal and surrounding area, where the godly influence of the hymn-writer, Gerhard Tersteegen, was still felt. Rationalism had not overcome the religious life there, as in other parts of Germany.[10] The first revival occurred in the Reformed Church through the ministry of Gottfried D. Krummacher, one of several evangelists of that family.[11] Karl A. Döring extended the movement by evangelism in the streets as well as the usual preaching.[12] In 1822, another revival swept the Wuppertal, its leaders being Immanuel Sander and Friedrich W. Krummacher, a nephew of his predecessor.[13] Sander was Lutheran pastor at Elberfeld.[14] Awakenings broke out in the Siegerland through the influence of the Wuppertal movement. Beginning after the Battle of Waterloo, revived believers met in fellowship in 'reading societies,' which shortly after became auxiliaries of the Rhenish Missionary Society. This lay movement was paralleled by the efforts of pastors, who instructed as many as two hundred inquirers each week.

In Baden, Aloys Henhöfer, yet another Roman Catholic priest, was converted through Bible reading. He preached with such power that Protestants as well as Roman Catholics flocked to hear him. He was persecuted, and an accusation brought imprisonment in 1822, with dismissal from the Roman Church.[15] He entered the Protestant Church where he contended with rationalism. The Grand Duke of Baden planned to move him from church to church, so regularly had revivals broken out. Church authorities discouraged this, but Henhöfer ministered widely just the same. Many younger clergy professed conversion under his ministry.[16]

Two of the forerunners of the German Awakening were Michael Hahn and Christian Pregizer, in Württemberg and in the Black Forest area, who evangelized the people at a time when dismal sermons by rationalists were emptying the churches.[17]

In German Switzerland, Basel was the headquarters for many of the activities of German-speaking revivalists. In St. Peter's Church in Basel, Gottlieb Blumhart, long-time secretary of the Deutsche Christentumsgesellschaft, exercised an evangelistic ministry. As early as 1804, the Basel Bible Society was founded; in 1815, a missionary training school was set up, developing into the Basel Missionary Society.[18] The revival began to touch Bern in the late 1820s, when a free church was founded, followed by an Evangelical Association. Zürich's Evangelical Society was formed later.

The Awakening touched many places in Bavaria. There was revival in Nürnberg and in other Bavarian communities. Thus Professor Christian Krafft, an indirect convert of the Roman Catholic Bavarian revival, became a leading light at Erlangen University, till then a domain of rationalism.[19] He was reproved for associating with pietists, cooperating with Bible and missionary societies, converting church members, and for distributing tracts. Several other professors were converted and helped make Erlangen an evangelistic place for a whole generation.

Ludwig Hofacker was converted at Tübingen, where he studied theology, and found fellowship in the conventicles of farmers in the district. His health was generally poor, but at Stuttgart in Leonhardskirche people flocked to hear him; in Reilingshausen successive revivals swept the community also; thousands were converted, but hundreds of thousands were influenced by his books.[20]

Rationalism was entrenched at the University of Giessen, in Hesse.[21] The rationalists tried to eradicate the earlier pietism with fanatical polemics. One professor taught his students that pietism was caused by trouble in the abdomen. When nineteenth century revivalists entered Hesse through Frankfurt-on-Main, insult and persecution followed. The revival moved many Hessians, the best-known preachers being Franz Joseph Helferich, another converted priest who later left the Church, and Bichmann von Lich, a Lutheran pastor.[22] In Kassel also the awakening was felt.

Revivals swept the Hanover area in the 1820s and 1830s. An outstanding evangelist in the revival around Minden was Johann Volkening, who preached so forcefully at Gütersloh from 1826 onwards that the Minden authorities suspended him.[23] G. L. D T. Harms, converted at Göttingen, became the outstanding evangelist in the Hanover area. Subsequent revival movements led him to found the Hermannsburg Mission.[24] There was also revival in Eastern Frisland, a movement having lasting results.[25]

In Bremen and Hamburg, historic seaports, the revival impulse came largely from Britain. In 1814, the Hamburg-Altona Bible Society was founded by British Bible agents, and eight years later the Lower Saxony Tract Society.[26] In 1825, the first German Sunday School was founded by Pastor Johannes William Rautenberg, prompted by a Tract Society agent, Johann Gerhard Oncken. The movement spread far and wide throughout Germany.

In 1810, after the restoration of Prussia, and especially after 1815, a revival of evangelical Christianity was enjoyed in Berlin and throughout its wide hinterland.[27] Its pioneers were Johannes Jänicke and Baron Ernst von Kottwitz. For thirty years, Jänicke had been pastor of Bethlehem Church in Berlin, where he proved to be a fearless preacher.[28] Von Kottwitz was a Silesian nobleman with a concern for social action as well as evangelism.[29]

August Neander and Friedrich Tholuck, two theological professors, exercised a remarkable influence in the Berlin awakening. Neander, born David Mendel, a Jew, professed a Christian faith in 1806 and became an ardent Christian through more faithful study of the Bible.[30] Tholuck, himself converted through Baron von Kottwitz, became a professor in 1823 in Berlin, and taught at Halle from 1829 onwards. He became an evangelist to the intelligentsia.[31]

The Berlin awakening was extended by the efforts of many laymen.[32] One, a tavern-keeper in Rixdorf, announced his conversion by pouring his supplies of brandy into the gutter and organizing a temperance society. Throughout all of Brandenburg, home meetings were held by new converts, whether school superintendents, village mayors, shepherds or farmers. In some cases, these little gatherings soon over-flowed and packed out large auditoriums.[33]

The awakening in Berlin spread to eastern Pomerania. In territory of landed proprietors, the evangelical message was propagated by noblemen on their estates. Gustav von Below returned from the battlefields in 1813, and found his faith through devotional reading, soon afterwards winning his brothers Karl and Heinrich to Christ.[34] In the 1820s, they conducted revival meetings which stirred the whole of the district, thousands attending the preaching which often went on until midnight. This attracted the attention of the authorities, who sent police to arrest and prosecute and imprison supporters. This only accelerated the movement, and converted ministers helped the laymen. Whole congregations between Stettin and Königsberg were quickened, and a spirit of public prayer fell upon the farmers. King Friedrich Wilhelm III, the Prussian monarch, interfered on behalf of the revival leaders, his officers convinced that the movement was inoffensive. Near Kammin, north of Stettin, a similar movement began on the von Thadden estate,[35] for Adolf von Thadden had been challenged by the Bavarian and the Berlin awakenings.

There was revival in West Prussia also. Various local pastors in Danzig engaged in biblical preaching, founded temperance associations, promoted mission classes, and circulated the Scriptures. Orderly camp-meetings were held in the forest, attracting thousands.[36]

Another of the converts of Baron von Kottwitz was Carl von Rappard, a landowner in Posen.[37] Von Rappard was confined to a wheelchair but, with a sympathetic wife, made up for his handicap in indefatigable service. After 1825, the whole area experienced a revival of evangelistic enterprise and a quickening of church life.

In Silesia, the agents of the British and Foreign Bible Society held revival meetings in the villages, but were soon hindered by church authorities.[38] The Count and Countess von Reden helped found a Silesian Bible Society, and after her husband's death, the Countess conducted meetings in Buchwald Castle for nearby parishioners.[39] The Countess helped her friends produce a Bible with commentary, and King Friedrich Wilhelm IV was so pleased with it that it was placed in all the national schools of Prussia. Bibles similarly were placed in all institutions of correction and welfare, thanks to the Breslau Bible Society.

Generally speaking, the German Awakening influenced the upper classes of the various Kingdoms and Duchies to launch a mission to the peasantry and working classes, a missionary movement rather than a spontaneous awakening of the masses of the people. Though there were many very ordinary people who responded, so often the leaders were men of either high breeding or education or both.

The intimate relations between Britain and the German States at the time were reflected in the close relations of British and German Christians.[40] Every British innovation produced by the British Awakening, whether the founding of missionary societies or Bible societies, was immediately taken up and put into operation in Germany. But the German Awakening fell short of the British movement in effecting the reform of a nation. It seemed that the German States were one generation behind in the progression of revival.

17

RENEWED AMERICAN REVIVAL, 1815–

The tide of revival, which had come to the full about the turn of the century, ebbed somewhat during the War of 1812, but started to return in the years after Waterloo. Churches in North America experienced little diminishing of spiritual power before another wave of blessing overflowed them.

The wholesomeness of previous local revivals was noted in the readiness with which congregations engaged in intercession for renewed awakenings. Undoubtedly the people of God regarded the revivals as Divine visitations, a crowning point of Christian experience.

The attitude of cautious and careful ministers towards these recurring revivals was displayed by a letter written by Dr. Alexander Proudfit, a Reformed pastor:[1]

> During the whole course of my ministry . . . this is the thirty-eighth year . . . I have never been favored with seasons more delightful in their recollection; none the results of which I anticipate with more joy on that day when the final account of my stewardship will be required.

The Concert of Prayer was continued into the decades of the post-war world, the Pax Britannica. The people of God needed no convincing of the power and efficacy of prayer in preparing the way for further times of refreshing.

The renewal of revival in the United States saw the rise of great evangelists, men whose reputation for success was such that their services were in demand far and near. One such evangelist was Asahel Nettleton, born in Connecticut in 1783.[2] He was converted in 1801, in a local revival. He graduated from Yale in 1809, was licensed to preach in 1811 and was ordained as an evangelist in 1817.

Before his health failed in 1822, Nettleton was involved in upwards of sixty more or less extensive awakenings in the parishes of Connecticut and in towns in Massachusetts and New York State nearby. The awakening in Saratoga Springs, in the latter named state, resulted in the 'hopeful conversion' of two thousand people in 1819. His work was outstanding in quality.[3]

Between 1815 and 1818, religious awakenings were being felt in many parts of the eastern United States. From Albany (at the head of the Mohawk), Joshua Bradley retailed the reports of six such movements in Rhode Island, fifteen in Connecticut, twenty-one in eastern New York, twenty-one in New Jersey, twenty-one in Pennsylvania, forty-five in Vermont, sixty-four in Massachusetts, and eighty in that part of New York up the river.[4]

On 15th October 1816, at the prompting of a church in Sheridan, the Baptist churches of Vermont engaged in a day of prayer and fasting, the object a return of the blessing of earlier years. Within a year, two thousand had been added, swelling the membership rolls.[5] There was a similar work of revival in New Hampshire and down east in Maine.

In Massachusetts, the Baptists began to pray for renewal in 1816, and almost immediately received a blessing. One pastor, Edward Barker, noticed a change in his congregation as early as January 20, then began to baptize candidates in ones and twos, doubling the numbers, and adding 228 to the church in six months.[6] Associational statistics showed that such a blessed increase was very general.

The revival affected the Congregational parishes as well. In Pittsfield, Massachusetts, an awakening began in 1820 under the ministry of Heman Humphrey, who received many converts into the church.[7] Asahel Nettleton, needing some rest and recuperation, came to visit his friends next spring, and was persuaded to preach, which he did earnestly and pungently. The results in the summer were unparalleled. Heman Humphrey became president of Amherst College but remained an evangelist and advocate of prayer for revival.

Churches which had experienced revival sought it again. The redoubtable Alvan Hyde, pastor of the Congregational Church in Lee, Massachusetts, reported a stirring again in 1820, with fifty additions 'from the world.' In the summer of 1821, the Lee church devoted itself to prayer and fasting, and became convinced of an impending blessing. Nettleton visited Lee at this juncture and preached five times to over-flowing assemblies. It proved to be a time of harvest, and hundreds responded to the evangelistic challenge. Dr. Hyde recalled the movement:[8]

> The Spirit of God came down upon us like 'a rushing mighty wind.' Conversions were frequent . . . At the suggestion of Mr. Nettleton, I now instituted 'inquiring meetings.' More than a hundred attended the first.

There was another awakening at Lee, Massachusetts, in 1827. It began with a sunrise service of intercession on the last Sunday of the previous year. A spontaneous revival ensued, instituting thirty new family altars and adding 125 to the membership of the church. Four years later, the same church enjoyed a still greater awakening, as simultaneously the churches throughout the Union were revived.[9]

In 1815, a revival began in the town of Salisbury, the first of a series in Connecticut; town after town, year after year, reported awakenings. Twenty-five out of thirty of the parishes in New Haven county, for example, were visited in 1820, with up to two thousand conversions.[10]

The year 1821, in Connecticut, was eminently a year of revival, for nearly a hundred congregations were affected in the Congregational Establishment, besides churches that possessed another affiliation, such as the Baptists. Thus in the First Congregational Church of Hartford, where earlier stirring Connecticut revivals had been felt, 'a work of great power' commenced in 1821 under the ministry of Dr. Joel Hawes.[11] Nearly two hundred were welcomed to fellowship, only a few of whom relapsed.

Among three dozen reports of local awakenings in all six states of New England, the Baptists in 1818 published a letter from David Benedict, afterwards a historian of note, describing an intense revival which began in Pawtucket in 1815 and continued for two years, providing him with the opportunity of baptizing more than a hundred candidates for church membership.[12] This was by no means the only such awakening among the Baptist churches of Rhode Island. In the city of Providence, the Congregationalist and Methodist churches shared in a general movement of revival with the Baptists and added large numbers to their congregations. Fully one-third of the students at Brown University made a profession of faith, besides seven hundred townspeople.[13]

There was renewal of revival in the Maritime Provinces. In Nova Scotia, evangelist Joseph Dimock reported a revival at Chester beginning late in 1819, characterized by general solemnity—quite in contrast to earlier movements—all the meetings crowded out, and many baptisms of believers.[14] A letter from Isaac Case told of hundreds being converted in Nova Scotia in 1824, while Joseph Crandall had baptized two hundred and fifty in New Brunswick.[15] Nova Scotian Baptists added 358 in a year during the awakening of the next decade, and there was a similar movement in New Brunswick.

As in New England, so also in the Middle Atlantic States. The movement was prepared by prayer, began quietly, was free of any extravagance, and accomplished much good of a lasting sort. Examples could be multiplied.

In 1816, Edward D. Griffin returned to Newark, New Jersey, and in December of that year a powerful revival broke out in the city and in towns nearby. Many converts were added to the churches round about.[16] Griffin carried to the presidency of Williams College a warm heart.

In Elizabethtown, New Jersey, the First Presbyterian Church was visited with 'a great revival of religion' in 1817 which commenced most signally as an immediate answer to the united prayers of God's people.[17] Special seasons for prayer were appointed to supplement the monthly concert of prayer, which was unusually full and solemn. When the revival came, it was marked by tears. Several hundreds in the meetings were impressed, and about 180 were admitted as communicants. Two years later, another revival was welcomed, resulting in the founding of another congregation in the town.

The Presbyterian Synod of New Jersey appointed a day of fasting and prayer in December 1825, its object a general revival in the churches.[18] It came, and lasted all of 1826.

The renewal of revival affected New York City churches. Dr. Gardiner Spring, a New York pastor, later reflected that the year 1814 was a trying one for him, his resources seemingly dried up; but in another season of refreshing, his Sunday services and weekly lectures and meetings for prayer began to increase during the summer; 1815 proved to be a blessing, the converts at the weekly lectures sometimes filling the aisle of the church, seeking admission. It proved to be the first of five such revivals before 1835; yet the session often administered severe discipline to maintain proper standards among professors of faith.[19]

In Salem, New York, an Associate Reformed church felt the operations of the Spirit in 1815, when 'a genial warmth appeared to pervade the whole church, to the joy of the generation of the righteous,' and at the same time multitudes were added to the company of believers. In 1824, a revival of different character was manifested, when people residing in different parts of town were suddenly smitten with deep conviction, stirring up the congregations and issuing in daily meetings for prayer and conference, generally overflowing with inquirers.[20]

In the winter of 1828-29, the Presbyterian churches of the city of New York united in a series of union, four-day, protracted meetings, and gained unusual benefit. Scarcely a church did not add a hundred new members to its rolls, and the impact was felt for a generation. Four-days series were promoted by Baptist, Methodist and other churches as a new means of evangelization.[21]

Great as were the awakenings before 1815, the religious upheavals in western New York State in the post-war years far surpassed all previous experiences, again affecting the Baptists, Congregationalists, Methodists and Presbyterians as well as German-speaking groups.[22] In 1818, for example, the Methodists alone gained 16% in membership. And ten years later, another movement running a dozen years or so provided a grand climax in the burned-over district.[23]

The Presbyterians, revived in the earlier movements, welcomed the Divine wind again blowing on their churches. In western New York State, the years 1816 and 1817 were 'peculiarly years of the right hand of the Most High. The revivals in those years were more numerous and of greater extent than in former years.'[24] A score of churches revived in 1819, thirty-five in 1826.

It was in the country south of Lake Ontario that the outstanding evangelist of the middle third of the nineteenth century arose to harness the movement of dynamic evangelism. Charles Grandison Finney was born in Connecticut in 1792. His family moving west, he studied law in western New York. He began to read the Bible with reference to the Mosaic legal code, and from this interest his familiarity with Scripture grew until he became convinced of the authority of the Word of God. He was converted, not through evangelistic witness, but by private study of Scripture and prayer. His conversion caused a great stir in his community, for he was already— at 29 years of age—a brilliant fellow, a splendid pagan who was impressive in personality, proudly conscious of his intellectual as well as his physical superiority.[25]

Finney's first evangelistic meetings were held in the tiny villages of western New York State.[26] In 1824, he preached in a hamlet named Evans Mills, but, after a score of sermons, there were still no responses. Finney announced his final message to those who were thus rejecting the message. It provoked a great concern and nearly everyone present professed conversion. In these tiny rural hamlets, he enjoyed increasing usefulness in times of sporadic revivals.

Charles P. McIlvaine, Episcopal Bishop of Ohio in later years, was impressed in the awakenings of 1815 onwards. In long retrospect,[27] he insisted that Episcopal churches under a more earnestly evangelical ministry were blessed of God with marked manifestations of the power of the Spirit. McIlvaine himself engaged in ministry at West Point among the military cadets, and saw a revival of religion there. One of the converts became a bishop in the western territories.

In 1815, 'a scene of wonderful interest occurred' at New Hampshire's Dartmouth College, at a time when there was trouble between president and trustees.[28] A general and an almost instantaneous solemnity prevailed, convicting the impenitent of sin, filling the chapel, the recitation room and every place of meeting. About sixty students were converted and not one relapsed, some becoming ministers and missionaries. Campus awakenings were repeated every few years.

At Williams College, in western Massachusetts, there was a college revival in the summer of 1815, the third such movement in the history of the college. In 1824, there were a dozen inquirers in the fourth movement, but only three seemed to persevere, one—William Hervey—becoming a missionary to India, another a minister at home, and another a professor at Williams. In 1825, another revival began, affecting almost the whole college. A dozen of the converts entered the ministry, and one joined Hervey in India. In 1827, a sixth revival began; in 1829, a seventh. In 1831, in the midst of general awakening everywhere, an eighth awakening occurred.[29] Revival had become a way of life.

At Amherst College, a second campus awakening began in the spring of 1827.[30] The 'noise and shaking among the dry bones' was sudden. In 1828, another revival swept the campus. In 1831, a period of declension was followed by a time of searching of heart, then a sudden awakening.

At Yale, there were recurring revivals in the years 1815, 1821, and 1831, the numbers of converts rising from twenty-five to sixty-nine. In 1832, the total number of the communicating Christians among the undergraduates was 190 of all denominations.[31]

At Princeton, in the second week of January 1815, without any alarming event, without any extraordinary preaching, without any special instruction, a campus revival swept the students and within four weeks impressed a majority of them. Of 105, forty were converted outright, another fifteen were inquirers, the remainder attending the means of grace.[32]

After the peace of 1815, land-hungry migrants poured through the Allegheny passes or down the water gap into the Ohio valley. The settlements were tiny, but revivals reached the settlers, as in Marietta, Ohio, in March 1818. By 1825, there were two-thirds of a million people in Ohio, seven thousand of them Baptists, to whom Joshua Bradley was adding hundreds in Ashtabula and Kingsville, on Lake Erie, besides a thousand on the Black River in Michigan on Lake Huron.[33]

In Upper Canada, or Ontario, sporadic revivals continued after the interruption of the War of 1812, which had caused resentment against some of the Methodist itinerants from south of the border. The Baptists began to plant churches, the Presbyterians also being evangelistically inclined, and subject to sporadic local awakenings.[34]

Daniel Baker emerged as an evangelist in the Southern States in 1816, and exercised a powerful ministry for forty years.[35] Born in Georgia, he graduated in the upper ranks of his class at Princeton, was licensed to preach for the Presbyterians in 1816, his first charge in Harrisonburg in Virginia in 1818. His successive pastorates were farther to the southwest, as far as the lower Mississippi. Baker preached to multiplied thousands through Virginia, Kentucky, Tennessee, the Carolinas, Florida, Georgia, Alabama, Mississippi, Louisiana, Arkansas and Texas, finally settling in the last-named State, a founder of Austin College.

In Virginia, the Baptists reported a reviving of churches in Prospect Hill, Spotsylvania, where in the summer of 1816 two elders who had attended the Triennial Convention called the congregation to prayer around the communion table. The silent weeping and the groan of penitents were noted at the time, but long remembered were the results of the revival, which were thorough and deep.[36]

In 1824, a movement of the Spirit added numbers to the different churches in Stevensville, Virginia, where John Bagley reported quaintly: 'I was at a baptizing on Sunday on the Rappahannock river, where I saw ninety-one buried in the liquid grave.' The revivals in Virginia during the year 1828 were particularly effective in Williamsburg and Norfolk and other tidewater towns.[37]

At Windsor, North Carolina, the town was 'entirely reformed' by a movement in 1824, in which four physicians and the high sheriff were among the four hundred and ten baptized and received into church membership.[38]

Movements of revival continued in South Carolina also. About 1820, the Methodists were maintaining three hundred churches to serve their sixteen thousand members in South Carolina; the Baptists ministered to fourteen thousand in a hundred and seventy churches; the Presbyterians served ten thousand in a hundred churches; the Episcopalians and the Lutherans each had eighteen clergymen, and eighteen hundred members between them.[39]

In Georgia, an intense revival began among the Baptists and Congregationalists in the Sunbury district in July 1822. In October, the first of several three-days' meetings were held, adding forty-seven white and black converts to the Baptists, sixty-six to the Congregationalists.[40]

In the years 1820 and 1821, there were no professing Christians in the University of Georgia at Athens. In 1822, seven young men who professed the faith initiated prayer meetings on campus, and these intercessory sessions were faithfully maintained for five years, until revival swept the campus in 1827.[41]

From 1820 onwards, a group of professors in Athens, in Georgia, attended a weekly prayer meeting to intercede with God for an awakening at Franklin College. In 1826, two popular students sickened and died, and impressed their colleagues to seek spiritual ends in life. In early fall of that year, a movement began which affected both town and campus.[42] Not only were many students converted, but the revival affected the Baptist, Methodist, and Presbyterian congregations nearby.

It was said that no general refreshing was experienced in Georgia until 1827, when a most remarkable and memorable revival broke out first in Eatonton, then spread over the State, adding fourteen thousand to the Baptist churches alone.[43] Similar movements touched the Methodists and the Presbyterians of Georgia.

It was estimated in 1824 that there were a thousand fully ordained Methodist ministers in the United States and four thousand local preachers; the Baptists were served by three thousand preachers, some educated and others uneducated; the Congregationalists had sixteen hundred, chiefly in New England, and the Presbyterians had thirteen hundred, in the main west of New England. Thus the evangelical churches had about eleven thousand active ministers. All others had approximately nine hundred. Baptists, Congregationalists, Methodists and Presbyterians multiplied by revival.

18

REVIVAL ON MISSION FIELDS, 1815–

In the forward missionary thrust of the 1791 Revival, Polynesia had become the first target of the missionary enterprise.[1] But the first mission to Tahiti met with sorry failure, and the project was abandoned in 1808.[2] In time, the missionaries returned from their Australian exile, and the work began to grow by twos and threes. Pomare II, who faced rebellion and war, declared his sympathy for the new faith, whose adherents were called derisively 'Bure Atua' or 'pray God.'[3] The crisis came late in 1815 when pagans massed to slaughter the Christians at worship and were defeated in battle by the king's forces.[4] A folk movement in Tahiti and nearby islands followed.[5] John Williams, converted in Britain in an 1814 revival, arrived and channeled the new-found enthusiasm into missionary outreach.[6]

In 1816, a Hawaiian youth Opukahaia (or Henry Obookiah) found his way to New Haven, Connecticut, and attracted the attention of Samuel J. Mills and his student colleagues.[7] In 1818, he died, but his friends determined to carry out his declared objective of evangelizing Hawaii, the first party arriving in 1820 to find an open field for service.[8] It was otherwise that year when the first Wesleyan missionary to Tonga tried to effect an entrance to the 'Friendly Isles.' In 1814, the first missionary party, Evangelical Anglicans, arrived in New Zealand, followed in 1819 by Wesleyans.[9]

In 1815, Joseph Carel Kam arrived in Indonesia and became the apostle to the Moluccas, where multitudes were ingathered.[10] In 1822, Dutch missionaries opened up a work in Minahassa, in northeastern Sulawesi.[11] And in 1820, the London Missionary Society entered Madagascar, peopled by an Indonesian-related race.[12] All these ventures led to great awakenings after the indoctrination of the converts.

These missionary enterprises were sparked and driven by the Concert of Prayer in the sending countries, where awakened believers met regularly to pray for the revival of religion and the extension of Christ's kingdom. The first missionaries were all products of the revival.

Missionary work in India was mostly pioneering in the days after Waterloo, as it had been since Carey's arrival, but after 1815 a folk movement crested at the tip of South India, on the Travancore side, and an Evangelical Anglican, Charles Mead, received three thousand Nadars into church fellowship in 1817.[13] A similar folk movement had taken place less than twenty years previously on the Madras side, when five thousand Nadars were baptized. (A revival may be described as the reviving of believers, an awakening as the winning of the related community, but a folk movement the ingathering of untaught outsiders along tribal, caste, linguistic or class lines.) The significance of these folk movements must be realised to understand the fact that, for fifty years, there were more evangelical Christians at the tip of India than in the rest of the sub-continent.

In 1793, William Carey and his colleagues had arrived in Calcutta, but received nothing but hostility from East India Company officials. Sheltering under the Danish flag at Serampore, they baptised their first convert in 1800.[14] The energy of the Serampore missionaries was astounding. Not only did they translate the Scriptures into various Indian vernaculars, but they taught school, introduced new crops, and sought social reforms. In 1808, Henry Martyn, the protege of Charles Simeon, arrived in India, noting in his diary: 'Now let me burn out for God!'[15] In six short years, his ambition was fulfilled. He was a disciplined man, in his duties as a chaplain being faithful, in his preaching to Hindus and Muslims, enthusiastic. The London Missionary Society sent out Nathaniel Forsyth in 1798, but he died in 1816,[16] by which time his colleagues were settled in Madras. In 1813,[17] the American Board placed its missionaries in Bombay, and in that decade the Church Missionary Society sent twenty-six missionaries to India, also beginning a Mission of Help to the ancient Syrian Church in Kerala.[18] In 1819, Wesleyans established their work in Madras,[19] and in 1821 British Baptists entered Orissa.[20]

The Baptist Missionary Society entered Ceylon in 1812, the Wesleyans in 1814, alas without their leader, great-hearted Thomas Coke who died on the way out.[21] In 1815, the American Board arrived,[22] and, in 1817, the Church Missionary Society.[23] Judson reached Burma in 1813.

Not only were these pioneers evangelical in conviction, but they were products of the 1791 Revival in Great Britain and the United States and in Germany.

The Second Great Awakening had missionary effects in another sub-continent, thanks to British imperialism. The Moravians reopened a mission to the Hottentots, closed by friction with Netherlands East India Company chaplains in 1743. After fifty years, they found traces of the pioneering work of Georg Schmidt, a German Moravian.

Within a few years of their return, the Moravians were witnessing a spiritual awakening at Genadendal: [24]

> A veritable hunger for the Word of God was apparent. The emotional Hottentots were moved to tears by the preaching of the Gospel . . . Those colonists who from time to time were witnesses of the work of God's Spirit in ignorant heathen, were moved to confess that they could hardly believe that such results were possible.

Van Zulch, another convert of Dr. Van Lier, proved so successful in his work among slaves and Hottentots near Wellington that he was able to build them a meeting-hall. M. C. Vos, an ardent evangelist, worked for the conversion of Hottentots not only by his own efforts, but through teaching farmers to teach their slaves and servants the Word of God daily in their own quarters.[25]

At the turn of the century, Jan Theodor van der Kemp arrived at the Cape to serve the London Missionary Society. He and his friends founded a mission for the Hottentots in the eastern Cape Colony.[26] His first wife having died in the Netherlands in a tragic accident, he married—not happily— a girl of mixed-blood, as did some of the other missionaries of the London Society.

After reviving their mission to Hottentots, the Moravians commenced in 1818 to evangelize the Bantu in eastern Cape Colony.[27] A Swede, Hans Peter Hallbeck, became bishop of of the Moravians, and the work went forward steadily.

In 1820, a vigorous Scottish minister, John Philip, was appointed superintendent of London Missionary Society work in South Africa. For a full generation he directed the work, embracing the viewpoint of the natives and exasperating the Afrikaner farmers by his advocacy of the rights of the non-Europeans. He lived a stormy life.[28]

So the work of the Christian missions went forward in a disintegrating society. The social benefits were obvious— instead of filthy sheep-skins, they wore good cloth; instead of illiteracy, they could read the Bible; instead of licentiousness, they had family life; instead of drunkenness, they were sober; they had cattle and wagons and houses.[29]

That was the impact of English-speaking missionaries at Bethelsdorp upon Hottentots. The same was true of those who spoke Dutch. The town of Philippolis, founded in 1823 on the recommendation of Ds. Abraham Faure of Graaff-Reinet to evangelize the Hottentots, was visited by Adam Kok, chief of the Griqua mixed-bloods who settled there. The Griquas then possessed 35,000 sheep, 3000 oxen, and 500 horses, and Griqua country was as Christian as the Cape itself.[30] The Griquas persisted in Christian civilization.

In 1813 and 1814, awakenings were reported from many of the stations of the London Mission. Many Hottentots repented of their sins and turned to God at Bethelsdorp, near Algoa Bay where the future Port Elizabeth was built. The movement was marked by strong conviction of sin and by tears, and it arose through strong preaching.[31]

Far away, at Griquatown beyond the Orange River, a great awakening began in June of 1813. The awakened settlers and the mixed-bloods began to confess their sins and to evangelize the unreached heathen in the immediate vicinity. One of the missionaries, William Anderson, described the movement as 'life from the dead.'[32]

The news of one awakening provoked many another. At Hooge Kraal, near George in the Cape Province, there was such conviction that the crying and sobbing drowned out the voice of the missionary.[33] The whole populace was transformed into a godly community commended by the local government.

In Namaqaland occurred similar happenings. News of the awakening at Griquatown stirred the people at Pella. There were many baptisms of heathen from the hovels around and lasting work was accomplished.[34]

The London Missionary Society workers gathered in Graaff-Reinet in August of 1814. They rejoiced to report hundreds of conversions.[35] The burghers of Graaff-Reinet were impressed by the good tidings of the workings of God among the heathen, and in high enthusiasm founded there an auxiliary missionary society.[36] Andries Waterboer, later to become a military leader and chief of the Griquas, himself preached in the meeting house.

Thus evangelization of the Hottentots was accomplished through the revival of the Christian folk in Dutch dorps and English towns. The general movement of the Spirit throughout Evangelical Christendom had resulted in the successful, lasting accomplishment of the task.

Of greater significance in winning the Bantu peoples of South Africa to Christ were the revivals among Methodists there. Arriving in 1816, their first minister encountered much opposition, his chapel being burned by a regimental colonel.[37] Presbyterians entering with Scottish troops met with less difficulty, thanks to establishment.

In 1820, more than five thousand British folk came out to South Africa and settled on the frontier between the Boers and the Bantu, founding Grahamstown and Port Elizabeth and creating the Eastern Province.[38] As picked artisans and farmers, they overcame initial hardships.

The official sponsors of British colonization were tardy indeed in providing official Anglican churches and clergy. The High Church S. P. G. and S. P. C. K. which followed the Church of England communicants and adherents into South Africa helped build Anglo-Catholic predominance, while by default (due to Anglican comity) Evangelicals were weak.

The early beginnings of the Baptist, Congregational and Methodist work as well as Scots Presbyterian in the Eastern Province demonstrated a measure of home-bred piety and evangelical zeal among British settlers—all voluntary.

It was among the Methodists that the first sign of revival was reported. The Reverend William Shaw, converted in Glasgow in 1812, came out as an immigrant pastor and began to preach the Gospel in the new settlements and, itinerating on horseback, organized a local preachers' band, dedicated to building churches in various places.[39]

Shaw had found conditions among the troops and settlers and hangers-on deplorably bad, the people often given over to drunkenness and debauchery. There was no ministry of any kind, Anglican or otherwise, for a thousand souls. Soon Shaw's powerful preaching and the kind of praying it provoked resulted in an awakening which cleaned up the community and began its civic reputation for a vigorous church and academic life. The Grahamstown Awakening of 1822 came not from special efforts but followed the usual means of grace in church life, producing many converts.[40]

With almost unanimous support, the Methodists erected a commodious chapel in Grahamstown, generously allowing the Baptists to use it for services, and even granting the Anglicans its use while the parish church was being planned and built—though the parish priest protested the Methodists ringing their own church bell for Methodist services as they willingly did for the services of their Anglican guests.[41]

George Lisle, an American Negro who fled to Jamaica in 1783, had been gathering converts of faithful preaching into Baptist churches.[42] Wesleyans opened their work in 1786.[43]

Before the end of the century, an awakening had begun in the West Indies, first moving Jamaica where, instead of a score or so, more than eight hundred were crowding out each chapel.   In St. Christopher, in 1802, the aisles of the chapels were wedged with black and white, who sat interspersed throughout the services.[44] In Tortola, four hundred new converts joined the Methodist society in 1802.   And in Antigua, there were eight hundred additions within eighteen months, sometimes 'the power of God descending' and many people prostrated thereunder.   Persecution soon followed, plantation owners objecting to the good done to their slaves. The Baptist Missionary Society sent out missionaries, in 1814, to help Lisle and his colleagues.[45]

In the first quarter of the nineteenth century, a Scottish agent of the British and Foreign Bible Society succeeded in gaining entrance to the South American republics.[46] He was an agent also of the British and Foreign School Society.

James Thomson sailed from Liverpool to Buenos Aires, reaching that port on 6th October 1818, after a voyage of three months. He was well received by the Government of Argentina, to whom he proposed the establishment of schools on the Lancasterian plan. Even the clergy gave him support, for just then the native-born clergy were open to new ideas; and within three years he had set up schools in Argentina and Uruguay with a total of five thousand pupils.[47] He was made an honorary citizen of Argentina, as he was of Chile.

Thomson arrived in Chile in mid-1821 and established schools on the same monitorial plan.   Some of the monastic orders were dispossessed of their convents to provide room for his schools. It seemed that his work had been established. No less a personage than the Liberator, San Martin, installed Thomson as first director of public instruction in Peru.[48] Navarrette, a local priest, was his best supporter. In Colombia, Thomson initiated a school system. In Mexico, ten primary schools became a thousand within a generation.

In Argentina, Chile, Peru and Colombia, Thomson's good start was lost both to education and evangelism. His well-organized school system and plans for extension and continuance languished for want of trained teachers. He lacked the organized support of British and American Churches. A greater factor was the unrelenting hostility of the Hierarchy.

19

AMERICAN OUTPOURING IN 1830

Although local revivals had continued for fifteen years after Waterloo, it seemed certain in 1830 that a further out-pouring of the Holy Spirit was imminent, as promising as anything experienced in the exciting times at the turn of the century. The American Home Missionary Society, founded in 1826, summarized its correspondents' reports:[1]

> With feelings of reverential gratitude, it becomes us to make mention of the blessings of the Most High poured out upon the churches of our country. From one end of the land to the other, points of light are appearing amid the darkness. In some districts, these luminous points are becoming so numerous as to blend their brightness so that the pathways of the Spirit may be distinctly traced by the glory which attends His visitation.

By the middle of 1830, the awakening had become general. The Presbyterians and Congregationalists were receiving reports of revivals from every quarter, east and west, north and south.[2] Thirty presbyteries west of the Hudson rejoiced in torrents of blessing. The General Associations of Connecticut and Massachusetts reported over-crowded churches, while the General Conventions of Vermont and New Hampshire told of 'great numbers turning to the Lord' and 'extensive revivals of religion.'[3] In Boston, metropolis of New England, it was said that God was raining down righteousness upon the people, the evangelical churches instructing six hundred inquirers, soon becoming fifteen hundred converts. It was noted that Methodists and Baptists were united with Congregationalist-Presbyterian colleagues in the work.[4] As generally the case in the initial outpouring of the Spirit, there was utter harmony.

Reports from Boston announced that there was a cloud of mercy resting over the city, and several churches were engaged in days of fasting and prayer.[5] In New York, souls were being added daily to almost all the churches, Baptist, Dutch Reformed, Methodist, and Presbyterian being noted with some Episcopalian congregations.[6]

Far to the northeast, in Maine, there were awakenings in the churches that principally moved the youth.[7] Many revivals were occurring in New Hampshire.[8] The awakening in Vermont was general, the small town of Poultney telling of 114 converts received, 63 by the Baptists, 36 by the Congregationalists, and 15 by the Methodists.[9]

Shaftsbury, Vermont, the base of a very evangelistic Baptist Association,[10] was early visited by a downpour of blessing, the meetings being still and calm, very solemn but with deep emotion, believers first moved, then sinners. In Massachusetts, one of the most thorough awakenings was occurring in Charlestown.[11] It began with prayer meetings for ministers, convened in the local Baptist Church. From the pastors' quickening, it spread to various churches. On Cape Cod peninsula, Massachusetts, the town of Hyannis was stirred by a thorough awakening which began, it was noted, among the children. More than two hundred people were converted, some of the instances being remarkable.[12]

The first intimation of a growing seriousness in the city of New York was not found in great congregations, nor in the ordinary assemblies of the saints, but in little praying circles that were discovered multiplying.[13] The movement was spontaneous and entirely interdenominational.

On Long Island, there were awakenings in many parts, including Southampton, West Hampton and Oyster Ponds. Up the Hudson river, the little towns were touched, and along the Mohawk westwards the revival was intense.[14] The most encouraging news came from Rochester.

The awakening in New York State was already considered 'a glorious work'—crowded churches, powerful intercession, convicting preaching, immediate conversions, encouraging additions in New York City, Albany, Troy, Utica, Rochester and a score of other towns.[15]

In Albany, capital city of New York, the revival swept the First, Second, Third and Fourth Presbyterian Churches, the ministers being Campbell, Sprague, Lockhead and Kirk. Many conversions occurred in these churches.[16] The impact of the movement gave William B. Sprague a lifelong interest in revival, his published lectures a standard work.[17]

A Rochester newspaper in the last week of 1830 told of unabated interest in spiritual things, observing that a large proportion of the recent converts were among the citizens of first intelligence and highest station.[18] Meetings in the churches were still crowded out.

The evangelist of the Rochester revival of 1830 was none other than Charles G. Finney.[19] His powerful preaching, his logical presentation of truth, and his appeal for immediate decision, given at a time when the Spirit of God was already moving in western New York and throughout the country, combined to produce one of the most fruitful local revivals of the time. Fully a thousand of the ten thousand inhabitants professed to be converted, 450 of whom joined Presbyterian churches that same year.[20] The revival reportedly reduced crime in Rochester, prosecutions lessened two thirds while the population trebled.[21]

News of the Rochester revival created quite a demand for Finney's evangelistic services throughout the States. Finney's autobiography has stated:[22]

> The very fame of . . . the work at Rochester . . . was an efficient instrument in the hands of the Spirit of God in promoting the greatest revival of religion . . . that this country had then ever witnessed.

The present research has shown that the 1830 Awakening was already effective throughout the States at the time of the local revival at Rochester.[23] Yet nearly all the historians have repeated the notion of its Rochester origin. Finney furthermore quoted Dr. Lyman Beecher as saying:[24]

> That was the greatest work of God, and the greatest revival of religion that the world has ever seen in so short a time. One hundred thousand were reported as having connected themselves with churches as the result of that great revival. This is unparalleled in the history of the church, and of the progress of religion.

Finney did not apply Beecher's words to his own work, but many writers have misread the quotation, including a devout German scholar who wrote: 'Der kritische Theologe Dr. L. Beecher beurteilt Finneys Wirkungen als „die grössten religiösen Erweckungen, die man jemals während einer so kurzen Zeit erlebte".[25] It is one's conclusion that the hundred thousand additions to the churches resulted from the general awakening already under way when Finney won a thousand in Rochester as part of the general movement. Finney went on to complete fifty years in evangelism and social service, in which he won his hundreds of thousands.

In 1832,[26] Charles Finney moved to New York City and engaged in a protracted work of evangelism which lasted two years, and resulted in the building up of the Tabernacle on Broadway, as well as a number of other churches.

A Philadelphia journal, dated 19th February 1831, carried the details of the awakening in Philadelphia which had begun the previous year.   It affected the churches of the evangelical denominations.[27] Finney had preached in Philadelphia in 1828, his 'new measures' in evangelism stirring up the ire of hyper-Calvinists in his own denomination.[28] The revival of 1831 there contributed more to the increase of dynamic evangelism than did the polemics of Finney.[29] There was a vastly different attitude displayed   by the church folk in the 1830s, thanks to the increase of the concert of prayer.

Again, the general awakening in the communities, like a line of thunderstorms, spawned a score of tornadoes in the colleges.[30] In Kenyon College, an Episcopalian institution in Ohio, there was a sweeping revival, with fifty volunteers for the ministry.   Union College in Schenectady   reported early morning and late evening prayer meetings.   Prayer meetings in Western Reserve were well attended. A spirit of grace fell upon the students at Jefferson College, with three dozen undergraduates inquiring after salvation.   The general awakening in Williamstown, Massachusetts, soon penetrated the college campus with encouraging results. In Yale, a college revival of great power brought more than fifty conversions at once, beginning in the senior class and spreading— as the movement in New Haven increased—till the college administration reported that one hundred only of three hundred and fifty were unaffected. At Brown University, it was noted that seventy of the student enrollment of 130 had been 'pious' before the revival, thirty had become 'pious,' and hope was expressed that the other thirty would experience a change of heart and become 'pious.'   A revival was felt at Amherst also. In Bowdoin, a revival swept the campus and a score of students professed new-found faith.   There was a revival in Ohio University. Hamilton College in New York State reported a stirring. There was an awakening also at Middlebury. No movement was reported from Harvard, but elsewhere revivals were the outstanding campus events.

In 1830, a great revival began in the town of Glasgow in Kentucky, where more than fifteen hundred joined the local Baptist churches.[31] There were no extravagances reported, nor any in the awakenings anywhere in Kentucky, Tennessee or camp-meeting country. Rather there were reports of a strange stillness in the trans-Appalachian country, in which sinners wept and trembled under conviction of sin. Yet none doubted that it was another outpouring of the Spirit.[32]

The rising tide of revival affected the Presbyterian cause in Kentucky, Tennessee, Virginia, North Carolina, South Carolina, and Georgia around about 1830. There were many thousands of conversions in Kentucky, and a general revival in Georgia, and stirring movements in every other state.[33]

The awakening reached its greatest effectiveness in the city of Richmond, Virginia, in July 1831. On the first Sunday there were thirty baptized in the river, twenty white and ten black; two weeks later, twelve white and ten black; but before many weeks, First Baptist Church had received 480 into fellowship, and Second Baptist Church 152.[34]

Among Baptists in Virginia were many ministers that were hyper-Calvinistic in theology and ultra-conservative in practice. William F. Broaddus, for example, opposed the use of 'means' in evangelism until he was persuaded to invite sinners to come forward in four-day meetings at Mount Salem.[35] In spite of anti-missionary opposition,[36]

> from that meeting may be dated the commencement of those glorious revivals with which most of the churches in the Shiloh Association were blessed in 1831 and 1832.

The Presbyterians in the South announced that the Lord was working wonders in Virginia and North Carolina, new churches being formed in South Carolina and Georgia to take care of the converts.[37] Specifically, North Carolinians informed their friends that they had never known a revival so general as the movement in Franklin County during the winter of 1830-31. These observers included many who had lived through the exciting days of thirty years before.[38]

In North Carolina, the churches of the Kehukee Baptist Association experienced the awakening in full strength. In what was described as a 'moral wilderness' a few years before, there was an astounding reformation of white and black society.[39] Local revivals continued.

Among the converts of the awakenings sweeping South Carolina during the 1830s was Richard Fuller, converted on 27th April 1832, afterwards becoming a worthy successor to Richard Furman in the leadership of South Carolinian Baptists, and, like him, an outstanding figure in American Baptist affairs.[40]

The effect of the awakenings of 1830 onwards among the Georgia Baptists was noticed in the state statistics, which showed 356 churches with 28,268 communicants in 1829, 583 churches with 41,810 communicants in 1835, and 971 churches with 58,388 communicants in 1845.[41]

The 1830 Awakening exercised a powerful influence in the evangelization of American Negroes. This was shown not only in reports of black conversions here and there, but in church statistics. For example, in 1797 there were 3715 white Methodists in South Carolina, and 1038 black; and this proportion was maintained in 1807 with 14,419 and 5111 respectively. But in 1818, the number of blacks had risen to more than half, 21,059 and 11,587 respectively; and in 1828, it was much the same, 35,173 and 18,475; but by 1838, the numbers were 24,016 white and 23,498 black.[42]

Sporadic revivals were altogether common in the Middle West, that westering frontier, during the years before 1830. In the burgeoning state of Ohio, in 1828, so many people crowded the meetings in the new settlements of Gallia County that temporary shelters were erected to accommodate fully a thousand people, and the crowds came. A revival was experienced in Worthington, Ohio.[43] Even far to the west, in Indiana, the congregations were unusually large in Hanover, where special meetings were held in October 1828. Settler communities were stirred in Illinois and Missouri.

In 1830, Ohio was dotted with little towns and new settlements, farmers clearing the forests for their fields. From every sector came reports of revivals, a startling stirring in the town of Cincinnati on the great river Ohio detailed.[44] In Indiana and Michigan there were movements also, and in 1831 the tiny towns of Illinois were awakened by the Spirit in the days of His power, causing the churches to rejoice, whether Baptist, Congregationalist, Methodist or Presbyterian.[45] The movement continued for several years. And in 1832, the tide of revival had reached the state farthest west, Missouri. Awakenings were touching the churches in towns named in French for saints, St. Louis, St. Charles, St. Francis, and roundabout.[46]

At that time, there were 5,322 Baptist churches, 3,467 ministers and 385,259 church members in the United States. In 1832, the Baptists were multiplying in the Middle West. Their statistics gave the numbers of churches, ministers and members as follows:[47]

Ohio	280	166	10,493
Michigan	17	13	667
Indiana	299	201	11,334
Illinois	161	123	4,622
Missouri	146	93	4,972
Other	101	42	3,380.

It is of interest, in view of the past popularity of the fallacious 'frontier' theory of revivals, that it was claimed that in the 1830 movement 'the cities and colleges have been the scenes of the deepest interest.'[48] This awakening did not begin on the frontier. Neither did the movement of 1792 in the United States. Nor did the 1858 Revival.

In 1832, there was a glut of revival news, the editors of evangelical magazines happily complaining that the 'joyful tidings of revivals' made it quite impracticable to notice them all.[49] From then on, news concerned items of novelty. Baptist editors decided that 'volumes might be filled with the delightful intelligence'[50] of revivals throughout the land. The opinion of editors at the beginning of 1833 was simply stated: 'Again the Spirit of God seems to be visiting the American churches.'[51] The Awakening was no longer news, it being taken for granted that revivals were widespread. In the opening weeks of 1834, it was feared at first that a withdrawal of the pervading influence of the Holy Spirit was in progress, but before many weeks had passed the editors were gladly acknowledging its return in all quarters.[52]

Examples of continuing local revivals may be multiplied. It was thought that an 1832 epidemic of cholera, that carried off many victims, and a severe tornado on 19th June 1835, that destroyed much property, had prepared the hearts of the people of New Brunswick, New Jersey, for an awakening. The Christian churches in this town in the Raritan valley —where more than a century before the works of grace under Freylinghuisen and Gilbert Tennent had begun—were the scenes of a startling awakening in 1837. The movement actually began in the Baptist Church in the month of April, during which the presence of the Holy Spirit was manifested in a remarkable way, affecting the other congregations.[53]

Much heartsearching arose in the Presbyterian Church which had reported discouraging conditions to presbytery, so a day of fasting and prayer was held; the people soon responded and a thoroughgoing revival was felt, in which not only were members revived but 149 converts joined the congregation, about a quarter of the total accessions to the churches of various denominations in New Brunswick.[54]

By summer, the revival had spread to Boundbrook which in September admitted 102 new converts, of whom 37 were publicly baptized, and a further 17 joined the church before winter, 125 in all.[55] Revival movements were also felt in Somerville, Piscataway and Plainfield.[56]

Baptist editors, analysing the Awakening of 1830, found among the furthering factors:[57] early morning and evening prayer meetings; protracted meetings; immediate repentance and faith; private conversation with seekers; Sunday School instruction; a more general effort to evangelize the community; and the zeal of younger converts in witnessing. The growth of the Baptists in the three periods of revival was demonstrated by their statistics: in 1790, there were 872 churches with 64,975 members; in 1812, there were 2633 churches with 204,185 members, a trebled total; in 1836, there were 7299 churches with 517,523 members, a 250% increase.[58] The Awakenings, and the congeniality of Baptist doctrine and practice thereto, were prime factors.

The General Conference of Methodists in 1832 heard the bishops' report with much rejoicing, that 'It has pleased the great Head of the Church to pour out His Spirit upon us in an extraordinary manner.'[59] In 1833, the aggregate increase was unusually large, 'the revivals having been very general and very powerful during the last year.'[60] Statistics told the story in the numbers of white and non-white members:[61]

1828	359,533	59,394	1832	472,364	76,229
1829	382,679	65,064	1833	519,196	80,540
1830	402,561	73,592	1834	553,134	85,650
1831	437,024	76,090	1835	564,974	85,694

The standstill in numbers of non-white membership was due to the shameful expulsion of the Indian tribes from their ancestral lands to west of the Mississippi. The decrease (-1860) in members in 1836 was attributed by Methodists to attraction of other evangelical denominations, and it caused much expression of humiliation, prayer and fasting—until the following decade, when there were great revivals in some parts of the country, notably where the agitation on the slavery question was not prominent. The 580,098 total in 1840 doubled by 1843 to 1,171,356.[62] Within a couple of years, Methodism was rent in twain.

In view of twentieth century preoccupation with the 'wild extravagances' of early nineteenth century revivals, the judgment of the Presbyterian General Assembly in 1831 is of value: 'The character of this work . . . has generally been . . . still, solemn, and in some cases overwhelming.' As before the 1830 Awakening, Presbyterian membership grew by 11,000 a year, the increase in 1832 alone was astounding —35,000.[63] A decline in membership after 1832 was due to affiliation of certain Presbyterians with Congregationalism.

In the wake of the 1830 Awakening, several small groups committed to a restoration of New Testament simplicity in doctrine and practice came together to form the Disciples of Christ denomination, also known as Christian Churches, or Churches of Christ. These restoration fellowships were thriving during the earlier decades of revival,[64] encouraged by denominational reaction and resistance to change.

Thomas Campbell, minister of a Presbyterian church in the North of Ireland, left home to seek better health in the American Colonies, arrived in 1807 in Philadelphia and was appointed to western Pennsylvania where his deep spirituality and his unusual abilities provided him with a widening ministry and a growing influence.

Thomas Campbell possessed a truly catholic spirit, and welcomed to the Lord's Table various believers who did not adhere to the Presbyterian organization to which he belonged. For this, he was censured and criticized so severely that he resigned from his ministerial affiliation.

Thomas Campbell convened a meeting of his friends and proposed a return to the teachings of the Word as the basis of truest unity. He held forth a maxim, 'Where the Scriptures speak, we speak; and where the Scriptures are silent, we are silent.' After discussion, it was decided to form 'the Christian Association of Washington,' a society to promote Christian unity and a pure evangelical reformation.

Thomas Campbell began to minister at large. Alexander Campbell, son of Thomas Campbell, had previously crossed to Scotland to study for the ministry of the Seceding Presbyterians.[65] In Glasgow, he had come under the influence of the brothers Haldane in whose ministry was blended revival and evangelism. The Haldanes had by then adopted congregational rather than presbyterial church polity. Alexander Campbell found that he had lost confidence in his own denomination. The younger Campbell took ship for America to find himself wholly in sympathy with his father. Alexander Campbell soon became the leader of the denomination, which within a century passed the million mark in membership.

For a while, Campbell's followers had been associated with the Baptists. Many of the believers following Barton Stone, squeezed out of the Presbyterian Church by rigid Calvinism, and James O'Kelly, squeezed out of Methodism by benevolent dictatorship, fused with the Disciples, who continued in the tradition of Christian reunion on the basis of New Testament practice, no longer interdenominational.

What of the German-speaking Lutherans and Reformed and Mennonites? Abdel Ross Wentz observed: [66]

> The German-speaking American Church in its two branches, the Lutheran and the Reformed, had felt practically nothing of the Great Awakening of 1740, and now at the beginning of the nineteenth century they were somewhat slower than the other churches to feel the quickening evangelical influences that swept over the other churches at that time.

Wentz cited language difference and conservatism as the reasons for the spiritual lag. But in the 1830s, Lutherans were influenced by the renewed revival, E. J. Wolf saying: [67]

> Symptoms of renewed spiritual life attested everywhere the presence of the Holy Ghost. The pulpit was marked by peculiar earnestness and pastors excelled in self-sacrificing fidelity in the catechism class and in house to house visitation. The congregations experienced 'an increased degree of spirituality,' . . . a warm spiritual life coursing through all the arteries of Christ's body.

But German-speaking folk were lost to evangelical groups such as the Evangelical Church and the United Brethren and the River Brethren, products of the impact of the 1792 revival upon the Mennonites and other German immigrants, starved of emotional involvement in their own cultural cocoons. [68]

Thanks to the energy of dedicated bishops and clergy, the Episcopal Church was recovering from the debacle of earlier days. One thrust was High Church, the other Evangelical, and after the Awakening of 1830, there was a line of cleavage through American Anglicanism and between it and others. [69]

After such an extraordinary experience of revival and church growth in the United States, it was inevitable that American observers would make comparisons of progress under a free church system with progress under state church establishment in Great Britain. In the 1830s, New York and Liverpool had approximately the same population, 220,000. The former had 142 ministers serving 31,000 communicants in 132 churches; the English sister-city had 57 ministers serving 18,000 communicants in 57 churches. Cincinnati, only forty years old and still in dense forest, possessed 30,000 citizens compared with Nottingham's 50,000. The Ohio city had twenty-two ministers and churches to compare with Nottingham's twenty-three, but there were 8555 active church members in Cincinnati to compare with 4864 in the English town with 60% greater population. [70]

20

BRITISH REVIVAL AND REACTION, 1830–

The Awakening in Britain which commenced about 1791 had affected not only Free Churches and Methodist Societies but the Establishment itself, making the Evangelical party therein the most influential force in England.

The returning wave of revival that crested in the United States in 1830 or thereabouts was to encounter opposition in Britain, not in the Free Churches nor in the Evangelical sector of the Church of England, but in the declining party of the Moderates in Scotland and in the advancing party of the Tractarians in the English Establishment.

In mid-summer 1833, John Keble preached a sermon in Oxford. Entitled 'National Apostasy,' it protested the action of Parliament in suppressing ten redundant bishoprics of the established Anglican Church of Ireland.[1] There followed a series of ninety Tracts for the Times, propounding the High Church viewpoint of a group of leaders around Keble, hence the designation Tractarians was given them.

Able scholars have published works on the Tractarian Movement, describing it as an Anglican Revival. It most certainly was a 'revival of religion,' but it was not—in the historical, theological, methodological or ideological sense — an evangelical awakening. It is true that evangelical awakenings were commonly called 'revivals of religion,' a term that could be applied to revivals of any kind of religion, Roman Catholic or Protestant, Christian or non-Christian. But the usage of the term 'revival of religion' in eighteenth and nineteenth century literature was restricted to specifically evangelical movements.

The essential element of an evangelical awakening was an outpouring of the Spirit upon believers in New Testament Christianity, more particularly those who had enjoyed the New Testament experience of conversion and regeneration following. This effusion issued in a spontaneous and general movement of believers to prayer, followed by conviction of sin, repentance and confession, soon leading to a burning concern for the salvation of the souls of men, near and far.

The Tractarian Movement did not resemble the Great Awakenings of the past. Instead of conversion followed by regeneration, it stressed baptismal regeneration which in practice was infant baptismal regeneration. It produced no spontaneous and general movement of believers to prayer, but was rather a confederacy of elitist scholars, fortified without doubt by a commitment to sacramental and liturgical devotion. It did not issue in evangelism, as understood by practioners of evangelism, though it did win commitment to a consistent churchmanship. It bitterly opposed the work of Evangelical churchmen, and, when a widespread awakening occurred twenty-five years later, its advocates set themselves in adamant opposition.

Although the Tractarians condemned 'the errors of the Church of Rome,' Evangelicals within and without the Church of England regarded the movement as Romeward, and were not at all surprised when John Henry Newman and others defected to the Roman Communion.[2]

None of this is meant to deny the very considerable contributions of the Tractarian or Oxford or Anglo-Catholic Movement to Anglicanism, nor to depreciate its missionary passion and social service. It is one's conclusion that, although the best authorities have asserted that 'The high church revival was not the antagonist but the supplement of the evangelical revival which preceded it,' this was not believed by the worldwide evangelical constituency—least of all by Evangelicals in the Church of England.

There were successive waves of revival in the growing Anglo-Catholic movement, issuing in— as was surely the case in the Roman Catholic revivals—the formation of orders and monastic communities. The pattern thus was medieval, rather than apostolic or reformational.

Anglican Evangelicals were moved to prepare for coming revival by the convening of the Islington Conferences in London, and, four years later, they erected Exeter Hall in 1831 for rallies of the Evangelical forces.[3] In 1833, Robert Aitken, an Anglican-ordained but interdenominationally experienced evangelist, began to devote himself to evangelism within the parishes of the Church of England.[4] William Haslam, whose conversion in an Anglican pulpit sparked a revival in Cornwall that lasted three years, continued as an Anglican missioner, one of many pastoral evangelists. Evangelicals were active in promoting missions among the poor and dispossessed as well as the better off.[5]

The decade of the 1830s produced another series of local revivals in Wesleyan Methodism in England, at the end of which the Wesleyan Conference declared: 'Some churches regard revivals of religion as gracious singularities in their history; we regard them as essential to our existence.' It is to be noted that these 'revivals of religion' were neither planned nor organized, except for prayer meetings.[6]

In 1834, an extraordinary revival began at Yeadon in Yorkshire. By the end of January, the whole town appeared to be brought under the religious influence. The spirit of conviction was so general that business was suspended for several days in some houses. So great was the number of penitents that prayer meetings were held from morning till night in the chapel. The movement spread to Guiseley and Rawden and doubled the membership there, but in Yeadon itself all six hundred members were revived and welcomed to their fellowship nine hundred new converts.[7]

Membership in the Wesleyan Societies passed the quarter of a million figure sometime in 1831. It had been rising each year by one or two thousands, but in 1832 the total had jumped to 256,272, an increase of more than seven thousand; in 1834, it jumped twelve thousand or so to 291,939, and thereafter rose a thousand or so annually until the end of the decade.[8] In the early 'forties, there came another period of revival, an overflow from American Methodism.

James Caughey was an Irish-born emigrant to the United States who was converted in the times of revival in 1830-31 and ordained to the Methodist ministry there shortly after. It was while engaged in pastoral ministry within the Troy Conference that he felt a definite call to return to the British Isles for a ministry of evangelism.[9] His work in Canada proved very successful, so he set sail for his native land.

After missioning in Dublin, Caughey crossed the Irish Sea and commenced his meetings for revival and evangelism in Liverpool, a city of quarter of a million population.[10] His ministry was most successful, for he preached a hundred and twenty times and turned over more than twelve hundred converts to the churches. The Methodists welcomed him to other cities and towns, where he reaped a harvest of converts as well as stirring the congregations to revival. His meetings were very fruitful in Nottingham, remembered in the records as being the place where a young man named William Booth professed conversion and took to street-preaching.[11] In all, Caughey claimed 22,000 converts.[12]

The ministry of James Caughey among the Huddersfield churches claimed 'thousands saved in pardon and purity.' The Methodist congregations reaped a harvest in revived believers as well as new converts.[13]

In the town of Goole, Caughey's ministry filled the local churches, with aisles and stairs as well as seating crammed to capacity.   The response was equally rewarding.[14]

Four months of ministry in Sheffield had produced no less than three thousand professed conversions, and half that number of those already believers entered into a vital experience of commitment. After a year had passed, there was no reaction against the movement reported.[15]

Three months in the old cathedral city of York produced nine hundred professed conversions, and three hundred restored from backsliding, and the circuit ministers noted a great work still progressing.[16]

Caughey's Chesterfield ministry resulted in both revival and evangelism, crowds upon crowds attending, nearly a hundred professing faith in one day. The circuit reported 369 converted 'out of the world,' 142 converted among the adherents of the societies, 88 backsliders restored, and 137 professing Christians making a full commitment of life.[17]

A London reporter described in detail Caughey's visit to Birmingham, where he preached in four Methodist chapels in both the east and the west circuits, attended by over-flowing audiences, with the Spirit of God outpoured upon the people, not only Methodists but Baptist and Congregational adherents becoming penitents.[18]

> We believe the revival in Birmingham has taken deep root and such an excitement has it created in the town on religious matters as was never before witnessed.

The largest Methodist church in Birmingham, seating two thousand or more, was densely crowded, the aisles and stairs and vestries as well as the pews being packed. So great was the number of penitents that the accommodation was altogether insufficient, and the large schoolroom was filled.   About six hundred professed conversion, the slain of the Lord—it was said—being 'heaps upon heaps.'

The revival left the barrooms and beershops 'vocal with lonely grumblers.' And Caughey reported that twenty-eight hundred were converted, half that total 'sanctified.' East Circuit in 1846 expressed 'devout gratitude for the remarkable outpouring of the Holy Spirit,' West Circuit claiming unprecedented prosperity, 285 added and 257 on trial.[19]

In the 1840s, Wesleyan Methodism increased its membership from 300,000 to 350,000, when dissension crept into the fellowship, controversy rent its councils, an uprising against Jabez Bunting occurred, and membership fell off by 50,000.

Wesleyan Methodists were cooling off in their concern for revival.[20] The people first reached by Methodism were from the lowest orders of society, but (as Wesley observed) the Methodists in every place grew diligent and frugal, and so moved up the social ladder. They grew less concerned with the evangelization of the masses.[21]

In this connection, it is important to assess the influence of Jabez Bunting, four times the president of the Wesleyan Conference, a president-maker, the dominant figure in the councils of Methodism for thirty years.[22] Bunting himself was the product of the Manchester revival prayer meetings, where he first exercised his ministry. But Jabez Bunting clashed with the more radical revival preachers, drove them out of the Wesleyan fellowship, and became a law and order man. It is interesting, if not ironical, that Bunting's own minister, John Barber, wrote him at ordination: [23]

> I am fully convinced that . . . the spirit of the revival is the spirit in which we shall all live, if we wish to be useful. But you will find that many of the rich, and all the lukewarm Methodists, will be against it, because they want a religion and a mode of worship that will meet the approbation of the world . . .

Within a few years, Bunting's whole outlook had changed, and the rest of his life was dedicated to proper ministerial pastorship and oversight of the flock which the Scriptures enjoined as universally necessary.[24] Bunting was a superb organizer, debater and churchman. He clashed with less order-oriented Methodists and drove them out into the Methodist splinter-groups. The rich and the lukewarm Wesleyans welcomed the institutionalizing of Wesleyanism, and supported Bunting. Insofar as Wesleyans won working class converts in the 1830s and 'forties, the revivals were mainly responsible, not 'respectable' Methodism.[25]

Of course, the Primitive Methodists, the New Connexion, the Bible Christians, and the others continued their outreach to the masses. The Primitive Methodists suffered a setback in 1828, largely due to over-expansion, but before 1830 the tide had turned again.[26] In the 1830s, the Primitive force of 250 preachers and 2500 local preachers adopted aggressive evangelism, local revivals giving greatest increase.

Meanwhile, local revivals continued in Wales, affecting all the denominations. An awakening began in South Wales, beginning in a prayer meeting held at Llanddeusant in Carmarthenshire. Empowered preaching followed, and the work spread throughout all the counties of the South. About two hundred and eighty converts were added to the church at Llanddeusant alone, two thousand to the congregations of Calvinistic Methodists in the county, and like numbers to the Baptists and Congregationaliats.[27]

At the time of the American awakening of 1830, Robert David of Brynengan was praying that the Lord would let him see at least one more revival.[28] John Elias preached at the Calvinistic Methodist Association rally in Pwllheli in the early autumn of 1831, pointing out the low condition of the Church and urging earnest and importunate prayer. The delegates and friends scattered to their homes, committed to prayer. In 1832, a powerful movement began to be felt at Brynengan. A Sunday School rally at Llanystumdwy was visited. Several months elapsed, and then the awakening spread throughout Carnarvonshire.

In 1840, more than two thousand people were added to the churches of Merionethshire in a movement which affected North Wales, Liverpool, and certain areas of South Wales. Charles G. Finney's lectures on the subject of Revival had been studied by the promoters of this work. Meetings for prayer were arranged, and district evangelization was then undertaken. This use of means distressed some of the older Calvinists.[29] An American visitor, the Rev. Henry Chidlaw of Ohio, was instrumental in stirring up much interest. A Day of Prayer was appointed by the Congregationalists of Carnarvonshire, 1st January 1840. The work was 'quiet and solemn.' Very few converts fell away.[30]

In 1849,[31] a great cholera epidemic afflicted South Wales, and concern impressed several thousand in a few months. The Congregationalist churches of Monmouth, Glamorgan, Brecknock and Carmarthenshires, numbering sixty-seven, added 9139 converts. So great was the rush into church membership that many feared that there would be a general falling away. Their fears were not realised, though some (of course) did not persevere.

The pattern of revival in Wales in the 1830s and 1840s was one of sporadic awakenings, sometimes affecting an entire county, sometimes all of North Wales or all of South Wales, the Free Churches the chief beneficiaries.

The early 1830s in Scotland saw the rise of a movement of far-reaching import. It was engineered by Evangelicals and directed largely by Thomas Chalmers, Thomson having died in 1831. It challenged the whole system of lay patronage and other abuses tolerated by the Moderates.

In 1834, the Church of Scotland General Assembly, led by Evangelical reformers, declared itself by a substantial and determined majority in support of the right of a congregation to veto the nomination of a minister thereto by a proprietor. It also initiated the creation of new parishes, Chalmers and his friends raising funds to build two hundred churches in seven years.[32] Scots Evangelicals were becoming powerful, but a tremendous crisis lay ahead.

Among the rising leaders of Evangelicalism were John, Horatius, and Andrew Bonar, ardent evangelists in pastoral ministry. Another was the saintly Robert Murray McCheyne in Dundee.[33] W. H. Burns ministered in Kilsyth. In Inverness was MacDonald of Ferintosh. Thomas Chalmers exercised the widest influence from his parish in Glasgow.

In Kilsyth, the Rev. W. H. Burns had found conditions in the parish in 1830 utterly deplorable, culminating in drunken brawls and unusual outbursts of sin. A day of fasting and prayer was set.[34] Prayer meetings had been carried on for ninety years, since the revival in 1742 in the days of James Robe's ministry; these were intensified for seven years or so in intercession for another great revival.

The ministry of prayer reached new heights in the later 1830s,[35] and a remarkable measure of interest in foreign missions was manifested as well as a burden for revival in Scotland. In the summer of 1839, the Rev. William Chalmers Burns, the minister's son, came to hold special meetings. He preached on: 'Thy people shall be willing in the day of Thy power.' As he told the congregation of the great work at Kirk of Shotts in 1630, he felt his own soul so moved that he began to plead with the people for instant response. All the while, the people were listening with rapt and solemn attention. Then their feelings broke restraint, and weeping and prayer drowned out the voice of the speaker.[36]

As the revival swept Kilsyth, the various denominations worked together in perfect harmony. The parish minister rejoiced that society was completely transformed. On 22nd September, more than twelve thousand people flocked to the town. The sabbath services went on all day and concluded at daybreak Monday. Multitudes professed conversion.

In the absence for reasons of health of Robert Murray McCheyne, William Chalmers Burns preached in Dundee on Tuesday 8th August 1839.[37] The phenomena of Kilsyth were repeated, and by Thursday evening the people were in tears.   Then followed three months of crowded meetings, night after night. In the autumn, more than six hundred inquirers were instructed in the faith. Before McCheyne returned to Dundee, there were thirty-nine meetings for prayer in the congregation. When the parish minister came home on 23rd November, the excitement had died down, 'but the number of saved souls is far beyond my knowledge,' he commented.[38]

Soon the awakening spread all over Scotland, Lowlands and Highlands. W. C. Burns was English-speaking, so he ministered in the great cities of St. Andrew's, Perth, and Aberdeen.   There was some opposition in the Granite City, the Aberdeen presbytery being unfriendly. A committee of Presbytery decided to investigate the results of the revival, reversed its attitude and heartily approved the awakenings, 'in hopeful progress in various districts of Scotland.' [39]

W. C. Burns was asked to minister in county after county, in the various parishes.[40] In many reports, reference was made to his preaching of the love of Christ in dying for sinners. A majority of the conversions occurred, however, during the seasons of prayer, and not at the end of sermons.

Leith, the port of Edinburgh, experienced a great revival during the winter of 1841-42.[41] The pattern was usual—much prayer beforehand, great expectation, deep conviction of sin, genuine repentance and transformation of character. The work spread to other churches in the Edinburgh district, as expected. There were movements also in Glasgow.

Revivals broke out quite independently of the leading revivalist. The town of Kelso was moved, Horatius Bonar reporting more than a hundred converted. An awakening was reported from Jedburgh.[42] Annan, on the Solway Firth, was mightily moved as the revival spread southwest. All over the Lowlands, great crowds attended the churches.

In the western Highlands, an extraordinary awakening occurred in Oban, in Argyllshire, so that people flocked to the meetings from the countryside around, some walking as many as twelve miles.[43] On 12th January 1843, a work of grace began at Lismore, where prayer meetings preceded the work of conviction, and neither farm-houses nor school-houses could contain the inquirers.[44]

In 1840, an extraordinary movement agitated the island of Skye from end to end, beginning with a wounded-pensioner, Norman MacLeod, whose farewell service at Unish deeply convicted the congregation, so that the people would not retire but continued all night, MacLeod staying with them for several weeks, services day and night. Fifty boats came from the coast around, and the movement lasted for months. In 1844, an awakening broke out on the island of Bute, and many scoffers were converted, some being deeply agitated. More than two hundred were converted in a little village. An unusual revival occurred on the island of Tiree, in the Congregational chapel. The island of Mull also was moved during this period of revival.[45]

Blairgowrie in the central Highlands experienced a stir. In the Breadalbane district in Perthshire, the minister was able to persuade W. C. Burns to visit his people. Prayer meetings had been maintained for a long time, and the local expectation was great.[46] Great was the realisation of hope, for many responded. There was an 'indescribable awe' in the meetings, some overwhelmed and even fainting.

In the northern Highlands, Dr. John MacDonald preached at a quarterly communion service in Tarbat, and a tide of deep spiritual emotion went over the congregation. On the Sunday following, MacDonald preached at a communion in Tain, farther north. Next day, the great congregation was melted by the power of the Word; a heart-rending cry arose from every part of the densely crowded church.[47]

In 1842, the General Assembly of the Church of Scotland, by a large majority, declared that while the civil courts had essential jurisdiction over civil cases, they had no right to interfere with the government and discipline of the Church. Sir Robert Peel, the Tory Prime Minister, persuaded the Parliament to reject the appeal of the Church. So, in 1843, Thomas Chalmers and a couple of hundred ministers walked out, reconvening to form the Free Church of Scotland, 474 ministers seceding, giving up churches and manses. The Free Church built more than six hundred churches within the next few years.[48] It founded New College in Edinburgh, and maintained all the overseas missionaries.

The shock to the Church of Scotland and its continuing 729 ministers seemed severe. Some ancient churches were nearly empty, as in Edinburgh. The Highlands supported the Free Church. But the Established Church recovered, and lay patronage was abolished by law thirty years later.

The effect of the awakenings in Scotland upon the lesser Presbyterian bodies was to draw them together, a majority of the Relief Church joining with the United Secession Church to form the United Presbyterian Church in 1847. Many of the uniting congregations derived from companies of praying people, opposed to the theological heresies and ecclesiastical abuses rampant in the Church of Scotland in the eighteenth century.[49]

James Morison, a Secession minister, was dismissed from the fellowship for preaching a 'whosoever will' gospel. In the revivals of 1839 onwards, Morison was extremely busy in evangelism, and from this activity sprang the 1843 Evangelical Union, which organized churches on the congregational plan.[50] This movement was quite distinct from the Congregational Union of Scotland, organized in 1812, a much more Calvinistic body, also augmented by the revivals, due in time to moderate its views and unite with the Evangelical Union before the end of the century.

The Baptists also gained from the revivals, not only from the ultimate accession of the Haldanes, but from the 1839 movement and the ecclesiastical turmoil in the Church of Scotland. A Baptist Home Mission (founded in 1826) was used to advance the cause.[51] The Christian Brethren also gained adherents in Scotland.

The non-conforming Episcopal Church of Scotland stood for a different order of churchmanship, and seemed to be untouched by the movements of evangelical revival, as were the few remaining Scottish aristocrats and the many Irish common folk pouring into Glasgow who adhered to the Roman Catholic Church.

The revivals greatly accelerated the growth of Scottish interdenominational societies, some of which were affiliates of worldwide movements begun in London, others having been founded in Scotland. David Nasmith, for example, had volunteered for missionary service overseas, but was not considered sufficiently educated for appointment. In 1826, he founded the Glasgow City Mission, followed by the Dublin City Mission, then he crossed the Atlantic to form the New York City Mission and the Toronto City Mission, tackling in 1835 the formation of the London City Mission.[52]

These were days of ample Scottish emigration overseas, and the revivals influenced the lives of many of those going abroad, making the Scottish contribution an evangelical one, including educators, schools and colleges.

At the beginning of the second third of the nineteenth century, Ireland's eight million population were divided in denominational loyalty between the Roman Catholic Church, with 6,427,712; the Church of Ireland and the Methodists, 852,064; the Presbyterians, 642,356; others, 21,808.[53]

In 1829, Catholic Emancipation brought relief to Roman Catholics suffering civil discrimination in Ireland. In the 1830s, the 'second reformation' was continuing to produce results in conversions of Roman Catholics, a process that was accelerated in the following decade by Alexander Dallas and Irish Church Missions, which built a score of churches and thirty schools in twenty years.[54] The Bishop of Tuam at mid-century averred that ten thousand had left the Roman Church in his diocese alone.

In 1832, Ireland was visited by an epidemic of cholera, killing thousands. Many Irish people became religiously concerned, and not a few were converted but were forced to emigrate because of persecution. Wesleyan Methodist membership rose from 22,000 in 1832 to 26,000 in 1835, and remained at that figure till the end of the decade.[55] Then in 1839, Fossey Tackaberry reported encouraging numbers of converts in Belfast, noting an absence of 'noise' but an occurrence of trembling and occasional prostration.[56] And in 1841, James Caughey preached 129 times in Dublin, seven hundred converts being turned over to the churches.[57]

The defeat of the Arians in the Presbyterian North gave the evangelical movement new life in Ulster.[58] A hundred new churches were built in the 1830s to meet the 'new spirit of seriousness throughout society.' In 1833, Presbyterians adopted measures for the dissemination of the Gospel in all of Ireland. The general reviving produced evangelism, and prayer meetings made possible the union of Synods in 1840.

In 1845, a blight affected the potato crop, a food staple in Ireland; and in 1846 the crop failed utterly, producing a great famine. Vast numbers died and many more were forced to emigrate to survive, the population diminishing by two million in five years or so. The disaster produced a turning to God, the effects of which were hard to see, for most of the converts decided to emigrate. The evangelism of the Methodists was so effective that its gains averaged the numbers of its losses by emigration. Local revivals broke out in the North, in Antrim, Ballymena, Limavady, Londonderry, Lurgan, and Randalstown in the years that followed the famine.[59]

21

REVIVALS IN SCANDINAVIA, 1830–

A British chaplain, George Scott, commenced in 1830 a
ministry that had a profound effect upon the religious life
of Sweden.[1] Born in Edinburgh in 1804, he was a Wesleyan
in his preaching but an interdenominationalist in his practice.
Although he did not have a drop of Swedish blood in his veins,
he fostered a love for the Church of Sweden, his ministries
raising up Swedish leaders who affected Christianity in the
kingdom for more than a lifetime.

Samuel Owen, a British industrialist, had opened a factory in Stockholm, and, being an ardent Methodist, he hit
upon the device of bringing a chaplain to Stockholm in 1826
to minister to his workmen. Scott was his second chaplain,
but he was not content to preach only in English, so he
mastered Swedish well enough within a year to preach also
in that language.[2] He secured the garden pavilion of Count
de Geer in Kungsholm, and held services that were obviously
in disregard, if not defiance, of the Swedish Conventicle Act
of a hundred years before.

In 1832, Scott's ministry was provoking a genuine revival
of evangelical Christianity among the Swedes.[3] The revival
made his name known to the masses, just as he was known
in aristocratic circles by diplomatic friendships. Soon he
was representing the British and Foreign Bible Society in
the city, helping organize and direct the Swedish Missionary
Society, and reorganizing the Evangelical Society founded
earlier by John Patterson in 1808.[4] Scott busied himself in
all sorts of good works, including schools for children and
a needed propaganda for temperance.

Sweden at that time was cursed by a national addiction
to brännvin, a liquor distilled from potatoes and grain.
The per capita consumption of alcohol in Sweden exceeded
that of every other country in Europe.[5] Even the clergy
supplemented their incomes by manufacturing the potent
drink. It became the customary beverage, supplanting tea
or coffee or even milk. Brännvin rendered the Swedes
stupid, besotted, and quarrelsome.

When an American temperance advocate, Robert Baird, visited Sweden, Scott lent his aid, and in 1837 a national temperance society was founded in Stockholm.[6] With his Swedish friends, Scott toured the country, addressing a crowd of three thousand in Norrland, sharing the platform with evangelical leaders such as Nyman and Wieselgren in Jönköping and Esbjörn in Hudiksvall.

During the revival of the 1830s, Carl Olof Rosenius was converted.[7] The son of a pastor in Norrland, Rosenius was moved to gather young men and boys for fellowship and service. With his bishop's permission, he began to preach in Piteå, farther north.[8] He studied at Uppsala, but gave up in disgust.[9] In Stockholm, he associated with Scott and soon joined with him in founding an evangelical periodical.

Scott's success earned him as many enemies as friends. The Church Consistory in Stockholm opposed the building of a church, a project on which the evangelist had set his heart.[10] With a measure of support from the press and the Crown, Scott won permission to build, and in October 1840 the English Church was opened. The opposition increased, and the church was closed finally in 1842, Scott leaving the country on the last day of April.

Rosenius had ministered in the English Church while his British colleague was visiting the United States to raise enough money to pay off the indebtedness on the building. When the church was closed, Rosenius took to the road and preached in conventicles. Many years passed before he returned to that pulpit, later called Bethlehem Church.

Meanwhile, the movement of the Readers— in various forms—received strong impulses from the reviving of the 'thirties and 'forties. Because the movement was barely tolerated, its leadership was haphazard, hence it developed peculiar manifestations.[11] Young people often went into a trance, and spoke of coming judgments, frightening those who heard them, but often effecting a transformation of life and character. The peculiarities were called 'the preaching sickness.' Some called it prophetic, others clairvoyant— and officialdom dubbed it 'madness.'

The 'preaching sickness' seemed to have originated in the hinterland of Göteborg.[12] It spread rapidly north and east, and affected all sorts of communities. The clergy and doctors, considering it some kind of epidemic, prescribed odd remedies. But the movement could not be restrained or controlled.

The extraordinary manifestations of the revival of the 1840s had much the same effect upon the general population as the frontier extravagances had had on American settlers beyond the Alleghenies. The odd manifestations were very disputable; reformations of character were irrefutable.

The revival preachers of the early nineteenth century were strong preachers of the law and gospel, with more emphasis upon the law; the later evangelical revivalists stressed free grace. Into the general movement, the 'free grace' preachers poured their time and talents. In due course, the revival movement took on a structured form.

The amorphous awakening of the 1840s continued into the 1850s. From one end of Sweden to the other, news was received of local revivals. In May 1850, Rosenius wrote: [13]

> Praise the Lord. Gladdening news is reaching us from many areas of our land of an awakening of spiritual need and life. The long dark winter of indifference...is yielding to the warm rays of the Sun of Righteousness.

A while later, Rosenius reported with greater gratitude still the news of spiritual awakenings from every province, calling for praise and thanksgiving. Year after year, the awakening continued. A sensation was caused by the lasting conversion of the 'Swedish nightingale,' Jenny Lind, who abandoned the stage as a career.[14]

George Scott had encouraged both Carl Olof Rosenius and Anders Wiberg, who had been students together at the University of Uppsala, both talented men. Another one of Scott's friends, F. O. Nilsson, became convinced by Baptist arguments and was baptized in Hamburg by the German Baptist, Johann Gerhard Oncken. In turn, Nilsson baptized Wiberg, who proceeded to the United States and returned to the land of his birth to become the leader of the Baptists in Sweden.[15] Rosenius's friends founded a society within the State Church, Evangeliska Fosterlandsstiftelsen, or, the National Evangelical Foundation, which stood for evangelical Lutheranism.[16] Thus the evangelical movement was divided.

Sweden was suffering from many economic and social problems at the time. The expanding population found but little room in the antiquated farming allotments. There came an emigration explosion, which took Swedes by the hundred thousands to the United States. Among them were many converts of the evangelical awakenings who found life in Sweden restrictive, not the least in its spiritual aspects, among them Lars Paul Esbjörn,[17] Augustana Synod founder.

Norway faced peculiar difficulties in its church life, for fewer than five hundred clergymen served almost a million people scattered in the valleys and on the coasts of fjords and on islands of a long, narrow land. The Haugean revival had raised up a host of lay preachers, or Readers, and the farmers and fishers welcomed their ministrations. But it was not till 1842 that the anti-conventicle law was repealed.

Hans Nielsen Hauge had been released from prison in 1814, and had devoted the remaining ten years of his life to a ministry of writing. The Haugean revival reached its greatest extent about the year 1824, its advocates stressing conversion and holy living, and soon numbering many very successful people among them. In 1825, there was revival of great power in the province of Sunnmøre.[18]

In 1833, there came a renewal of awakening all over the country.[19] At the beginning of the century, there had been only one non-rationalist bishop in Norway, Johan Nordal Brun of Bergen. His grandson, Pastor Lyder Brun faced a crisis of the spiritual life in Bergen, and emerged as a great revival preacher there and in western Norway.[20]

A few years later, Gustav Adolf Lammers was appointed pastor of the parish of Skien in southern Norway.[21] He was converted about 1848, and began to preach the experience of repentance and conversion, a great revival in the district ensuing. In the following decade, Lammers and some of his friends were impelled by conscience to separate from the State Church, forming a free church in Skien. It seemed that the movement would progress outside the Establishment, but it split, and Lammers sought to return.

In the 1840s, Gisle Johnson was studying in Berlin, and Leipzig, and Erlangen, and was much impressed by Neander and other leaders of the German Awakening.[22] His return to Norway brought about a fresh surge of awakening in the State Church. His ministry resembled that of Charles Simeon, for not only did he preach a powerful message, but he helped renew the parsonages of Norway, his talent and learning in his professorship of theology at Oslo (Christiania) inspiring many a younger man.

The awakenings of the 1840s and 'fifties, which produced the Inner Mission, Luther Foundation, and other evangelical agencies, and which accelerated the interest in missionary enterprise, was clearly part of the general revival of the second quarter of the nineteenth century. It was reinforced by Rosenianism from Sweden, welded to Haugeanism.[23]

The Danish awakenings which had appeared about 1800 maintained the evangelical witness of the earlier Pietists and Moravians in the country. The coming of European peace in 1815 was followed by further movements. On the island of Fünen, Kristen Madsen was converted in 1819 and won in turn Anders Larsen and Peter Skræppenborg who hepled in the spread of the movement.[24] Immediately, the forces of repression struck them, and several of the leaders were imprisoned. Johan Nielsen, a lay preacher, was fined more than thirty times. Members of the nobility and some of the pastors interceded on behalf of the evangelists, who won a measure of royal tolerance, hence the conventicles continued on the islands and Jylland.

The leaders of the awakening looked in vain for support from high places in the Church. From 1834 to 1854, Jakob Peter Mynster served as bishop of Sjæland.[25] He had turned away from rationalism and romanticism, but was opposed to the Awakening, with its emphasis on sin and repentance. Nicolai Frederik Severin Grundtvig, a truly remarkable Dane,[26] had also repudiated rationalism and romanticism, but showed little sympathy for the message of the awakening calling for repentance and conversion. Instead, he tended to stress the sacramentarian way of life, but supplemented this ministry with a consistent effort for social betterment, an emphasis borrowed no doubt from the social activists of the awakenings in England, which he visited many times. Grundtvig tended to neglect the Bible, which, of course, was the foundation on which the evangelical revivalists built.

It was during these times that Sören Kierkegaard began his spiritual pilgrimage as a forerunner of existentialism. His name became more widely known than that of Mynster or Grundtvig, for his philosophy was rediscovered in the twentieth century.[27] In his day, Kierkegaard had little to do with the evangelical awakenings in Denmark.

The Baptist expression of evangelical awakening was introduced to Denmark in the 1830s, J. G. Oncken of Hamburg having baptized Julius Köbner as a converted Jew.[28] The first Baptist church in the country was organized in Copenhagen in 1839, stirring up the opposition of the State Church which sought to counteract the appeal for believer's baptism by requiring by law all parents to have their infants baptized, a demand supported by Mynster but opposed by Grundtvig. The evangelical awakening in Denmark seemed weaker than that progressing in Norway, Sweden, or Finland.

When peace came to Finland after the Russian annexation, the evangelical awakening under Paavo Ruotsalainen was still continuing,[29] Ruotsalainen remaining active until 1857. In 1820, two young Lutheran priests, Jonas Lagus and Nils Gustav Malmberg, were converted and began to preach in the Swedish-speaking country of the southwest. There was a great awakening throughout the area, and in the 1830s it spread over all of the country. In Helsinki, the movement captured the interest of the university students and of the cultured classes.

In central and northern Karelia, which were Finnish-speaking districts, Henrik Kukonnen—his Swedish name was Renqvist—became the leader of a Karelian revival which not only promoted evangelism but the distribution of evangelical literature.[30] British and Foreign Bible Society agents gladly collaborated with Kukkonen.

.   As in Scandinavia proper, the laws against conventicles were strict, and the Russian officials began to apply them against the revivalists, so much so that there was a decided recession in the 1840s. After the rise of Carl Olof Rosenius to leadership in Sweden, there came another surge of revival in Finland, Fredrik Gabriel Hedberg becoming the leader. Many other younger Lutheran pastors throughout the Swedish-influenced South and West supported the movement.[31]

More than in Denmark, more than in Sweden, as much as in Norway, the evangelical awakenings permeated the life of the people in Finland, producing a national Church which was loyal to Lutheranism but molded by pietism in its more modern forms. Finland enjoyed a measure of autonomy granted no other part of the Russian Empire, and nationalism grew, evangelical influences supporting it. The tension between Swedish-speaking and Finnish-speaking citizens waxed and waned, but in times of revival the awakenings tended to draw the constituencies closer together.

Looking at the Scandinavian countries as a whole, it is clear that the general awakening at the turn of the century affected them all, but in varying degrees. In Norway and in Finland, the lay leaders of the revival wrought a thorough transformation of the national Church; in Sweden, the work was opposed by church authority to a greater degree; in Denmark, the anti-evangelical forces were stronger still. It is noteworthy that this response to evangelicalism has persisted into the twentieth century, Norway and Finland being the more evangelistic countries, the others less so.

22

THE ISLANDS AWAKENINGS

The evangelization of Polynesia provided a remarkable example of the impact of evangelical awakening upon pagan cultures. Evangelical revival provided the intital dynamic for missionary enterprise, the Polynesian missions being thrust forth and reinforced by the awakenings from 1790 till 1840. Secondly, evangelism of an extraordinary kind issued from exactly the same kind of awakenings on the field as in the sending countries—prayer, preaching, repentance, confession and conversion. Thirdly, revival-awakenings in the Islands repeated the pattern, for neither missionaries nor Islanders were content to found churches only, but strove to establish missionary churches which sent out heroic pioneers and well-taught teachers to other distant islands.

In the vast reaches of the Pacific, during the 1830s, the work of God continued to prosper under pioneering British Wesleyans, who preached for decision. Peter Vi became converted through the ministry of Nathaniel Turner, experiencing conviction of sin and joy of forgiveness. Taufa'ahau (a young chief on Habaii) experienced a radical conversion under the preaching of Peter Vi, the first Tongan evangelist, and the missionary Thomas, removing to Habaii, found a ready audience.[1] Taufa'ahau became convinced that he must confront his god and priestess, so he prepared a club from the soft stalk of a banana tree, and smote the priestess a soft blow and sent her (still under god-possession) reeling to the ground. The onlookers were amazed.[2]

Some plotted to kill the 'sacrilegious' chief, but the conspiracy was uncovered. The chief in turn adopted a forgiving attitude toward would-be murderers, but vented his indignation on the gods and their shrines. The priests tried to poison Taufa'ahau, but missionaries saved his life by administering emetics, while a company of Christian natives prayed all night for his recovery.

Taufa'ahau crossed to the island of Vavau to try and win a related chief to the Christian faith. His kinsman, Finau, gathered together his idols and addressed them thus:[3]

> I have brought you here to prove you. I will tell you
> beforehand what I am going to do, so that you may have
> no excuse. I am going to burn you. If you be gods,
> escape!

None of the gods moved, so Finau ordered their holy
dwellings to be set afire. The weather being damp, it took
four days before they were consumed. The affrighted people
sat by in fear and trembling, dreading retribution. None
came. The reign of the gods had ended.

Such happenings were bound to be noticed. On all the
islands of Tonga, people turned from idolatry and sought
Christian instruction. It proved more than the turning of a
people towards a superior religion, for phenomenal revival
broke out. A veteran Tonga missionary, J. Egan Moulton,
commented in retrospect:[4]

> While Christianity was said to have been embraced,
> true conversion was wanting. And this was a matter of
> concern to the missionaries. In 1834, the 'baptism
> from above' came.

The spiritual awakening to righteousness that followed
the mass turning to Christianity bore the marks of evangelical revival. It was marked by an intense conviction of sin,
weeping, public confession of sins and joyous conversions.
The movement spread rapidly to the other islands.

The Tongan Pentecost resulted in nine thousand people
becoming full members in six years. The awakening began
at Vavau and spread to the islands of Habaii and Tongatabu,
a couple of thousand being radically converted within a few
weeks in either place.[5]

The missionaries and their native converts gathered for
prayer each noonday, and there were prayer groups in the
scattered villages, in one of which they prayed all night.
The life of the villages was disrupted and then transformed
into that of Christian communities.

Public confessions of wrongs were made and old enemies
were reconciled. Polygamy began disappearing almost over-
night. Turner on Vavau was leading six meetings a day.
Tucker on Habaii was conducting four mass meetings daily;
and he recorded a glimpse of the movement:[6]

> As soon as the service began, the cries of the people
> commenced . . . One thousand or more have bowed
> before the Lord . . . and praying in agony of soul. I
> never saw such distress, never heard such cries for
> mercy, or such confessions of sin before . . .

A Tongan convert, Joeli Bulu, observed that the work went on from house to house, and from town to town, strangers also from other islands carrying it home with them. The Tongan kingdom rapidly became Christian, and continued thus, generation after generation.

The Tongan Revival had its critics. None could gainsay the good effected, but 'strangers to grace' in its historic evangelical form criticized both the manifestations and the doctrines proclaimed.

One, Basil Thomson, a British Colonial official with a bias against evangelical Christianity, described the revival as 'hysterical enthusiasm.' His criticism was based upon hearsay, for the movement had occurred before he ever set foot upon the islands.[7]

A trained anthropologist, the Australian Alan R. Tippett, assessed the emotional overflow as an accompaniment of a 'work of grace' succeeding a work of formal conversion and he cited the statistics of transfer from probationary association to full membership to show the significance of what had happened on Vavau:[8]

1829	31	1830	72
1831	516	1832	1422
1833	3456	1834	7451

These figures denote tried and tested church members, and do not include the generally larger numbers of converts from paganism on probation.

The immediate outcome of the Tonga Revival was the evangelization of other island chains by Tongan missionaries who risked their lives daily to accomplish what no European could do.

In 1846, yet another evangelical revival began in Tonga. The great awakening of 1834 had stamped indelibly on the minds of the Christians the importance of prevailing prayer and spiritual power in the warfare of the saints. Nathaniel Turner wrote of the 1846 movement:[9]

> For some time previous, our local preachers, leaders, and some of our members had been manifestly growing in grace. The spirit of piety had been deepening and spreading for two or three months . . . This was particularly the case at a prayer meeting held with the local preachers and leaders once a week. At one of these meetings the presence of God was signally manifested. . .

The actual outbreak of revival occurred on Vavau and spread throughout the islands. Back in Hihifo, in an ordinary worship service, the 'most solemn awe pervaded the place' before the crowded chapel was filled with suppressed sighs.

> When many chiefs met together for the transaction of business, they were unable to proceed, and were obliged by an influence from above to change the meeting for business into a meeting for prayer.[10]

As a result of the revival, sinners were truly converted, church members in a low state of grace were quickened and the ruling class of chiefs experienced a blessed moral transformation. The churches were equipped for service at home and abroad.

Calvinistic Congregationalism was rooted in Tahiti while Wesleyan Methodism was grounded in Tonga, and the overflow from each met in the Central South Pacific in a new and promising mission field.

John Williams was eager to evangelize Samoa from the east.[11] He joined forces with a Samoan Christian chief, Fauea, and sailed for Samoa. Fauea was settled on Samoa as an evangelist, and found the times ripe for his work. In 1830, many factors were combining to turn the interest of the Samoans towards Christianity. Williams returned in 1832, when Fauea's teachers had built a church, a number of folk including chiefs having embraced the faith. In every village, Williams met with the inquirers and converts who called themselves 'Sons of the Word.' So hastily Williams sent for missionaries from Britain; it was 1836 before they arrived, but native interest was increasing all the while. Williams pushed the work of evangelism and translation meantime, planning for the future.

A Samoan had visited Tonga in 1828 and had become converted, returning to Samoa to begin a spontaneous work of building little churches. While Williams was gone, the Samoans petitioned Tonga for teachers. The Samoan chief Tuinaulu, who had presented the petition to the Tongans, returned to become an ardent evangelist. So quite a few Samoans were converted between 1833 and 1835, while the Tongan revival was raging; the Wesleyan impact on Samoa, a Congregationalist field, had begun.[12]

Thus far, no Wesleyan missionary had trespassed on the L. M. S. field in Samoa. It was a domestic development. In 1834, Peter Turner arrived in Samoa. His arrival heralded a great awakening, gathering at first two thousand and then winning thirteen thousand to the faith. Eighty churches were built in eighty villages.[13]

It was quite a shock to Peter Turner to be told by the arriving Congregationalist missionaries that the previous comity arrangement made it wise for him to withdraw from Samoa. Turner first refused to consider it, and fought for his work. He left Samoa in bad grace after the Wesleyans in London had sustained the L. M. S. point of view.[14]

The thirteen thousand Methodist converts were left in an awkward situation. There were enough differences with Congregational Calvinism to be an embarrassment. Less than twenty years later, the Australian Methodists (who had taken over British responsibility) sent their missionaries to reclaim their work in Samoa.[15]

There were further outpourings of the Spirit on Samoa in 1840, under Congregationalist prayer direction, when many nominal Christians experienced what was called a reconversion, as elsewhere in the Pacific. Two thirds of the whole island population showed anxious 'concern.' These Samoan awakenings paralleled the related Scottish Revivals of the 1830s and 1840s, and movements in Wales and England.

In Tahiti, in spite of the fact that the Christians were known as a praying people, that they were instructed in the Word by faithful teachers, that they possessed the Scripture in their own tongue, there was nothing like a classic revival for twenty years. True, there had been a folk movement of startling proportions, but until 1835 the reports of London missionaries gave no evidence of the repentance unto tears.

Just before an 1835 awakening, there were revivals of the unwanted kind—a syncretistic admixture of Christian rites and exercises of immorality, with dangerous and visionary heresies combined. Between 1831 and 1833, the cultists dominated Bora Bora.[16] The congregation at Maupiti were seduced by Teao and Hue, leaders of the Mamaia cult, and engaged in drinking bouts, lustful dancing and fornication.

In 1835, a genuine evangelical revival began at Papara on Tahiti.[17] It was marked by unusual praying, by intense conviction of sin, by repentance and confession. Groups of people participated, but it was not a folk movement in the accepted sense of the term. Henry Nott, a veteran pioneer from the first landing, noted that the response fell into three categories: nominal believers who had abandoned heathenism but lacked spiritual experience; teen-agers who had been baptized and catechized now registering personal commitment; and backsliders who had been disciplined for misconduct. They were instructed accordingly.

At the beginning of the 1830s, there were only 577 church members throughout the Hawaiian Islands. But the tide of spirituality was rising, and not only were believers being prepared, but the masses were developing an interest.

All around the world, there were people praying for a general awakening. The missionaries in Hawaii gathered each year for discussion and united prayer. In 1835, they were moved to make an appeal to Christians in the United States to pray for a baptism from on high for the Hawaiian field, just as they were praying for the whole world.[18]

At Hilo on Hawaii there was stationed Puaaiki, a blind preacher, the leader of the 'praying ones' in the Islands. In 1835, Titus Coan, an associate of Finney and Nettleton, the American evangelists, moved to Hilo also.[19] It was here that the Great Awakening of Hawaii first manifested itself. It began in 1837 at Hilo and continued for five years, a total of 7557 converts being received into one church, 1705 of them in one day.[20] Titus Coan won thirteen thousand in all in his preaching ministry up until 1870.

Coan itinerated through the Islands.[21] On the western shore of Kaui, he preached three to five times a day to vast crowds, who remained till close to midnight and were back again at cock-crowing. Coan himself described the work:

> The sea of faces, all hushed except when sighs and sobs burst out here and there, was a scene to melt the heart. The word fell with power and sometimes, as the feeling deepened, the vast audience was moved and swayed like a forest in a mighty wind. The Word became like the 'fire and hammer' of the Almighty, the Spirit, quick and powerful.

All over the islands, the movement was felt.[22] Among the commoner manifestations of conviction, a trembling and shaking occurred, and likewise prostrations to the ground. Missionaries tried to control the meetings and to prevent them getting out of control. Sometimes the scoffers were smitten. On other occasions, weeping drowned out the voice of the preacher. The New England missionaries frowned on such manifestations, but Titus Coan seemed unafraid of them, and became greatly beloved by the people.

The movement at Hilo continued into 1838, and news of similar awakenings came from all the islands. Attendances at Hilo were so great and so sustained that something like a two years' camp meeting was in progress. Sometimes the inquirers walked more than fifty miles to attend.[23]

On Molokai, a first sign of revival was noted at Kaluaaha in the rising of intercessors before daybreak to pray for an outpouring of the Holy Spirit. This voluntary gathering increased in numbers and in solemnity before the blessing came. The island churches were revived and augmented.[24]

On the populous islands of Oahu and Maui, as on Hawaii, the congregations averaged between two thousand and six thousand. Women held their own meetings in places, and even little children interrupted their play in the cane fields and banana groves to hold devotional meetings, and often surprised their parents by rising early for prayer out in the fields together.[25]

The missionaries were thorough in the care of converts. They divided the inquirers by age group, and instructed them in the faith and encouraged them in discussion and prayer.[26] They were placed on probation, and when their testimonies by word and deed were deemed satisfactory, they were admitted to membership.

Titus Coan received 1705 into membership after a long probation and a careful examination.[27] He admitted 5000 in a single year. The number of backsliders was extremely small, possibly one in sixty of the inquirers counselled. On Oahu, there was a relapse into drinking by some, but this was countered by a day of humiliation and prayer, soon followed by another outpouring of the Spirit.

Between 1837 and 1842, more than twenty-seven thousand converts after thorough probation were received into the membership, about one-fifth of the population of the islands. In 1843 alone, 5296 were admitted; 19,679 were in good standing twenty years later in spite of the decline in the Polynesian population due to epidemics of alien diseases. The nation, regarded as Christianized, was granted a Bill of Rights by King Kamehameha III in 1839.[28]

Meanwhile, the sons of the early missionaries played an unusually influential part in the affairs of Hawaii—building up the economy, harvesting new crops, developing industry. This provoked a later jibe, 'The missionaries came to the Islands to do good, and did very well.' Few missionaries abandoned their sacrificial missionary work for gain and their sons rendered Hawaii a notable service.

An influx of non-Christian stock from the Orient changed the Christian and Polynesian majorities into a minority which, through its own Hawaiian Evangelical Association, began to win the newcomers, often from Buddhist faith.[29]

Far to the southwest in the vast expanse of the Pacific lay the Fiji Islands, populated by a mainly Melanesian folk. War between tribes and villages was common and life was cheap.   Widows were strangled on the death of husbands, and sick and aged were killed. Cannibalism was so common that social rank was gained by the number of humans eaten.[30]

The first rays of hope for Fiji shone from farther east. The progress of the gospel encouraged Tongans to take the Good News to other islands, including the Fijian Lakemba. In the significant year, 1835, when so much was happening elsewhere in the world, the Wesleyans landed two British missionaries on Lakemba, where they encountered a rough reception. But their mission succeeded and nearly 300 were baptized within twelve months.[31]

In 1835, a terrible epidemic raged on Ono, another Fijian island, where a local chief—despairing of pagan rites— offered worship to God of whom he had vaguely heard. A Tongan teacher visited the island, and enlightened people further, and in 1839 two hundred converts were baptized by a Wesleyan missionary.[32]

As the missionaries penetrated the islands to the west, they were compelled to witness numerous horrors—the killing and cooking and eating of a dozen captives, and the like.   They persisted with preaching and teaching for many years, a full decade from their first landing in Fiji.

In 1845 a revival-awakening began, marked by conviction of sin and transformation of life.[33] The work of grace in Fiji included typical folk movements, in which the heathen turned from idolatry to the worship of God, and revival-awakenings, in which nominal Christians underwent a deep change for the better and their kinsfolk professed faith in Jesus Christ. There were successive revival movements of heart-felt conviction, followed by conversions.

In 1854, before a second decade of evangelism ended, the Fijian king Thakombau openly espoused the Christian faith, perhaps influenced by a letter of appeal by Taufa'ahau of Tonga, known as King George of Tonga.[34] Cannibalism came to an end, as did widow strangling; and the tribal warfare dwindled and ceased.

The Fijian churches grew steadily by evangelism and by local folk movements.   The Wesleyan Methodists provided the missionaries, at first from Britain and then from the Australian colonies.   Before 1860, another period of revival accelerated the Christianizing of the Fijian people.

The most significant factor in the evangelization of the Indonesian Archipelago in the first quarter of the nineteenth century was the awakening in the Netherlands in Napoleonic times, with its revival of believers and missionary outreach —still continuing throughout the first quarter of the century. The most significant factor in the second quarter of the nineteenth century was the awakening in the Netherlands known as 'Het Reveil,' which was paralleled by revival and missionary zeal among Hollanders in the Indies, and by movements among Indonesian people towards Christ.

Missionaries of the Netherlands Missionary Society had entered the island of Celebes (Sulawesi) in 1822. While the revival was moving the sending country, a folk movement of great proportions swept Minahassa, the northeastern peninsula of Celebes, resulting in an ingathering which was to make that field Christian in a couple of generations.[35]

The growth of the churches in the Moluccas continued into the second quarter of the century. Amboina was soon to become as Christian as the sending country in Europe. In 1835, the Rhenish Missionary Society entered the island of Borneo, contending against the greatest difficulties. In the next decade, the Church Missionary Society supported a work begun by an Oxfordman, McDougall, in Sarawak, a British-protected part of the same great island.[36]

Meanwhile, persecution raged on Madagascar. Queen Ranavalona I was determined to stamp out Christianity utterly. All public worship, together with the teaching and circulating of the Scriptures, was banned. A young woman was martyred in 1837; in 1840, nine believers were speared to death; others were done to death by the ordeal of poison and by spearing in 1842; fourteen Christians were thrown over a cliff and four more burned to death near the royal palace in 1849; in 1857, twenty-one were stoned to death and others were killed in various ways calculated to strike terror into Christian hearts; thousands of Malagasy folk who professed the faith were flogged, or deprived of their rank and property, or sold into slavery; others fled to the British island of Mauritius.[37]

Malagasy Christians continued to meet in secret. They cherished the reading of the Scriptures, which had been translated into court Malagasy before the persecution began. They waited patiently for liberation from oppression, and for the evangelization of their country; but a full quarter of a century passed before their prayers were answered.

23

AWAKENINGS IN SOUTH AFRICA, 1830–

It has been demonstrated that the evangelical awakenings were a prime factor in sending out dedicated pioneers to the mission fields. What is not so readily apprehended is that not only folk movements of uninstructed people turning to God helped build the churches on the field, but that real revivals of believers and awakenings of communities played a very vital part in getting the younger churches under way. The 1830s and 'forties in India, Africa and Oceania presented examples of the Spirit at work on the opened mission fields.

In South Africa, in 1831, a second season of revival was enjoyed in Grahamstown and district.[1] It began in the local Wesleyan Church and spread to other towns and farms.[2] Many young people were converted to God, and a number entered the Christian ministry.

Minutes of the District Meeting of Methodist ministers and local preachers in Albany (Grahamstown) District noted:[3]

> Throughout the past year, the English congregations have been large, and from want of room in the chapel, great inconvenience has been experienced . . .
> It has pleased the Head of the Church to grant us a gracious revival of religion in our Grahamstown congregation, in the early part of last year, principally among our young people. . . we have a clear increase of fifty-six members.

As among the Dutch-speaking congregations, the revival of the European Christians produced a vital interest in the evangelization of the heathen. Demonstrating the essential oneness of the work of God, there were outbreaks of revival everywhere, an inter-racial and interdenominational work.

In the first quarter of the nineteenth century, the Dutch Reformed folk in South Africa were suffering from a dearth of clergy. The Awakenings had already moved Scotland, but not the Netherlands, so a Governor of the Cape succeeded in persuading a number of Scottish ministers to emigrate to the colony to minister to its Dutch-speaking people in dorp and veld.[4] The experiment proved a happy one.

Among these Scots came the elder Andrew Murray, who not only quickly identified himself with his adopted people but prayed earnestly for an evangelical awakening in South African churches similar to the movement stirring Scotland, a habit which he continued until his death.[5]

This Andrew Murray sent his sons John and Andrew to study in Scotland, where they were deeply moved by the awakening begun with W. C. Burns, whose preaching had stirred Dundee. Both young men decided to enter the ministry, and went on to Utrecht for their theological studies. The Awakening provoked by the visit of Robert Haldane to Geneva was already spreading, since 1820, from France to the Netherlands. Their involvement in the Revival both in Holland and Scotland had lasting results in South Africa, yet another example of the interplay of evangelical awakenings across time and space.[6]

Not only was Evangelicalism the major influence in the Dutch Reformed Church, but it predominated in the English-speaking Churches also, in the Baptist, Congregationalist, Lutheran, Methodist, Presbyterian, and others. This is confirmed in standard histories of South Africa, as in the writings of Walker, Cambridge historian,[7] and Latourette, missions historian at Yale, who said:

> The main recruitment of the clergy came through the missionary societies. The Wesleyan movement, the Evangelical revival in Great Britain, and the Lutheran revival in Germany had put new life into Protestantism ... had even affected the far-distant Cape ... welcome support to the incoming evangelical missionaries.[7]

Evangelicalism had its own distinctive type of ecumenism, one which began at the grass-roots between individuals who shared the same spirit of brotherhood, concern and cooperation. The ministers of the Dutch Reformed Church in the days preceding the quickening at the Cape were often jealous of Moravian, Lutheran, Anglican and other workers in the vineyard. What a vital difference of attitudes in the early nineteenth century when the Church of England clergy held their services in the Groote Kerk,[8] Wesleyan and Lutheran congregations happily sharing the Cape Town constituency with Reformed parishes. This evangelical ecumenism was reflected in the founding of the Cape of Good Hope Church Missionary Society, in a meeting presided over by the good Sir Benjamin D'Urban. It came to an end with the arrival of Churchmen with a non-Evangelical view of the Church.

An attractive people with a musical language, Bantu folk were possessed of a tribal organization capable of withstanding the impact of European colonists. It must be recognized that they lacked some elements of civilization, whether of the West or the East. Their bravery, even their chivalry in battle was unquestioned, but many of their tribal customs were considered barbaric by European and Asian observers.

The first quarter of the nineteenth century had produced a military genius among the Zulus who attacked and decimated three hundred tribes, butchering and burning so that it was said that not a single square mile of what is now Natal was left unsodden by the blood of his victims. Shaka and his impis (including runaway rebels against his tyranny) desolated a wide swathe of territory that lay as comparatively empty as the southwestern veld where the Bantu folk were unknown.[9]

The 1831 awakening among the British settlers— chiefly Wesleyan in character—moved Christians in evangelizing the Bantu as well as Hottentots. Near the Buffalo river, the Rev. Samuel Young was preaching in the Wesleyville station, when a man began to cry aloud until the whole congregation became affected, beginning a thorough revival.[10]

These local awakenings often continued for months on end. The Methodist missionaries were delighted to win so many of various racial and tribal origins, and one of many chiefs converted was Kama, a first fruit of Bantu Christian chiefs.

Among the converts of the awakening stirring the 1820 Settlers was Joseph Warner, who went forth as evangelist among the Tembu, and who gave two sons to the Methodist ministry. Another was Henry H. Dugmore, who became a superintendent, ministering to Europeans and Bantu folk.[11]

Joseph Williams, of the London Missionary Society, took the message to the Xhosa-speaking folk who represented the first great wave of Bantu advance to the southwest. His converts survived his premature death, thriving in the faith.[12]

Robert Moffat, another Scot, devoted himself to evangelizing the Bantu tribes of Botswanaland.[13] When he and his wife Mary arrived at Kuruman, they found 'not a ray of light' in the darkness of local social and spiritual conditions.[14] A spiritual awakening began in 1829. Within five years, the population of the station had risen to 727, with 115 scholars being taught in the school; the attendances at worship on Sundays rose to 340, weekdays to 130, and 29 were regular communicants.[15] Robert Moffat, unbelievably to some, won the notorious chief, Africander, to a vital Christian faith.

The awakening in Botswanaland continued. A report of 1832 from the Plaatberg Circuit claimed that the average attendance for many months was five hundred and sometimes rose to a thousand in Christian worship.[16]

There was similar blessing in the Transkei, where the inhabitants were Xhosa-speaking. At Butterworth, the local Methodist missionary read a letter from Wesleyville:[17]

> Cries at this time became general throughout the chapel so that my voice and the voices of those who prayed were drowned; and when we were compelled to break up the meeting, many went away from the chapel sobbing.

Most of the Wesleyan stations in the Transkei and other Bantu areas experienced a visitation. The manifestations of the awakenings in the homelands were being seen in Africa, among people not so long indoctrinated.

Before the end of 1834, the Sixth Kaffir War had broken out; within a few days, invading Amaxhosa impis murdered many settlers and destroyed hundreds of homesteads and many mission stations, scattering the missionaries.[18]

Another extraordinary awakening began in 1837, again in Grahamstown, the large chapel being crowded for prayer night after night, many professing to find faith, more than two hundred in number.[19] In its membership, the European Circuit increased from 315 to 609 in a single year. The awakening spread to the Bantu congregations, taxing every bit of space. Probationers increased in number rapidly, accredited members more slowly.

In the same quarter of the century, another product of the Awakening in Scotland arrived in South Africa, a significant event. David Livingstone married Moffat's daughter, Mary. At first he took his wife and children on his long, dangerous journeys. After losing his youngest child and almost losing the others, he sent them home and pursued his extraordinary explorations alone. His heroic exploits pointed a way to the evangelization and civilization of Africa.[20]

Scotsmen were not only well represented in the London Missionary Society, but also in national societies. Scottish Presbyterians contributed a major benefaction to the education of Bantu folk by founding, along with other schools, the Lovedale Institution in 1841.[21]

Anglicans were somewhat tardy in their outreach to the Bantu, their belated ministry chiefly to English settlers and officials absorbing their energies until the coming of Bishop Gray, a dynamic High Church leader, in 1847.[22]

In 1835,[23] the Congregationalist American Board entered Natal to evangelize the Zulus. In 1829, the Paris Evangelical Missionary Society—a product of the Revival in France— sent its first missionaries to South Africa; and in 1833 they entered Lesotho and founded an abiding work. Their greatest pioneer was François Coillard,[24] himself a revivalist whose heart had been kindled by the ministry of Haldane in France.

Another revival-sparked society, the Rhenish Mission, sent its first missionaries to South African Hottentots and Bantu folk in 1829. It was followed by its sister Berlin Missionary Society in 1834.[25]   Yet another missionary product of the revival in Europe, begun through the awakening in 1848 in Hanover, was the Hermannsburg Mission to Africa.[26]

The Awakening in Norway under Hans Nielsen Hauge led to the sending of Hans Schreuder and a Norwegian Mission to the Zulus of Natal in the years following 1843.[27] Schreuder was a forerunner of several Scandinavian enterprises.

It is an inescapable conclusion that pagan tribespeople in South Africa were being evangelized by missionaries thrust forth in the awakenings in South Africa and the overseas motherlands, and that these same kind of awakenings were used to win great numbers of pagans to Christ in a remarkably fruitful beginning of the evangelization of Africa.

Johann Ludwig Krapf of Württemberg was an obvious product of the post-Napoleonic revival in Germany. Receiving his training at Basel, he entered the service of the Church Missionary Society in Africa. After several attempts to enter closed doors, he moved southward to Zanzibar and Mombasa to preach, becoming proficient in Swahili. Krapf dreamed of a chain of mission stations across the breadth of Africa.[28] The fulfillment of such a dream awaited the coming of recruits from the next series of evangelical awakenings.

What of the remainder of Africa, south of the Sahara?   It was indeed a Dark Continent. First European contacts with Black Africa had come through the nefarious slave trade in which the professedly Christian nations followed the Arab example in abetting raids on innocent tribes.

In the early nineteenth century, the slave trade was suppressed, but settlements around the coast begun for trading purposes continued.   Explorers and missionaries began to traverse the continent. Then there followed the 'scramble for Africa' in which European nations carved up the continent's mass. In many instances, missionaries preceded the flag; in others, they followed it.

24

STIRRINGS IN THE EAST, 1830–

Historical records have demonstrated a general concern among the evangelical missionary societies thrust forth by the early nineteenth century Awakening for the ancient but languishing Christian communities of the Near and Middle East. One society after another embarked upon a 'mission of help' to these Christian minorities, whether Armenian in Asia Minor, or Coptic in Egypt and Ethiopia, or Nestorian in Mesopotamia and Persia, or Syrian in India.

Thus in the 1830s the American Board of Commissioners for Foreign Missions opened up permanent stations in the metropolis of Istanbul (Constantinople), in Asia Minor and in Armenia[1]. Their missionaries found the Muslim Turks intransigent, but they were welcomed by the Armenians, to whom they introduced evangelical doctrines and evangelistic methods[2]. There was no intention of setting up a separate denomination of Evangelicals, that term being used simply to describe one who held the right to read the New Testament and to follow its teachings within the fellowship of his church.

The Erasmus of the Armenian reformation was a clever teacher named Peshtimaljian, who maintained a school for candidates for the priesthood in the capital. Many younger priests became influenced by the Scriptures, and progress was made[3]. In Nicomedia, close to the Sea of Marmora, a local revival broke out in 1838, followed by another nearby at Adabazar in 1841. Inevitably, the conservative clergy began to persecute the evangelical 'ecclesiola in ecclesia,' the Patriarch in 1839 ordering the arrest and imprisonment of its leading men; and in 1846 a bull of excommunication was issued[4]. Persecution was intensified, accelerating the progress of the Gospel. The Evangelicals were forced to establish an Armenian Evangelical Church[5]. As the work spread, revivals of religion in the Armenian minority also increased, even in southern cities such as Aintab and Aleppo. In due course, the tensions between the Gregorian Church and the Evangelicals subsided, the latter often being asked to preach in the older churches and teach in their colleges[6].

Evangelical Christians were convinced that, in western Asia, there was little hope of converting Muslims while the Oriental Christians appeared no better in daily living than the Muslims, who regarded them as worse than themselves —hence claimed that the teachings of the Koran proved far superior to those of the Bible.[7]

The American Board established its mission in Persia (Iran) also, with a strong base at Urumiah, on the shores of the lake of that name in the northwest.[8] As early as 1844, an unusual interest in vital Christianity commenced among the Nestorians, 'a refreshing from the presence of the Lord.' A large village, Geog Tapa, was particularly moved.[9] By 1846, the awakening at Urumiah had developed all the usual characteristics of genuineness and thoroughness, quite as much so as in the revivals witnessed by the missionaries at home.[10] The Nestorians were amazed by the work, and the missionaries were 'filled with wonder, as well as joy unspeakable.'[11] The revival was characterized by suddenness, deep conviction, lack of animal excitement, lack of gossip, while no extraordinary means were used to effect the work, which first moved the older rather than the younger.[12] A year later, the outpouring was still effective in revival, with an absence of opposition from any quarter, least of all the priests, several of whom were converted to God.

In 1849, a second awakening occurred. Geog Tapa was moved; in Seir, scarcely a person was unaffected; in other places, there were large attendances and happy results. In 1850, a third revival began, again stirring the schools. In Iran, there was not as much opposition as encountered among the Armenians, hence the Assyrian Evangelical churches that were formed retained membership in the ancient Church until 1870, when the mission became Presbyterian.[13]

Likewise, the Church Missionary Society attempted to renew the Coptic Church in Egypt, and received a friendly welcome. There was no secession, and some reforms were effected.[14] The United Presbyterians from North America in a succeeding generation entered the field and built up a following among the Copts. Ethiopia remained closed.[15]

The Church Missionary Society established a 'mission of help' to the ancient Syrian Church of Malabar in South India. It translated the Scriptures into Malayalam, established a college and printing press, and promoted vital evangelism. In 1836, tension brought about a separation, but the leaven continued to work,[16] later producing the Mar Thoma Church.

In 1830, Scottish Presbyterian missionaries arrived in India, their noted leader being Alexander Duff, a product of the nineteenth century awakening in Scotland, his family influenced by Simeon, himself a protege of Chalmers.

Alexander Duff proved to be one of the most influential men to reach India. Not only did he leave his imprint upon the educational systems of India, including State schools, but he worked as an evangelist with a care for souls.[17]

Another famous Scottish missionary, John Wilson, had arrived in India the same year as Duff, under the auspices of the Scottish Missionary Society.[18] He too was a product of the Revival of the early 1800s in the Scottish border country, and he too became a famous educator as well as an evangelist. He helped found the University of Bombay, but his monument was Wilson College.

Stephen Hislop, yet another Scots convert of the Revival in the border country, arrived in India during the 1840s and continued in educational work and evangelism in the Central Provinces.[19] The Scots also founded a college in Madras.[20]

Anthony Norris Groves of the Open Brethren brought out a dozen missionaries to India in 1836.[21] Christian Brethren, be it noted, were thrust forth by the British Revival.

After the triumph of Ulster Evangelicalism in 1840, the Irish Presbyterians began a work in Gujerat,[22] gathering their converts into villages. Welsh Presbyterians, hitherto working through the London Missionary Society, sent their own missionaries to the Khasi hill tribes of Assam in 1841, winning converts and founding little churches.[23]

After 1840, American Presbyterians entered the Punjab, while John Scudder and missionaries of the Reformed denomination in America were gathering congregations at Arcot in the Madras area under the American Board of Missions,[24] later supported by the Reformed Church.

In 1832, the fervent preaching of Deerr and Jenner, of the Church Missionary Society, won five converts in the Nadia district in Bengal, but between 1838 and 1840 a folk movement of Karta Bhojas to the Gospel gathered 1200 into the fold. Bishop Wilson of Calcutta[25] was 'full of thankful ecstasy.' After this, the Nadia Church seemed to institutionalize its Christian life.

In the second third of the century, American Lutherans entered India[26] and operated a mission in Telugu country. The Evangelical Lutherans, later known as the Leipzig Mission,[27] entered the Indian field through Madras in 1840.

Lutherans, through the Basel Mission, opened a work on the Malabar coast at Mangalore about that time.[28] One of the German missionaries who came out to serve in India was Samuel Hebich, whose remarkable zeal gained him 'an honourable mention' in Bishop Stephen Neill's history of Christian missions.[29] Son of a pastor, Hebich was converted in 1821 and, after a business career, volunteered for the mission field, arriving in Calicut in 1834.

Hebich preached a simple Gospel, evangelical and direct, an outstanding success with the officers of British regiments stationed nearby. His vocabulary of English words scarcely exceeded five hundred, but his methods were witlessly naive and devastatingly effective. Scores of officers responded to his challenge and lived as true men of God in the service of the Queen.

In August 1847, Samuel Hebich had gone with a European congregation to Chirakal to attend a meeting. The Indian catechists at the meeting were so filled with the Spirit and spoke so searchingly that many Europeans were in tears. Two Indian boys made confession of their sins and declared their new-found faith before the Chirakal congregation.[30]

The 'fire' spread to Cannanore. Europeans made public confession of their faults in the prayer meetings, while the Indians came in groups, confessing to Hebich as to a priest. Hebich, during this revival season, was almost beside himself. One day he rode to Tahy, the hamlet of fishermen, his soul all afire. When he entered the village, he called out to all: 'Repent! Repent! The day of the Lord is at hand.' The effect of this message was overpowering. None of the people dared look up and all were silent before God. When he came to the mission house, he called out: 'Who will repent?' The people came crowding to the missionary, confessing their sins and praying for forgiveness.

On 6th October, he rode to Tellicherry and confessed his many failings and faults to his German brethren, who were not pleased at first. Then they followed his example. He told the national church of the revival in Cannanore. That evening, after he had returned to Cannanore, a revival began in Tellicherry that spread to Calicut and far around; everywhere the revival meetings continued far into the night. The heathen were filled with a spirit of great awe; nowhere was the voice of mockery now heard; but they would not attend the revival meetings, though a few who did were converted in defiance of caste.

By the mid-century, the number of Protestant Christian Indians had reached a hundred thousand, half of whom were residing at the tip of India, where successive folk movements and awakenings and revivals were occurring. Undoubtedly, the civil and military power of Britain in the sub-continent, while never directly applied to the support of missionaries, accelerated the growth of Christianity there.

The missionary volunteers of the Second Awakening also tackled the lands of the Buddha, but met with resistance except among their animistic minorities.

The London Missionary Society had landed a party of missionaries on the island of Ceylon (Lanka) but gave up its mission in 1818.[31] The Baptists reinforced their 1812 excursion in 1830. The Wesleyans extended their 1814 mission to several parts of the island. And the Church Missionary Society, from their initial landing in 1817, also developed a work in various areas.[32] The American Board tackled the Tamil-speaking area around Jaffna.[33] Revival was reported among the converts being instructed in little churches.

In Burma, Adoniram Judson had concentrated upon the Burmese language and people. His colleague, George Dana Boardman, who arrived after 1825, became interested in the Karens, and baptized Ko Tha Byu, a Karen murderer and robber.[34] The new convert became a dynamic evangelist to his own people, just at a time when the Karens were proving most responsive. A folk movement followed, the first fruits of the Christianizing of the Karens and other non-Burmese tribes. Converts multiplied by hundreds, then by thousands.

At the time of Carey's arrival in India, the Emperor of China was announcing to the western world that it was forbidden to propagate the 'English religion' within his domain. The Serampore missionaries, hoping for a change in circumstance, prepared translations of the Scriptures into the Chinese ideographs.[35] Robert Morrison, converted in 1798 in Northumberland, arrived in Canton as an interpreter and was appointed official translator by the East India Company. He completed a translation of the Bible in 1819, but five years earlier, he baptized his first Chinese convert, just after receiving a helper from Scotland, William Milne, also a convert of the general awakening.[36]

Only a tiny foothold in China was secured for the Gospel, but a beginning had been made. Korea and Japan remained closed, but in China the door was forced ajar by political considerations, not of missionary choosing.

In the 1830s, the American Board sent its first missionaries to China, as did the American Baptists.[37] American
Anglicans and Presbyterians followed, choosing the port of
Canton as a base of operations.[38] Karl Gützlaff, a graduate
of Jänicke's school in Berlin, toured the coasts of China in
the 'thirties, distributing literature.[39]

The shameful Anglo-Chinese War of 1839-42 opened up
additional Chinese ports to the residence of foreigners, so
that missionaries, however they felt about the evil of opium,
were enabled to find further opportunities for the gospel.
Hong Kong was ceded to Great Britain, many missionaries
settling there, and at Shanghai, and other treaty ports.

Gützlaff gathered about him a staff of Chinese preachers
and colporteurs who were reported to be distributing the
Scriptures and gathering converts in most of the Chinese
provinces. He was discouraged to find that many of his co-
workers were thoroughly dishonest double-crossers.

Society after society entered the treaty ports of China,
Shanghai becoming a strategic place. In 1847, W. C. Burns
(whose revival ministry had challenged many who became
missionaries) himself came out to China.[40] For more than
six years, he travailed without a convert in Amoy. As soon
as some were won, he moved on as an evangelist to other
treaty ports. Burns impressed many, nationals as well as
missionaries, by his transparent saintliness.

A Hakka villager in South China, Hung Hsiu-Chuan by
name, came into touch with Christianity in the 1830s.[41] He
had strange visions of power, and out of his preaching came
a movement in the mountains of Kwangsi. In the 1840s, he
renewed his contacts with Protestant missionaries, but in
unknown ways he converted his movement into an army and
overran China from the South to the middle Yangtse, setting
up a capital in Nanking. Shortly after the second Anglo-
Chinese War, in which France joined, the Imperial Chinese
armies, with foreign help, crushed Hung and his Taipings.

In the main, the entrance to China was made by missionaries of societies raised up by the nineteenth century revival
movements.[42] As yet, no breach was made in the uniform
Chinese resistance to the Christian faith, converts being few
in number. Revivals in China came many decades later.

Although the intrepid Gützlaff visited ports in Korea and
Japan, both these kingdoms remained tight-closed against
the gospel until the second half of the nineteenth century,
evangelized only by the worldwide Concert of Prayer.[43]

25

SOCIAL OUTCOME OF REVIVAL

The impulse for social action in the nineteenth century was derived from the impact of the eighteenth century revival but the personnel to implement it were recruited from the awakening of the late eighteenth and early nineteenth century worldwide. This is not seen in the historical treatments of England before and after Wesley,[1] which generally ignore the worldwide recession at the time of the French Revolution and the awakenings that began just after Wesley's death.

Europe and America were convulsed by war in the days of Napoleon, hence it was to be expected that the flowering of social reform would follow the coming of peace after the battle of Waterloo. Peace made possible a way for social improvement not only in Great Britain and parts of Europe but also in the United States. The first period of impact came to an end about the time of the abortive revolutions of 1848 and the Crimean and American Civil Wars, and the second one commenced in the 1860s.

The first social impact was felt in the emancipation of slaves, in the protection of prisoners, in the care of the sick and wounded, in the betterment of the standards of workers, in the defending of women and children and helpless animals against abuse, and in extending systems of education.

By far, the greatest social evil was that of human slavery. Inter-tribal wars provided opportunities for slavery, which was the lot of the captured, not only in Africa but in many other parts of the world. The Arabs first introduced war for the capture of slaves for the Near Eastern market as a way of life in Africa, Europeans introducing the same objective (directly and indirectly) into West Africa for the overseas, rather than the overland trade. There is no escaping the responsibility for the active promotion of inter-tribal war, although (of course) such a state of affairs could not have occurred in the nominally Christian homelands, even then. The feudal system, with its institution of serfdom, a form of slavery, had passed away in most European countries, though persisting in the most backward.

179

The slave trade was a diabolical affair. African chiefs often raided nearby villages at night and set fire to the huts, slaughtering the very old and very young and dragging the survivors in shackles to the coast. In the overseas trade, it was estimated that one in eight died during the voyage in which they were packed like logs in stinking holds, and that another one in twenty died in the port before reaching the auctioneer's block, twenty per cent dying within ten weeks of embarking, with no more than fifty per cent reaching the plantations. Likewise, in the overland trade, ten lives were lost for every slave who reached the coast and fifty per cent never reached a slave market,[2] according to Livingstone.

Thirteen years before the formation of the Committee for the Abolition of Slavery, John Wesley published his thoughts on slavery in a direct and penetrating argument against the inhuman traffic in human beings: 'Can human law turn darkness into light or evil into good? Notwithstanding ten thousand laws, right is right and wrong is wrong still.'[3]

Wesley declared all slave-holding absolutely inconsistent with any kind of natural justice, let alone Christian ethics. He declaimed that the whole business was hypocritically greedy, that slavery bred other vices. Men-buyers, he said, were no better than men-stealers. He denounced the wealthy slave-merchants as the mainspring that put into motion the slave-captains, slave-owners, kidnappers and murderers. They were all guilty.

These were strong words to use in 1774, when plantation slavery was protected by law, when philosophers of old and statesmen of the time were quoted eagerly to justify the outrageous institution. Wesley followed the example of the Quakers, who had spoken against slavery in the seventeenth century. George Whitefield declared less opposition. But the anti-slavery advocates were only a small, enlightened minority in both Britain and the American Colonies. Their voices were scarcely heard at first.

Slavery, though not practised in Europe, was prevalent in European colonies in the New World as well as in most Asian and African countries. In the nineteenth century, slavery was practised mainly in the plantation communities of the South in the United States and in the West Indies, as well as in the Ibero-American colonies. Yet the control of the machinery of slavery lay in the efficient shipping organizations of England, Old and New. And naval police power lay in the hands of the British Admiralty.

The pioneer advocates and engineers of the abolition of slavery within the British Empire were almost all activists of the evangelical awakening. William Wilberforce and his colleagues were Evangelicals, many of them the pillars of the then-derided, now-extolled Clapham Sect, the group of Church of England Evangelicals with Free Church adherents holding greater concern for the souls and bodies of men than for current ecclesiastical strife.[4] As the abolition movement gained strength by spiritual persuasion, great men such as William Pitt, Edmund Burke and Charles James Fox, and others of like rank, joined the Evangelicals in their grand objective, as did liberals with ethics inherited from their own Christian forebears.[5]

From the time that Lord Mansfield declared in a famous case in 1772 that any slave brought to England was automatically free, anti-slavery agitation made progress; and so the slave trade was abolished in 1807.[6]

That abolition of the slave trade had been achieved in Britain was of utmost importance. Had another country so decided, only a good example at the least would have been forthcoming. After Trafalgar, however, Great Britain's naval might was unchallenged for a century, and it was used to dissuade other nations from slave-trading. The nations at the Congress of Vienna agreed that the slave trade should be abolished, hence country after country took legislative action until it was internationally outlawed by the civilized nations, and by some less-civilized countries as well.[7]

At first, the patrol action of the British navy against the slave-ships in the Atlantic and Indian Oceans had the effect of worsening conditions on the voyage to slave-markets, for up to two-thirds of the human cargoes were lost, some being thrown overboard to avoid detection and capture. And thus the dwindling supply of slaves caused much overwork in the West Indian plantations.[8]

Sir William Fowell Buxton led the agitation, until in 1834 emancipation of the slaves came into law throughout all the British Empire.[9] No less than 750,000 in the West Indies alone were proclaimed free men, their chapels being crowded at midnight 31st July, while the day of liberation, far from being one of bloodshed as predicted, became a day of order, reverence and rejoicing, the Negro having been prepared for his liberty through the influence of evangelical missions. Parliament cheerfully paid twenty million pounds sterling to recompense the slave-owners.

It took another thirty years to bring about the emancipation of the slaves in the United States. The successes in the early nineteenth century of the British emancipation had dealt a staggering blow to the American institution of slavery, but it took more agitation by indignant reformers and convicted Christians and yet another evangelical awakening, before a majority of the people were ready to abolish slavery. Many of the Northern evangelists, including Finney, conducted an anti-slavery agitation in their writing and preaching.[10]

In prisons was held another reservoir of human misery. Already in the eighteenth century significant prison reform was under way. The conditions of life in prisons were at that time indescribably foul. Old, decrepit buildings were commonly used as prisons; strait-jackets, irons and chains were added for security on the slightest excuse. The prisons were dens of despair with disease, drunkenness, indecency and debauchery forced on their inmates. Not only were the vicious criminals so incarcerated but also first offenders, and even persons already declared not guilty of any crime.

An Evangelical, John Howard, took up the challenge and gave his life as well as his private fortune.[11] John Howard received the official thanks of Britain's House of Commons. He was recognized[12] as the father of modern prison reform, inspiring others to take up the task only barely begun in his lifetime. Evangelicals took the lead, followed by the free-thinkers, who tackled the reform of the penal code.[13]

A young Quaker mother who raised eleven children became burdened for the women, desperate and depraved, whom she found in the notorious Newgate prison that Wesley had called the earthly equivalent of hell. Elizabeth Fry not only read the Scriptures and prayed with these unfortunates, but also opened successful prison schools for them.[14] In 1817, Mrs. Fry founded a society for prison reform, dedicated to those principles now taken as elementary; separation of the sexes, classification of criminals, useful employment, secular education, and religious instruction with a view to restoring the prisoners to society.

One of those directly influenced was Theodor Fliedner, born in the first month of the year 1800, son of a Lutheran pastor.[15] Unconverted, he had attended the Universities of Giessen and Göttingen, but his faith was deepened elsewhere, a greater influence on his life being the evangelical impact of Halle,[16] the university where August Francke had served. He dedicated his life to the ministry.

Theodor Fliedner was called to the cure of Kaiserswerth, a Protestant parish situated in the midst of a Roman Catholic population.[17] A threat of foreclosure of a mortgage sent him off to Holland and England to collect funds. It was in London that the effects of the Revival dispelled finally any trace of rationalism in Fliedner's mind.[18] In 1823, Theodor Fliedner met Elizabeth Fry in the British capital.[19]

> I learned to know a whole host of institutions that minister to the bodies and souls of men. I inspected their schools and prisons. I observed their homes for the poor and the sick and the orphaned. I studied their missionary societies and Bible societies and their societies for the improvement of prisons, and so forth. And I particularly noted that practically all of these institutions and organizations were called into being by a living faith in Jesus Christ and that nothing but this vital faith sustains them.

On his return to Germany, Fliedner requested voluntary imprisonment, but was refused. In 1826, he organized a prison society, the first of a series of philanthropic ventures. He built a home for discharged women prisoners, another for men, another for orphans, a hospital for the sick, an asylum for the insane. He urgently needed nurses to help, but in those days an educated woman would not stoop to empty a bucket. Fliedner decided that, if a farmer's daughter could care for helpless animals, she could care for sick folk. He put girls in uniform and called them deaconesses.

Florence Nightingale, an English gentlewoman, was much intrigued by a report of the ministry of Theodor Fliedner at Kaiserswerth where the sick were lovingly cared for by the German deaconesses, all of them of peasant stock, as were Elizabeth Fry's, nursing being regarded as too low for ladies. Soon she took her training in nursing at the obscure village on the Rhine.[20] Looking back years later, she deplored the backwardness of the hospital but commended its tone as 'excellent,' affirming that she never had met a purer devotion. With evangelical zeal, she applied the lessons learned.

Before she died at the age of ninety, the 'lady with the lamp' had revolutionized the life of the private soldier. She became generally regarded as the founder of modern nursing. And historians have conceded not only her training at a school born of evangelical revival but her debt to Evangelicals for her lifelong simplicity of purpose. Daughter of a Unitarian, she took an evangelical view of the Deity of Christ.[21]

Great Britain was the first of the countries of the world to become industrialized. The industrial revolution brought about a sorry exploitation of the toiling masses, for whom deism had done little, evangelical revival much.[22]

Converted as a boy in the days of revival before Waterloo, Ashley Cooper, 7th Earl of Shaftesbury, called himself 'an Evangelical of the Evangelicals.'[23] He embarked on a crusade for the betterment of humanity, giving unparalleled demonstration of Christian love, rather than of class hatred, love harnessed to improving the lot of the working poor.

Until Lord Shaftesbury's reforms, workers were caught in a treadmill of competitive drudgery which served to keep them straining for sixteen hours a day. Shaftesbury and his friends put an end to that by legislation limiting operation of factories to ten hours a day, introducing a Saturday half-holiday, and abolishing all unnecessary Sunday work.[24]

Shaftesbury's Mines and Collieries Act made impossible any further exploitation of women or children in coal mines where they had been used to drag coal in heavy wagons along darksome tunnels. His Chimney Sweep Acts prohibited the use of little boys to clean narrow factory chimneys of soot; many a child had suffocated at the task and others had been maimed therein. He also delivered children in the country from an agricultural exploitation as terrible as that of the factories. Shaftesbury, by his Lunacy Acts, transformed the lot of the insane from abused prisoners to patients.[25]

Shaftesbury promoted public parks, playing fields, gymnasia, garden allotments, working-men's institutes, public libraries, night schools, choral and debating societies, and other opportunities of self-help.

Even Kenneth Scott Latourette in his weighty volumes confessed that there was not enough space to list more than a few of the reformers and reforms impelled by evangelical motivation.[26] Nine out of ten of Lord Shaftesbury's colleagues in social and industrial reform were as much the products of evangelicalism as the Earl himself. A cotton-mill owner, John Wood, provided most of the money needed for the Ten Hours' Crusade. Richard Oastler, who did so much for the factory children, was a Methodist lay preacher. Others in the crusade were active in the lay preaching of the gospel. The Ten Hours' Act proved to be the Magna Carta of the liberty of industrial workers, closing factories at 6 p.m., keeping them closed for twelve hours, preventing workers from being robbed of evening and Sunday leisure.[27]

Critics of the failure of the Churches to reach the working classes of England nevertheless conceded that 'in so far as Methodism gained new adherents among the working classes between 1800 and 1850,[28] revivals were mainly responsible.' As the Wesleyans through affluence lost their contact with the masses, the Primitive Methodists gained theirs.[29] When a rally was held in Durham on 20th August 1831 to consider grievances, many speeches were larded with Bible texts, as most speakers[30] were Primitive Methodist local preachers. Sidney Webb, Fabian socialist, conceded that Primitive lay preachers took the lead and filled positions of influence in trade unionism.[31] This action long predated the rise of the Christian Socialist movement at the mid-century.

British trade unionism owed much to the six Dorchester farm-hands who were transported to Australia for seven years penal servitude.[32] Their crime was that of forming an agricultural union to resist further depression of their wages, already cut to a below-subsistence level of a shilling a day. They were guilty of no violence, no intimidation, not even a strike. In 1834, all six were seized, condemned and shipped, ten thousand miles to Tasmania.

These Dorchester farm-hands, often called the Tolpuddle martyrs,' included three Methodist local preachers and two others active in the Tolpuddle Methodist Chapel. A sixth professed no religious convictions, but was so impressed with the religious life of one of his companions who slaved with him in a convict gang that he became a Christian and a Sunday School superintendent in later life. An aroused public opinion forced the early pardon of these working-men and their transportation home. The trade unions had won a round in the battle for working men's elementary rights.

The Liberal Prime Minister, David Lloyd George, paid an unusual tribute to evangelical influence thus:[33]

> The movement which improved the condition of the working classes, in wages, hours of labour, and otherwise, found most of its best officers and non-commissioned officers in men trained in institutions which were the result of Methodism ... John Wesley inaugurated a movement which gripped the soul of England, that deepened its spiritual instincts, trained them and uplifted them; the result is that when a great appeal is made to either England or America, there is always the response . . . and it is due to the great religious revival of the eighteenth century.

The decades following 1830 in American life have been called by writers [34] 'The Sentimental Years,' for they were times when organized good works flourished as never before. There was scarcely an object of benevolence that lacked a dedicated society or institution,[35] and all of the organizations ---whether church-related or not—were directly indebted to the evangelical awakening of the times.[36]

In the United States, there were societies to promote education, to reform prisons, to stop prostitution, to colonize Africa with freed slaves, to advance the cause of peace, to provide social and spiritual amenities for sailors in port-— not to mention the multitude of home and foreign missionary societies, Bible societies and tract societies, associations of Sunday Schools, and temperance clubs.[37]

Out of the Revival in Britain came the monitorial school system of Lancaster and Bell, a prelude to mass education. Schools and high schools and colleges were founded in the United States as a result of the Awakenings of 1800 onward in many churches and colleges, awakenings which provided not only founders but teaching staffs. Most of the denominational schools and high schools gave way to free public school systems in turn. Latourette declared: [38]

> Even more important, the initiative and the early leadership in the creation of the system of free public schools supported by the state came largely from those who seem to have caught their inspiration from the Protestant wing of Christianity.

In the United States, therefore, the public conscience had been stirred by the private example of committed Christians, so that there was no longer the urgent need of originating schools for the masses. There was a great need of training an elite for leadership, of providing higher education for all aspirants to service in the professions.

The impact of the college awakenings was felt in the founding of colleges and academies throughout the West. The principal dynamic behind the college founding movement was undoubtedly evangelical religion, for realization by the once fearful churches that the sceptical and rowdy revolutionary students were being converted by the hundreds on campuses certainly fired enthusiasm for establishing new colleges.

Of 180 denominational colleges in the West in 1860, 144 or so were founded and maintained by the more evangelistic denominations.[39] Led by teachers with strong convictions, it is not surprising that college revivals recurred often.

The Christians' conscience in many parts of the United States was troubled regarding the problem of the Negro in their society. In 1816, the American Colonization Society was formed to colonize some part of Africa (or other place to be designated by Congress) with free blacks. In this, the example of Anglican Evangelicals in initiating the settlement of Sierra Leone by liberated slaves was followed—but there was a difference, for few of the Sierra Leone settlers had been born in Britain, if any. Samuel J. Mills, the student evangelist, died on the homeward voyage from exploring a site in West Africa.[40] A result was the founding of Liberia, but the major problem of freedom and slavery remained.

There were many evangelicals in the North and West who agitated against slavery, and not a few non-evangelicals too. But the institution was intrenched in the plantation economy, and many of evangelical affiliation in the South sought to find biblical justification for it. To many in the North, abolition by gradualness meant compromise, and indignation led to violent declamation, met in the South by defiance.

In the North, there were hopeful projects—often prompted by evangelical conviction—for the education of the Negroes, but fear that literacy might lead to insurrection led some legislatures in the South to veto elementary black education. It was easy for uninvolved evangelicals in England and New England to denounce slave-holdong, but harder for those who owned slaves to manumit them, which many did.

In Britain, Evangelicals supported agitation for radical restriction of capital punishment, Sir Thomas Fowell Buxton being an outstanding example.[41] He also assisted in founding the Royal Society for the Prevention of Cruelty to Animals in 1824, the first of its kind. Not only did it seek to stamp out cruelty, but it offered free veterinary service. It is not surprising to learn that the founder of the Society was an Anglican Evangelical clergyman, Arthur Broome, assisted also by Wilberforce and Mackintosh.[42] This was a fitting climax to an Evangelical campaign against cruel sports, bull-baiting, cock-fighting and other matches that caused pain to animals.[43] In the United States, brutal sports were repressed by the spread of camp-meeting evangelism; and in Britain by 'humanitarianism and religiosity' (Trevelyan).

The evangelical social reformers did not wait to persuade their own denominations of the rightness of reform—they went straight to the seat of civil power, without rioting in the streets. Their record was impefect, but gratifying.

The missionaries who invaded India with the Good News of Jesus Christ were agents neither of imperialism nor commercial enterprise. The East India Company provided the major opposition to their entry and penetration of the country. Nor were they there for self-interest. A quick glance around the graveyard in Serampore indicates the terrible toll of disease and death paid by pioneer missionary families.

Slavery was abolished in 1833 in all British possessions. Untouched was the Indian social order based on maintenance of caste,[44] by which the lowest level of the population lived in a serfdom akin to outright slavery, and the lower castes were held in limited bondage. Even the higher castes suffered a regimentation of privilege far removed from the blessings of personal liberty in a free society.

Among converts, the Indian Christians themselves found that conversion and caste were wholly incompatible, and their former caste associates confirmed this by rejecting them from fellowship. In effect the Christians had become a new caste in the sight of the general public, a caste difficult to place in order of rank.

In 1833, the Anglican Bishop Daniel Wilson declared that 'the distinctions of caste must be abandoned decidedly, immediately and finally' in the churches.[45] The Sudras who had been sitting apart from lesser castes defected to the Lutherans. Caste was persisting in Christian society.

But distaste and intolerance of caste in the churches grew more and more, and in later decades the influx of lower caste and outcaste folk into the churches demonstrated the real impact of Christianity upon the caste system, uplifting the lower classes and educating them, their children better equipped for life than some of those who despised them.

The missionaries soon felt compelled to act against the degrading cruelty that marked some of the great idolatrous festivals. The East India Company levied a pilgrim tax on those coming to some of the great shrines, using the money for the upkeep of temples and idols, priests and acolytes.[46]

The missionaries appealed over the heads of the Company officials to public opinion in Great Britain. Some missionaries tended to exaggerate the evils associated with such adulation of idols at Jagannath, and Company officials tended to minimise them. From 1814 to 1831, a profit of about a hundred thousand pounds was made by the Company through the Jagannath tax alone. In 1833, the missionaries' agitation ended the pilgrim tax as uncalled-for support of religion.[47]

William Carey at Serampore became concerned with the practice of some parents of sacrificing infants to the gods in sacred waters at the mouths of the Ganges.[48] This practice was outlawed. It took much longer for the Government to outlaw 'satisahagamana,' the 'voluntary' burning of widows on the funeral pyre of their husbands.[49] Suttee, thus named, aroused the anger of civil servants, but missionaries led a campaign against it, again stirring up friends in London— such as Wilberforce and Buxton. It was abolished in 1829.

Aware of the suffering of Indian women, ill-treatment of widows, the marriage of children, seclusion of women, the missionaries determined to end the more glaring evils, but they realised that education was needed for enlightenment.

One of the greatest of all educationalists in India, Sir Philip Hartog, a Jew, appreciated the missionaries' work:

> ... imbued from the first with a zeal not only for religion but for spreading secular knowledge in the vernacular as well as in English ... a great and inspiring influence in Indian education in all its stages ... As one who belongs to another faith, I desire to bear my testimony to the noble and unselfish work of Christian educators in India, men and women.[50]

Through the influence of Grant, Wilberforce, Macaulay, and other Evangelicals, the East India Company set aside a sum of a hundred thousand rupees annually for the revival of literature and introduction of science in India.

Yet in forty years' time, the total number of educational institutions managed, inspected, or aided by the Company was no more than 1474, in which 67,569 pupils were being instructed. In the same period, the evangelical missionary societies alone raised their total of schools to 1628 (exclusive of 1867 Sunday Schools) with 64,043 pupils (exclusive of Sunday School pupils).[51]

The Evangelical Awakening in Scotland sent out men who were to influence educational policy in India. Alexander Duff introduced far-reaching new methods in the missionary approach, developing Christian institutes of higher learning using English with an expectation of attracting young men of the higher castes, desirous of a European education. And the occasional converts of these colleges provided an educated leadership for many emerging Indian churches. Duff advocated schools for women too, the missions obliging. In other places, Scottish educators built influential colleges to educate the leadership of India.[52]

In Africa, missionaries were pioneers of health and sanitation, clinics and hospitals.   The first evangelical medical missionary to land in Africa was J. T. van der Kemp.[53] As early as 1823, the Moravians established a leper colony.[54] In the midst of incredible hardships, David Livingstone found time to report upon disease and medicines.[55] And from the compassionate efforts of the pioneers, a complex of mission hospitals and medical service ultimately grew.

From the beginning, the missionary societies declared war upon the slave trade. At times, whole communities of rescued slaves came under the jurisdiction of ordinary missionaries, who used every possible means to protect their charges. The same missionaries further sought to influence all civilized governments to assume responsibility for controlling and abolishing the slave trade. At home, their boards brought pressure upon the legislative conscience of parliaments and upon the executive compunction of governments.

Missionaries of the various societies tried to deliver primitive tribespeople from the unchecked terrors of their own tyrannical chiefs or scheming witchdoctors, opposing the smelling out of witches, trial by ordeal, brutal torture, or execution at the whim of a chief.

Next to preaching the Good News, the chief missionary method was elementary education, considered the beginning of modern civilization. Bantu folk had developed a system of education through puberty rites to equip the young for life in the tribe, but there was no 'reading, writing or arithmetic.' At the time of the missionary contact, a majority of Bantu folk south of the equator possessed no alphabet or other form of writing, no set of numerals, no almanac or calendar, no notation of time, no measurement of length or capacity or weight.[56] The missionaries tackled the educational deficiency and found pupils as eager as any in the world.

As a matter of course, missionaries played their part in reducing the languages of the Africans to writing.   They prepared translations of the Scriptures, taught the people to read and write, opened schools for the youth, established hospitals for the sick, introduced arts and crafts, and built up law-abiding Christian communities.

The missionary enterprise in Hawaii conferred benefits on the people, influencing legislation to build up morality, defying the opposition of other foreigners who preferred a lack of moral discipline, in fifteen years enrolling a sixth of the Islands' population in their schools.[57]

SUMMARY

THE SECOND AND THIRD AWAKENINGS
1792—1842

The infidelity of the French Revolution represented the greatest challenge to Christianity since the time preceding the Emperor Constantine. Christians had endured the threat of the northern barbarians, the assault of the armies of the crescent, the terror of the hordes from the steppes, and an eastern schism and a western reformation. But, until 1789, there had never been such a threat against the very foundations of the Faith, against believing in the God revealed in the Scriptures. Voltaire made no idle boast when he said that Christianity would be forgotten within thirty years.

In France, even the Huguenots apostasized. Deism rode high in every country in Europe, and so-called Christian leaders either capitulated to infidelity or compromised with rationalism. The infant but sturdy nation on the American continent was swept by unbelief, so that the faithful trembled. Between the mailed fist of French military power and the insidious undermining of faith, there seemed no escape.

The spiritual preparation for a worldwide awakening began in Great Britain seven years before the outpouring of the Spirit there. Believers of one denomination after the other, including the evangelical minorities in the Church of England and the Church of Scotland, devoted the first Monday evening of each month to pray for a revival of religion and an extension of Christ's kingdom overseas. This widespread union of prayer spread to the United States within ten years and to many other countries, and the concert of prayer remained the significant factor in the recurring revivals of religion and the extraordinary out-thrust of missions for a full fifty years, so commonplace it was taken for granted.

The outbreak of the Revolution in France at first encouraged lovers of liberty in the English-speaking world to hope that liberty had truly dawned in France. When the Terror began, and when military despotism rose, they were fearfully alarmed. The British people decided to fight. In the second year of the Revolution, John Wesley died.

The revival of religion, the second great awakening, began in Britain in late 1791, cresting in power among the Methodists who seemed unafraid of the phenomena of mass awakening. It was also effective among the Baptists and the Congregationalists, though manifested in quieter forms. It accelerated the evangelical revival going on among clergy and laity of the Church of England, strengthening the hands of Simeon and his Eclectic Club and those of Wilberforce in his Clapham Sect—an Evangelical party in the Anglican Establishment which soon became dominant in influence.

At the same time, the principality of Wales was overrun by another movement of revival, packing the churches of the various denominations and gathering unusual crowds of many thousands in the open-air. The revival accelerated the growth of the Baptists and Congregationalists, increased the number of Wesleyan Methodists, and caused the birth of a new denomination, the Calvinistic Methodist Church of Wales, now the Welsh Presbyterians, who separated from the Church of Wales because of its failure to provide either ministers or sacraments for its societies.

Phenomenal awakenings also swept many parts of the kingdom of Scotland, raising up such evangelists as the Haldanes, and such pastoral evangelists as Chalmers in Glasgow and MacDonald in the North. The Scottish revivals began in the teeth of majority opposition in the Church of Scotland but within a generation had evangelized the auld Kirk. The coverage of the Scottish Revival was patchwork, its occurrence sporadic, because of the desperate state of the country. The light prevailed over the darkness.

Not for the first time, nor the last, the unhappy kingdom of Ireland, a majority of whose inhabitants were disfranchized, was rent asunder by turmoil that boiled over into the Rebellion of 1798. In the midst of strife, local awakenings occurred among the Methodists, affecting the evangelical clergy of the Church of Ireland. The Presbyterians of the North were fully occupied contending for orthodoxy against a Unitarian insurgency. Revival brought forth societies for the evangelization of Ulster and the renewal of church life.

This period of revival in the United Kingdom brought forth the British and Foreign Bible Society, the Religious Tract Society, the Baptist Missionary Society, the London Missionary Society, the Church Missionary Society, and a host of auxiliary agencies for evangelism. It produced also some significant social reform, even in wartime.

Before and after 1800, an awakening began in Scandinavia, resembling more the earlier British movements of the days of Wesley and Whitefield, though borrowing from the later British awakening in adopting its home and foreign mission projects, its Bible societies, and the like. In Norway, the revival was advanced by a layman, Hans Nielsen Hauge, who made a lasting impact upon Norway as a nation. Another layman, Paavo Ruotsalainen, expedited the movement in Finland. There were several national revivalists operating then in Sweden, but the influence of George Scott, a British Methodist, later exceeded them all. In Denmark, the revival seemed less potent and was sooner overtaken by a Lutheran confessional reaction, which inhibited the renewal of revival in the 1830s—unlike Norway, Sweden, and Finland, which experienced extensive movements up until the mid-century, Gisle Johnson and Carl Olof Rosenius being the outstanding leaders in Norway and Sweden respectively.

In Switzerland, France, and the Netherlands, the general awakening was delayed until the defeat of Napoleon. A visit to Geneva by Robert Haldane triggered a chain reaction of revival throughout the Reformed Churches of the countries named, raising up outstanding evangelists and missionary agencies. In Holland, the movement was somewhat delayed, and was sooner cramped by confessional reaction among the Dutch Reformed, some of whom objected to state control as well as evangelical ecumenism.

In the German States, the general awakening followed the defeat of Napoleon, and raised up scores of effective German evangelists, such as the Krummachers, Hofacker, Helferich, von Kottwitz, and the von Belows; German theologians, such as Neander and Tholuck; social reformers, such as Fliedner; and noteworthy home and foreign missionary agencies. As in other European countries, the complication of state-church relationships provoked confessional reaction among Lutherans who repudiated the evangelical ecumenism of the revivalists in general. Next to British evangelical pioneers, the German revivalists achieved the most lasting social reforms. Close collaboration between British and German revivalists existed in home and foreign mission projects.

Confessionalism in Europe, whether Anglo-Catholic in England, Lutheran in Germany and Denmark, or Reformed in Holland and Switzerland, inhibited the renewal of revival in the 'thirties, unlike the United States, where the free church system accelerated it.

In the United States and in British North America, there were preparatory movements of revival in the 1780s that raised up leaders for the wider movement in the following decade. Conditions in the United States following the French Revolution were deplorable, emptying churches, increasing ungodliness and crime in society, infidelity among students. Sporadic revivals began in 1792. Then Isaac Backus and his friends in New England adopted the British plan for a general Concert of Prayer for the revival of religion and extension of Christ's kingdom abroad. Prayer meetings multiplied as church members devoted the first Monday of each month to fervent intercession.

In 1798, the awakening became general. Congregations were crowded and conviction was deep, leading to numerous thoroughgoing conversions. Every state in New England was affected, and every evangelical denomination. There were no records of emotional extravagance, and none among the churches of the Middle Atlantic States, where extraordinary revivals broke out in the cities of New York and Philadelphia as well as in smaller towns. In the western parts of New York and Pennsylvania, there were more startling displays of excitement. The population of these eastern States was three million, and the extent of the revival therein was three times more considerable than in the frontier territories, with three hundred thousand people.

In 1800, extraordinary revival began in Kentucky, long after its manifestation east of the Alleghenies. Among the rough and lawless and illiterate frontiersmen, there were extremes of conviction and response, such as trembling and shaking—described as 'the jerks,'—weeping for sorrow and shouting for joy, fainting. Extravagances occurred among a comparative few, but were exaggerated by critics out of all proportion, so that twentieth century historians have stressed the odd performances and ignored the major thrust of the awakening in the United States, even pontificating that the awakening actually began, extravagantly, on the frontier— an obvious misreading of history. It cannot be denied that the revival transformed Kentucky and Tennessee from an utterly lawless community into a God-fearing one.

On the frontier, there were minor schisms following the awakening, due largely to defects inherent in denominational organization than to the revival, which raised up voluntary evangelists among the laity. Reaction against evangelical ecumenism and lay evangelism forced some people out.

The awakening spread southwards into Virginia, North and South Carolina, and Georgia, again—as in Kentucky and Tennessee—attracting crowds so huge that no churches could possibly accommodate them, hence five, ten or fifteen thousand would gather in the forest clearings. The Negroes were moved equally with the whites.

In the Maritime Provinces of British North America, the revival of the 1780s was renewed among the Baptist and New Light Congregationalist churches. In Upper Canada— now Ontario—the Methodists promoted revival meetings and grew very rapidly, as did some Presbyterians and (later) the Baptists. American itinerants were most active in the movement, anti-American Churchmen and secular leaders most opposed to it. The war of 1812 interrupted the work, which resumed with the coming of peace, though still discouraged by conservative British leaders.

As the influence of infidelity had been so strongly felt in the American colleges, so the blessing of revival overflowed in collegiate awakenings. Timothy Dwight, erudite president of Yale, proved to be the greatest champion of intelligent evangelical Christianity on campus, but the movement among students soon became a spontaneous, inter-collegiate union. The revived and converted students provided the majority of recruits for the home ministry, educational expansion, and foreign missionary effort.

Revived Americans duplicated the formation of various evangelical societies in Britain, founding the American Bible Society, the American Tract Society, the American Board of Commissioners for Foreign Missions, the Foreign Mission of the American Baptists, and society after society. The order and extent of missionary organization reflected in some measure the degree of involvement of denominations in the Awakening.

The Dutch colony of 30,000 at Cape Town experienced an awakening under the ministry of Dr. Helperus Ritzema van Lier, and thrust out local missionaries to evangelize the Khoisan (Hottentot and Bushmen) in the Cape hinterland. A revival broke out in British army regiments in 1809, the Methodist soldier-evangelists gaining a hearing after an earthquake of great severity had shaken the Cape. There was little in the way of a free constituency to be revived in Australia, but the first chaplains to the settlements were Anglican Evangelicals, and revived congregations in Great Britain sent out evangelistically-minded laymen as settlers.

There is no doubt that the general awakening of the 1790s and 1800s, with its antecedents, was the prime factor in the extraordinary burst of missionary enthusiasm and social service, first in Britain, then in Europe and North America. Thomas Charles, whose zeal for God provoked the formation of the British and Foreign Bible Society, was a revivalist of first rank in Wales. George Burder, who urged the founding of the Religious Tract Society, was a leader in the prayer union for revival. William Carey, a founder and pioneer of the Baptist Missionary Society, was one of a group who first set up in England the simultaneous prayer union that spread throughout evangelical Christendom and achieved its avowed purpose in the revival of religion and the extension of the kingdom of Christ overseas. The London Missionary Society and the Church Missionary Society grew out of the prayers of other Free Church and Church of England Evangelicals in the awakening. Methodist missions came from the same source, as did other Scottish societies and the Church of Scotland missions. The revival provided dynamic.

The participation of Germans and Dutch in the Church Missionary Society and the London Missionary Society had its origin in the revival prayer groups in those countries, as did the proliferation of national missionary societies. A student prayer meeting in Williams College, the Haystack Compact, led to the foundation of the American Board and the American Baptist Missionary Union. The origins of the other denominational societies lay in the general revival.

It is all the more amazing to realise that these unique developments took place in Britain while that country was engaged in a titanic struggle with Napoleon, supported by ten times as many people. And the eager readiness of revived believers in Europe and North America transcended the political divisions and upheavals between them and Britain. The coming of peace in 1815 brought about a renewal of the revival in Britain, the rise of the Primitive Methodists to undertake an outreach to the masses somewhat neglected by Wesleyans. In the Church of England, Charles Simeon was at the height of his influence, and the Church Building Society with government help was building hundreds of parish churches. The Baptists and Congregationalists were active in revival in England, and in Wales there were local revivals in many places. In Scotland, local awakenings and pastoral evangelism and social service built up the Church of Scotland Evangelicals. Revivals occurred in Ireland.

As in Great Britain, revival was renewed in the United States and Canada after 1815, and for fifteen years there were revivals reported here and there. This renewal saw the emergence of outstanding evangelists, such as Asahel Nettleton in New England, Daniel Baker in the South, and Charles Finney in the 'burnt-over' area of western New York.

On the mission fields, the pioneers encountered three types of response to their evangelistic outreach and prayer: folk movements of unindoctrinated people, awakenings of instructed communities, and revivals of believers, in such places as South India, South Africa, Indonesia and Polynesia.

It seemed almost too good to be true that another general awakening of phenomenal power swept the United States in 1830-1831. Whether in the eastern, western or southern States, it was without reported extravagance. The movement began in Boston and New York and other cities in summer-time, 1830. It began in Rochester, New York State, with Finney's ministry, in autumn, and reached its peak in mid-winter 1830-31, winning a thousand inquirers at the same time that a hundred thousand others were being enrolled in other parts from Maine to the borders of Texas. Finney, as a national evangelist, was made by the revival of 1830-31, not vice versa. In these years, several smaller bodies of evangelistic folk unchurched by their denominations united in the virile Disciples of Christ movement.

The revival of the 1830s was effective in Great Britain also, provoking local movements of great intensity among the various Methodist bodies in England, strengthening the Anglican Evangelicals and Free Churches. It was inhibited somewhat by a confessional reaction, the Tractarian movement, which stressed a sacramental-sacerdotal churchmanship and opposed the evangelism of the awakenings. James Caughey, an American evangelist, won many thousands in a series of campaigns in England—including William Booth.

First South Wales and then North Wales were moved in awakenings in the 1830s. Another general revival stirred Wales in the 'forties, influenced by Finney's philosophy of revival. In Scotland, revivals increased in number in the 1830s, culminating in an extraordinary outburst at Kilsyth under the ministry of William C. Burns, who witnessed a like revival in Dundee, then in various parts of Scotland, as spontaneous revivals broke out in the Highlands from 1839 onwards. This Scottish Awakening prepared the way for the Disruption and the formation of the Free Church of Scotland.

So great was the interest in Ireland that bishops of the Church of Ireland were talking about 'a second reformation' somewhat prematurely, for the converts of the time were lost to Ireland by emigration following the potato famine. In the North, Evangelicalism triumphed over Arianism among Presbyterians, who soon expanded their congregations.

The ministry of George Scott precipitated lasting revival in Sweden, and Scandinavia in general experienced renewal. The movement in Germany continued in strength, though encountering a confessional reaction among Lutherans.

The 1830s were marked by some extraordinary revival-awakenings in Polynesia. In 1834, a phenomenal movement began in the kingdom of Tonga, described by the Wesleyan missionaries as a 'baptism from above.' In 1837, a similar movement began in the kingdom of Hawaii, Titus Coan taking in 1705 tested converts in one day at Hilo, 7557 in one church during the movement. Revivals were felt in other parts of Polynesia, and a movement in Tonga in the 1840s paralleled a great ingathering in the Fiji Islands, among a Melanesian folk fearfully addicted to cannibalism.

In the 1830s, there were renewed revivals in Grahamstown in South Africa, and an overflow to the Bantu folk round about. Robert Moffat witnessed an ingathering in Botswanaland. At the same time, pioneers were pouring into southern Africa from missionary societies renewed or founded in the movements going on in the sending countries.

Missions of help to the Oriental Churches in the Near and Middle East resulted in revivals and awakenings, sometimes in disruption and reformation. Missionaries were flocking to India, opening up area after area. A folk movement to Christ among the Karens of Burma followed the conversion of Ko Tha Byu in Baptist evangelism. Pioneers from the churches revived in Britain, Europe, and North America gained barely a foothold in China, where resistance to the foreign faith was strong. Japan and Korea remained closed to missionary enterprise.

Emancipation of slaves, protection of prisoners, care of the sick, improvement of working conditions, safe-guarding of women and children, and extension of popular education, prison reform, hospitals, asylums, orphanages, schools, high schools and colleges stemmed from the Revivals. The work of Wilberforce in Britain and the work of Fliedner in Germany were outstanding. The most evangelistic Methodists in England gave leadership to the trade unions. In the United

States, there were numerous good causes which were the object of evangelical benevolence. On the mission fields, wherever possible, missionaries became social activists in education, medicine, and other fields.

It is not commonly realised in Britain that the period of the First Great Awakening was followed by a decline which marked the late 1770s and early 1780s. The beginnings in the English Midlands of the Union of Prayer for a revival of religion and the extension of Christ's kingdom overseas prepared the way for the general revival which was greatly accelerated by the French Revolution in its challenge to Christianity. While some pioneers derived their inspiration from the First Great Awakening, they achieved objectives during the Second Great Awakening, which raised up a host of evangelical reformers and accomplished untold good.

The preoccupation of American historians with excesses of emotion on the frontier must be attributed to interest in the sensational or to ideological prejudice. The Second Great Awakening started in New England and the Middle Atlantic States without extravagance of any kind, and was accelerated by the Concert of Prayer for a revival of religion and the extension of Christ's kingdom overseas. It appeared on the frontier after ten years of movement in the eastern states, whose population was ten times greater. But all the attention has been given the excitable tenth of the frontier tenth, not only concerning the extravagances of emotion, exaggerated out of all proportion, but even to denying a social conscience to the Second Great Awakening. Why should anyone look to Logan County in Kentucky for the manifestation of a social conscience, and ignore the extraordinary developments of social reform in the hub of the English-speaking world? It has been said that the Second Great Awakening left converts too preoccupied with personal salvation and holiness of life. The camp meetings in Britain produced resurgent Methodists (the Primitives, nicknamed the Ranters) who were certainly preoccupied with personal salvation and holiness of life but who provided leadership for trade unions struggling for social justice. The Evangelicals of the Second Great Awakening were second to none in pioneering social reform.

These Great Awakenings, which got under way in 1792, ran for fifty years, after which there came a decline; but after fifteen years of declension, there came another great awakening, which surpassed the previous movements in its extent, wholesomeness, effects, and lasting impact.

There was nothing new in the theology of the 1830 Revival. All of its teachings were derived from the New Testament, its strong points the doctrines recovered in the Reformation and re-emphasized in the Evangelical Awakenings of the early and later eighteenth century.

Out of the evangelical ecumenism of the 1830s and 1840s came the Evangelical Alliance, founded in 1846 by leaders of the movement on both sides the Atlantic. Its doctrinal basis reflected the views of a majority of Protestants between 1810 and 1910 before broad church and high church partisans entered the cooperative movement.

> I. The Divine inspiration, authority and sufficiency of the Holy Scriptures, and the right and duty of private judgment in the interpretation thereof.
> II. The Unity of the Godhead, and the Trinity of Persons therein.
> III. The utter depravity of human nature, in consequence of the Fall.
> IV. The incarnation of the Son of God, His work of atonement for sinners of mankind, and His mediatorial intercession and reign.
> V. The justification of the sinner by faith alone.
> VI. The work of the Holy Spirit in the conversion and sanctification of the sinner.
> VII. The resurrection of the body, the judgment of the world by the Lord Jesus Christ, the eternal blessedness of the righteous, and the eternal punishment of the wicked.

The Evangelical Alliance had adopted a final statement of faith—that of the Divine institution of the Christian ministry and obligation and perpetuity of the ordinances of baptism and the Lord's Supper. The records of the Awakenings reveal no departure from the points listed above, but they do indicate the participation of preachers and teachers, such as Brethren and Quakers, whose view of Christian ministry and ordinances differed from the other denominations.

In those times, the Roman Catholic and Greek Orthodox Churches offered no cooperation, but often persecuted the Evangelicals. Apart from the Anglican, Lutheran, Reformed and other neo-confessionalists, Protestants used the Alliance idea of Christian unity so widely that it led to a practice of fraternal fellowship having the force of a major doctrine. The revivalists, evangelists, pastors and missionaries at home and abroad worked together in evangelical comity.

NOTES

Notes on Chapter 1: REVOLUTION AND INFIDELITY

1 A. H. Newman, MANUAL OF CHURCH HISTORY, Vol. II, p. 487.
2 T. Murray, THE LETTERS OF DAVID HUME, p. 497; cf. CHRISTIAN OBSERVER, London, 1815, XIV, p. 633.
3 See Jean Leflon, LA CRISE REVOLUTIONAIRE, 1789-1846.
4 C. S. Phillips, THE CHURCH IN FRANCE, 1789-1848, p. 18.
5 Robert P. Evans, 'The Contribution of Foreigners to the French Protestant Reveil, 1815-1850,' Ph.D. Dissertation, University of Manchester, 1971.
6 B. C. Poland, FRENCH PROTESTANTISM AND THE FRENCH REVOLUTION, appendices; ENCYCLOPEDIE, Volume VII, p. 94.
7 A. F. Beard, THE STORY OF JOHN FREDERIC OBERLIN.
8 G. M. Trevelyan, ENGLISH SOCIAL HISTORY, p. 355.
9 George Smith, HISTORY OF WESLEYAN METHODISM, Volume II, p. 289.
10 Cf. G. M. Trevelyan, ENGLISH SOCIAL HISTORY, p. 468; & George Smith, Volume II, p. 125.
11 George Smith, Volume II, pp. 673ff.   12 Volume II, p. 674.
13 Alexander Haldane, THE LIVES OF ROBERT AND JAMES ALEXANDER HALDANE, pp. 122ff; G. M. Trevelyan, p. 459.
14 J. S. Reid, HISTORY OF THE PRESBYTERIAN CHURCH IN IRELAND, Volume III, p. 293.
15 A. G. Edwards, LANDMARKS IN THE HISTORY OF THE WELSH CHURCH, pp. 161ff.
16 See Christian Wolff, EIGEN LEBENSBESCHREIBUNG.
17 M. G. Hansen, THE REFORMED CHURCH IN THE NETHERLANDS, pp. 276ff.   18 Alexander Haldane, p. 396.
19 G. M. Stephenson, THE RELIGIOUS ASPECTS OF SWEDISH IMMIGRATION, p. 17;   cf. Ernst Newman, p. 133.
20 J. du Plessis, THE LIFE OF ANDREW MURRAY, pp. 63ff.
21 CHRISTIAN OBSERVER, London, 1804, p. 58.
22 K. S. Latourette, A HISTORY OF THE EXPANSION OF CHRISTIANITY, Volume III, p. 454.
23 L. W. Bacon, A HISTORY OF AMERICAN CHRISTIANITY, p. 430.
24 P. S. Foner, COMPLETE WRITINGS OF PAINE, II, pp. 786ff.
25 F. G. Beardsley, A HISTORY OF AMERICAN REVIVALS, p. 80.
26 G. M. Trevelyan, ENGLISH SOCIAL HISTORY, p. 255.
27 A. B. Strickland, THE GREAT AMERICAN REVIVAL, p. 40.
28 F. G. Beardsley, A HISTORY OF AMERICAN REVIVALS, p. 80.
29 Stated by Joel Parker, in REVIVAL SERMON, 1794.
30 B. R. Lacy, REVIVALS IN THE MIDST OF THE YEARS, p. 65.
31 L. W. Bacon, A HISTORY OF AMERICAN CHRISTIANITY, p. 430.
32 William Speer, THE GREAT REVIVAL OF 1800, p. 12.
33 Daniel Dorchester, THE PROBLEMS OF RELIGIOUS PROGRESS, pp. 182-183.
34 See F. Rudolph, THE AMERICAN COLLEGE AND UNIVERSITY, pp. 38-39.   35 Timothy Dwight, TRAVELS, IV, pp. 376ff.
36 Lyman Beecher, AUTOBIOGRAPHY, Volume I, p. 43.
37 Letter of Ashbel Green, 10 April 1832, in William B. Sprague, LECTURES ON REVIVALS OF RELIGION, p. 342.
38 A. B. Strickland, THE GREAT AMERICAN REVIVAL, pp. 32-33.
39 S. E. Morison, THREE CENTURIES AT HARVARD, p. 185.
40 F. Rudolph, THE AMERICAN COLLEGE AND UNIVERSITY, p. 38.

41 T. J. Wertenbaker, PRINCETON, 1746–1896, pp. 134–137.
42 See C. P. Shedd, TWO CENTURIES OF STUDENT CHRISTIAN MOVEMENTS, pp. 20 & 53.
43 T. J. Wertenbaker, pp. 134–137.
44 C. C. Tiffany, A HISTORY OF THE PROTESTANT EPISCOPAL CHURCH IN THE UNITED STATES, pp. 289n, 388, 394–395.
45 H. E. Jacobs, A HISTORY OF THE EVANGELICAL LUTHERAN CHURCH IN THE UNITED STATES, Chapter XIX.
46 ACTS & PROCEEDINGS, Presbyterian General Assembly, 1798.
47 W. W. Sweet, THE STORY OF RELIGION IN AMERICA, pp. 241ff.
48 R. B. Semple, A HISTORY OF THE RISE AND PROGRESS OF THE BAPTISTS IN VIRGINIA; Methodists lost 11,160 members in 1793, 1794 & 1795; see MINUTES.
49 William Speer, THE GREAT REVIVAL OF 1800, p. 11.
50 S. D. Clark, CHURCH AND SECT IN CANADA, pp. 69–70.

Notes on Chapter 2: REVIVAL IN ENGLAND, 1790—

1 George Smith, HISTORY OF WESLEYAN METHODISM, Volume I, p. 451.   2 George Smith, Volume I, p. 474.
3 ARMINIAN MAGAZINE, London, 1784, Volume VII, pp. 211ff.
4 John Wesley's JOURNAL; see George Smith, Volume I, p. 496.
5 Albert D. Belden, GEORGE WHITEFIELD, p. 200.
6 Helen Knight, LADY HUNTINGTON AND HER FRIENDS, p. 251.
7 A. C. H. Seymour, LIFE AND TIMES OF SELINA, COUNTESS OF HUNTINGTON, Volume II, p. 490.
8 H. C. Vedder, A SHORT HISTORY OF THE BAPTISTS, p. 256.
9 A. H. Newman, A MANUAL OF CHURCH HISTORY, Volume II, pp. 688–689.   10 See S. Pearce Carey, WILLIAM CAREY.
11 Jonathan Edwards, THE WORKS OF PRESIDENT EDWARDS, Volume III, pp. 429–508.
12 E. A. Payne, 'The Evangelical Revival and the Beginning of the Modern Missionary Movement,' CONGREGATIONAL QUARTERLY, 1943, XXI, pp. 223ff.
13 DICTIONARY OF NATIONAL BIOGRAPHY, XX, p. 310; cf. John Ryland, THE LIFE AND DEATH OF ANDREW FULLER.
14 R. P. Beaver, 'The Concert of Prayer for Missions,' ECUMENICAL REVIEW, 1957–58, X, pp. 420ff.
15 See METHODIST MAGAZINE, London, 1798, pp. 240ff.
16 See ANNUAL BAPTIST REGISTER, London, 1790–1799.
17 ANNUAL BAPTIST REGISTER, 1798–1801, p. 1.
18 New Road Baptist Church, Oxford; ANNUAL BAPTIST REGISTER, 1798–1801, p. 29.
19 ANNUAL BAPTIST REGISTER, 1798–1801, p. 33.
20 Cf. EVANGELICAL MAGAZINE, London, 1794, pp. 30, 78, 118.
21 R. W. Dale, LIFE AND LETTERS OF JOHN ANGELL JAMES.
22 R. W. Dale, ENGLISH CONGREGATIONALISM, pp. 583–584.
23 James Sigston, A MEMOIR OF THE LIFE AND MINISTRY OF WILLIAM BRAMWELL, pp. 65ff; & George Smith, HISTORY OF WESLEYAN METHODISM, Volume II, pp. 225–226.
24 METHODIST MAGAZINE, London, 1801, p. 528; James Sigston, A MEMOIR OF WILLIAM BRAMWELL, pp. 72ff.
25 George Smith, Volume II, pp. 242–243, 358.
26 ARMINIAN MAGAZINE, London, 1794, pp. 603ff., 649ff.
27 James Sigston, A MEMOIR OF WILLIAM BRAMWELL, pp. 100ff.
28 George Smith, Volume II, pp. 246ff.

29 MINUTES OF THE METHODIST CONFERENCES, Volume I, London, 1813, pp. 230, 244, 257, 273, 292, 311, 338, 373, & 410.

30 MINUTES, Volume I, pp. 229, 243, 256, 272, 291, & 311.

31 MINUTES, Volume I, pp. 229, 243, 256, 272, 291, & 311.

32 METHODIST MAGAZINE, London, 1801, p. 110.

33 J. W. Etheridge, THE LIFE OF THE REV. ADAM CLARKE, p. 78; George Smith, Volume II, pp. 253-257, 308.

34 MINUTES OF THE METHODIST CONFERENCES, Volume I, London, 1813, pp. 229, 243, 256, 272, 291, 310, 337, & 372.

35 METHODIST MAGAZINE, London, 1798, p. 162.

36 Baptists, Congregationalists, Presbyterians and Quakers were counted as Dissenters in England.

37 ANNUAL BAPTIST REGISTER, 1790-1793, p. 524.

38 See F. W. Cornish, THE ENGLISH CHURCH IN THE NINE-TEENTH CENTURY; H. D. Trail & J. S. Mann, editors, SOCIAL ENGLAND, Volume V, pp. 320-321; H. D. Morgan, Bampton Lecture, Oxford, 1819, p. 279.

39 CHRISTIAN OBSERVER, London, 1805, pp. 592ff.

40 J. H. Overton, THE EVANGELICAL REVIVAL IN THE EIGH-TEENTH CENTURY, p. 161.

41 G. R. Balleine, A HISTORY OF THE EVANGELICAL PARTY IN THE CHURCH OF ENGLAND, p. 39.

42 See John Newton, THE WORKS OF JOHN NEWTON, Volume II, p. 135; G. R. Balleine, p. 77.

43 G. R. Balleine, p. 46.

44 Cf. L. E. Elliott-Binns, THE EARLY EVANGELICALS; and G. R. Balleine, pp. 63, 77, & 98.

45 Eugene Stock, THE HISTORY OF THE CHURCH MISSIONARY SOCIETY, Volume I, p. 57.

46 BAPTIST ANNUAL REGISTER, 1801-1802, p. 657.

47 United Kingdom Census, 1801.

48 CHRISTIAN OBSERVER, London, 1802, p. 335.

49 ANNUAL BAPTIST REGISTER, 1801-1802, p. 657.

50 J. S. Stamp, METHODISM IN BRADFORD; see George Smith, Volume II, pp. 418ff.

51 METHODIST MAGAZINE, London, 1819, p. 9.

52 WESLEYAN METHODIST MAGAZINE, 1818, p. 401.

53 C. C. Sellers, LORENZO DOW, pp. 101ff.

54 W. E. Farndale, THE SECRET OF MOW COP, p. 26.

55 H. B. Kendall, A HISTORY OF THE PRIMITIVE METHODIST CHURCH; cf. Ms. Journal of Hugh Bourne, 13 & 14 March 1804.

56 MINUTES OF THE METHODIST CONFERENCES, Volume I, London, 1813, Resolutions of July 1807, Liverpool.

57 Joseph Ritson, THE ROMANCE OF PRIMITIVE METHODISM.

58 W. E. Farndale, THE SECRET OF MOW COP, p. 48.

59 METHODIST MAGAZINE, London, 1802, pp. 323ff.

60 EVANGELICAL MAGAZINE & MISSIONARY CHRONICLE, 1814, XXII, p. 241.

61 George Smith, Volume II, pp. 551-552.

62 METHODIST MAGAZINE, London, 1814, pp. 547-551.

63 MINUTES OF THE METHODIST CONFERENCES, Volume III, 1813; Volume IV, 1814 & 1815.

64 See G. C. B. Davies, THE FIRST EVANGELICAL BISHOP.

65 William Carus, MEMOIRS OF THE LIFE OF THE REV. CHARLES SIMEON, p. 10.

66 William Carus, pp. 123ff.

Notes on Chapter 3: AWAKENINGS IN WALES

1 David Jones, LIFE AND TIMES OF GRIFFITH JONES, p. 4.
2 WELCH PIETY, Accounts of the Circulating Schools in Wales, published annually from 1740 onwards, edition of 1748-1749, p. 113.
3 Eifion Evans, WHEN HE IS COME, p. 12.
4 Henry Hughes, DIWYGIADAU CREFYDDOL CYMRU, pp. 166ff.
5 Eifion Evans, WHEN HE IS COME, p. 13.
6 D. E. Jenkins, THE LIFE OF THOMAS CHARLES OF BALA, Volume II, pp. 89-94.
7 Mary Duncan, HISTORY OF REVIVALS OF RELIGION IN THE BRITISH ISLES, p. 121.
8 ANNUAL BAPTIST REGISTER, 1790-93, pp. 221 & Evans, p. 12.
9 Eifion Evans, WHEN HE IS COME, p. 14.
10 Paxton Hood, CHRISTMAS EVANS, THE PREACHER TO WILD WALES; William Williams, DICTIONARY OF NATIONAL BIO-GRAPHY, XXI, pp. 464-465.
11 WELSH MAGAZINE, 1828, p. 313. (Letter of Edward Jones) cf. George Smith, HISTORY OF WESLEYAN METHODISM, Volume II, pp. 354-355.
12 Thomas Burgess, DICTIONARY OF NATIONAL BIOGRAPHY, Volume III, pp. 313-314.
13 A. G. Edwards, LANDMARKS IN THE HISTORY OF THE WELSH CHURCH, pp. 202-209.
14 D. E. Jenkins, THE LIFE OF THOMAS CHARLES OF BALA, Volume III, p. 115.
15 EVANGELICAL MAGAZINE, London, 1805, p. 235.
16 John Hughes, METHODISTAETH CYMRU, Volume I, p. 346.
17 Mary Duncan, HISTORY OF REVIVALS OF RELIGION IN THE BRITISH ISLES, pp. 121ff. cf. Eifion Evans, pp. 14-15.

Notes on Chapter 4: SCOTTISH REVIVALS, 1790—

1 See 'Inner Divisions, 1750-1800,' Chapter III, John Macinnes, EVANGELICAL MOVEMENT IN THE HIGHLANDS OF SCOTLAND, 1688-1800.
2 CHRISTIAN OBSERVER, London, 1802, pp. 82-83.
3 Alexander MacRae, REVIVALS IN THE HIGHLANDS AND IS-LANDS IN THE NINETEENTH CENTURY, pp. 21-22.
4 Alexander Haldane, THE LIVES OF ROBERT AND JAMES ALEXANDER HALDANE, pp. 1-41.
5 Robert Haldane, 'Address on Politics,' Edinburgh 1800, cited in Alexander Haldane, pp. 78ff.
6 Alexander Haldane, pp. 138ff.
7 John Kennedy, THE APOSTLE OF THE NORTH: THE LIFE AND LABOURS OF THE Rev. Dr. MACDONALD, London, 1867.
8 Neil Douglas, JOURNAL OF A MISSION, quoted in Macinnes, EVANGELICAL MOVEMENT, p. 142.
9 Alexander Haldane, pp. 260ff.
10 See Glasgow Tract Society, NARRATIVES OF REVIVALS OF RELIGION, V; cf. W. J. Couper, SCOTTISH REVIVALS, pp. 88ff.
11 Mary Duncan, HISTORY OF REVIVALS OF RELIGION IN THE BRITISH ISLES, pp. 321ff; cf. Glasgow Tract Society, Tract V.
12 See John Macinnes, THE EVANGELICAL MOVEMENT IN THE HIGHLANDS OF SCOTLAND, pp. 164-165.

13 Mary Duncan, pp. 340ff.
14 Alexander MacRae, REVIVALS IN THE HIGHLANDS AND IS-
    LANDS IN THE NINETEENTH CENTURY, pp. 71ff.
15 Alexander Haldane, pp. 143ff.
16 Alexander MacRae, p. 188.
17 John Macinnes, THE EVANGELICAL MOVEMENT, p. 292.
18 Alexander Stewart, ACCOUNT OF THE LATE REVIVAL OF
    RELIGION AT MOULIN, p. 13.
19 W. J. Couper, SCOTTISH REVIVALS, pp. 78-87.
20 Alexander Stewart, p. 13; and Glasgow Tract Society, Tract
    VI, p. 4.
21 J. Sievewright, MEMOIR OF ALEXANDER STEWART; cf.
    Mary Duncan, HISTORY OF REVIVALS OF RELIGION IN THE
    BRITISH ISLES, p. 304ff.
22 George Smith, THE LIFE OF ALEXANDER DUFF, p. 2.
23 Alexander Haldane, THE LIVES OF ROBERT AND JAMES
    ALEXANDER HALDANE, pp. 177ff.
24 John Kennedy, OLD HIGHLAND DAYS, p. 42.
25 Mary Duncan, HISTORY OF REVIVALS OF RELIGION IN THE
    BRITISH ISLES, p. 341.
26 See General Assembly of the Church of Scotland, V, 1799; cf.
    Alexander Haldane, pp. 201-202.
27 Alexander Haldane, THE LIVES OF ROBERT AND JAMES
    ALEXANDER HALDANE, pp. 203-204.
28 See General Assembly of the Cqrch of Scotland, XII, 1799.
29 MISSIONARY MAGAZINE, Edinburgh, 21 July 1800.
30 Alexander Haldane, p. 272.
31 Robert Haldane, 'Address on Politics,' Edinburgh 1800, p. 201.
32 See Hugh Watt, THOMAS CHALMERS AND THE DISRUPTION,
    Edinburgh, 1943.
33 Andrew Thomson, DCTIONARY OF NATIONAL BIOGRAPHY,
    XIX, pp. 714-715.
34 D. Mackichan, THE MISSIONARY IDEAL IN THE SCOTTISH
    CHURCHES, pp. 74ff, 105-106.

Notes on Chapter 5: REVIVAL AND TURMOIL IN IRELAND

1 ARMINIAN MAGAZINE, London, Volume IX, 1786, pp. 54ff,
   97ff, 152ff, 209ff, 260ff; cf. Volume XIV, p. 413.
2 R. R. Madden, THE LITERARY REMAINS OF THE UNITED
   IRISHMEN.
3 Irish Address, 20th July 1798, to the Methodist Conference, 1798.
4 See David Stewart, THE SECEDERS IN IRELAND, p. 105; cf.
   J. S. Reid, HISTORY OF THE PRESBYTERIAN CHURCH IN
   IRELAND, Volume III, p. 416.
5 A. R. Scott, 'The Ulster Revival of 1859,' pp. 18-19: University
   of Dublin, Ph.D. dissertation, 1962.
6 David Stewart, THE SECEDERS IN IRELAND, p. 228.
7 William Carus, MEMOIRS OF THE LIFE OF THE REV.
   CHARLES SIMEON, p. 563.
8 See BRIEF MEMORIALS OF THE REV. B. W. MATTHIAS,
   Dublin, 1842.
9 W. D. Killen, ECCLESIASTICAL HISTORY OF IRELAND, Volume
   II, p. 389. 10 James Morgan, MY LIFE AND TIMES, p. 17.
11 See R. J. Roden, THE PROGRESS OF THE REFORMATION IN
   IRELAND, p. 33.

12 MINUTES OF THE METHODIST CONFERENCES, Volume II, 1800 & 1801, pp. 55 & 96.
13 C. H. Crookshank, HISTORY OF METHODISM IN IRELAND, Volume II, p. 170; cf. M. McDonagh, BISHOP DOYLE, p. 91.
14 METHODIST MAGAZINE, London, 1802, p. 216; 1803, p. 375.
15 M. McDonagh, BISHOP DOYLE, p. 91.
16 C. H. Crookshank, Volume II, p. 339.
17 METHODIST MAGAZINE, London, 1800, p. 317.
18 C. H. Crookshank, Volume II, p. 285.
19 C. C. Sellers, LORENZO DOW, pp. 51ff.
20 Thomas Armitage, A HISTORY OF THE BAPTISTS, p. 571; H. C. Vedder, A SHORT HISTORY OF THE BAPTISTS, pp. 275ff.
21 ANNUAL BAPTIST REGISTER, London, 1794-97, p. 208.
22 Letter of James Haldane, MISSIONARY MAGAZINE, Edinburgh, December 1801; cf. Alexander Haldane, p. 281.
23 M. McDonagh, BISHOP DOYLE, pp. 342-343.
24 CHRISTIAN OBSERVER, London, 1807, p. 406.

Notes on Chapter 6: SCANDINAVIAN MOVEMENTS, 1790—

1 Frederick IV of Denmark supported a German Pietist Mission in India, see H. M. Zorn, BARTHOMAEUS ZIEGENBALG.
2 See Hal Koch, DANMARKS KIRKE GJENNOM TIDERNE, pp. 90ff.
3 Einar Molland, CHURCH LIFE IN NORWAY, pp. 73ff.
4 Sverre Norborg, HANS NIELSEN HAUGE, pp. 45ff.
5 Einar MOLLAND, PASSIM: Sverre Norborg, pp. 132ff.
6 Sverre Norborg, HANS NIELSEN HAUGE, pp. 226ff.
7 Einar Molland, CHURCH LIFE IN NORWAY, p. 12.
8 Sverre Norborg, HANS NIELSEN HAUGE, pp. 255ff.
9 J. C. Kjaer, HISTORY OF THE CHURCH OF DENMARK, pp. 77ff.
10 Hal KOCH, DEN DANSKE KIRKES HISTORIE, Volume VI 1800-1848, p. 104.
11 W. Canton, HISTORY OF THE BRITISH AND FOREIGN BIBLE SOCIETY, Volume I, pp. 164-166.
12 J. O. Andersen, SURVEY OF THE HISTORY OF THE CHURCH IN DENMARK, pp. 43-44.
13 cf. James Lumsden, SWEDEN: ITS RELIGIOUS STATE AND PROSPECTS, pp. 25ff.
14 Gunnar Westin, DEN KRISTNA FRIFORSAMLINGEN I NORDEN, p. 24.
15 W. Canton, Volume I, p. 201.
16 See H. Hägglund, HENRIC SCHARTAU.
17 H. Holmqvist, SVENSKA KYRKANS HISTORIA, VI, pp. 42-43.
18 G. M. Stephenson, THE RELIGIOUS ASPECTS OF SWEDISH IMMIGRATION, pp. 31ff.
19 Gunnar Westin, GEORGE SCOTT OCH HANS VERKSSAMHET I SVERIGE, Volume I, pp. 29ff.
20 J. Wordsworth, THE NATIONAL CHURCH OF SWEDEN, p. 370.
21 See Bengt Jonzon, STUDIER I PAAVO RUOTSALAINEN; cf. G. O. Rosenqvist, FINLANDS KYRKA, pp. 8ff.
22 O. Hallesby, Introduction to Juhani Aho, DE VAKTE (Norwegian edition of a Finnish original).
23 See Evald Uustalu, HISTORY OF THE ESTONIAN PEOPLE. W. Canton, Volume I, p. 178.
24 Alfred Bilmanis, THE CHURCH IN LATVIA; cf. W. Canton, Volume II, p. 259.

1 Letter of Dr. Wood, Boscawen, N. H., in Heman Humphrey, REVIVAL SKETCHES, pp. 167-168.
2 William Speer, THE GREAT REVIVAL OF 1800, p. 17.
3 C. L. Thompson, TIMES OF REFRESHING, p. 75.
4 N. S. Woods, HISTORY OF THE FIRST BAPTIST CHURCH OF BOSTON; cf. H. C. Fish, HANDBOOK OF REVIVALS, p. 56.
5 CONNECTICUT EVANGELICAL MAGAZINE, I, pp. 136ff; 177ff.
6 Heman Humphrey, REVIVAL SKETCHES, pp. 123ff; cf. Charles Roy Keller, SECOND GREAT AWAKENING IN CONNECTICUT, New York, 1942.
7 S. B. Halliday, THE CHURCH IN AMERICA AND ITS BAPTISMS OF FIRE, p. 91; cf. Heman Humphrey, pp. 118ff.
8 CONNECTICUT EVANGELICAL MAGAZINE, I, pp. 378ff; 420ff.
9 Bennet Tyler, NEW ENGLAND REVIVALS, pp. 23ff; Heman Humphrey, pp. 150ff.
10 Heman Humphrey, pp. 153ff.
11 CONNECTICUT EVANGELICAL MAGAZINE, I, pp. 23-27, 60-67.
12 Bennet Tyler, NEW ENGLAND REVIVALS, pp. 17ff.
13 CONNECTICUT EVANGELICAL MAGAZINE, I, pp. 131-136; cf. Sermon of President Griffin, Williams College, September 1828.
14 Heman Humphrey, REVIVAL SKETCHES, pp. 135ff.
15 Bennet Tyler, NEW ENGLAND REVIVALS, pp. 112ff; Heman Humphrey, pp. 139ff.
16 H. C. Fish, HANDBOOK OF REVIVALS, p. 59; Bennet Tyler, pp. 149ff; Heman Humphrey, pp. 145ff.
17 Heman Humphrey, REVIVAL SKETCHES, pp. 168ff.
18 Letter of John Preston, Rupert, Vermont, July 1804; in Heman Humphrey, pp. 171ff; & C. L. Thompson, p. 77.
19 Letters of Messrs. Ledoyt & Seamans, in Heman Humphrey, p. 166.
20 Letter of E. D. Griffin, 20 January 1832, in William B. Sprague, LECTURES ON REVIVALS OF RELIGION, p. 360.
21 Letter of Edward Payson, 29 May 1821, pp. 289-299.
22 G. G. Smith, THE LIFE AND LABORS OF FRANCIS ASBURY, pp. 191-192. The records mentioned no extravagances.
23 Heman Humphrey, REVIVAL SKETCHES, pp. 166-167; Letter of Philip Milledoler, 3 April 1832, Sprague, pp. 320ff.
24 Letter of Archibald Maclay, in Heman Humphrey, pp. 225ff; cf. BAPTISTS IN NEW YORK, 1809-1822.
25 See Samuel Buell, A BRIEF ACCOUNT OF THE REVIVAL OF RELIGION IN BRIDGHAMPTON IN 1799 and 1800.
26 William Speer, THE GREAT REVIVAL OF 1800, pp. 51ff.
27 Whitney R. Cross, THE BURNED-OVER DISTRICT, pp. 9ff.
28 Letter of Edward D. Griffin, 20 January 1832, William B. Sprague, LECTURES ON REVIVALS OF RELIGION, p. 361.
29 Letter of E. D. Griffin to Ashbel Green, Heman Humphrey, p. 178.
30 Letter of John McDowell, 5 March 1832, Sprague, pp. 283ff.
31 Cf. S. B. Halliday, THE CHURCH IN AMERICA AND ITS BAPTISMS OF FIRE, p. 85.
32 Letter of Philip Milledoler, 3 April 1832, Sprague, pp. 320ff.
33 Heman Humphrey, REVIVAL SKETCHES, pp. 181ff, 192ff; cf. William Speer, THE GREAT REVIVAL OF 1800, pp. 21-24.
34 CHRISTIAN OBSERVER, London, 1804, pp. 55ff; see William Speer, THE GREAT REVIVAL OF 1800, pp. 65-66.
35 William Speer, THE GREAT REVIVAL OF 1800, p. 72.

1 CHRISTIAN OBSERVER, London, 1804, p. 113; see the United States Census, 1791 & 1801.
2 A. B. Strickland, THE GREAT AMERICAN REVIVAL, pp. 44ff.
3 W. P. Strickland, editor, THE AUTOBIOGRAPHY OF PETER CARTWRIGHT, pp. 24-27.
4 See W. H. Foote, SKETCHES OF VIRGINIA, p. 427; SKETCHES OF NORTH CAROLINA, Chapter XXVII: 'Rev. James McGready and the Revival of 1800.'
5 NEW YORK MISSIONARY MAGAZINE, 1802, pp. 74-75: James McGready, 'A Short Narrative of the Revival of Religion in Logan County.' Narrative continued in pp. 151-155, 192-197, 234-236.
6 METHODIST MAGAZINE, London, 1803, pp. 181-184: Letter of the Rev. James McGready to Dr. Thomas Coke.
7 NEW YORK MISSIONARY MAGAZINE, 1802, pp. 151-155; cf. METHODIST MAGAZINE, London, 1803, Letter of McGready.
8 John B. Boles, THE GREAT REVIVAL, 1787-1805, Chapter V, 'Kentucky Ablaze.'
9 Barton W. Stone, 'A Short History of the Life of Barton Warren Stone,' in James R. Rogers, CANE RIDGE MEETING HOUSE; Catherine C. Cleveland, THE GREAT REVIVAL IN THE WEST, 1797-1805, pp. 183-189, Eye-witness account by John Lyle.
10 Leonard W. Bacon, A HISTORY OF AMERICAN CHRISTIANITY, p. 236. Cf. W. W. Sweet, REVIVALISM IN AMERICA, p. 132.
11 Barton W. Stone, 'A Short History of the Life of Barton W. Stone,' in J. R. Rogers, THE CANE RIDGE MEETING-HOUSE, pp. 157ff.
12 See special note:
13 George Howe, HISTORY OF THE PRESBYTERIAN CHURCH IN SOUTH CAROLINA, Volume II, p. 114; Lorenzo Dow, HISTORY OF COSMOPOLITE, pp. 201ff.
14 W. P. Strickland, AUTOBIOGRAPHY OF PETER CARTWRIGHT; Levi Purviance, BIOGRAPHY OF ELDER DAVID PURVIANCE, p. 249. The crack of the whip needs to be demonstrated.
15 John B. Boles, THE GREAT REVIVAL, 1787-1805, p. 68.
16 cf. J. H. Spencer, HISTORY OF THE KENTUCKY BAPTISTS, and David Benedict, A HISTORY OF THE BAPTIST DENOMINATION IN AMERICA, Volume II, p. 256.
17 W. W. Sweet, REVIVALISM IN AMERICA, p. 132.
18 David Rice, A SERMON ON THE PRESENT REVIVAL OF RELIGION, Kentucky, 1803, p. 45.
19 Elkhorn Baptist Association, MINUTES OF 1875.
20 Elmer T. Clark, editor, JOURNAL AND LETTERS OF FRANCIS ASBURY, Volume III, p. 187.
21 NEW YORK MISSIONARY MAGAZINE, 1802, p. 87: Letter of George Baxter to Dr. Archibald Alexander. See W. W. Woodward, SURPRISING ACCOUNTS OF THE REVIVAL OF RELIGION IN THE UNITED STATES, Philadelphia, 1802.
22 W. W. Sweet, THE STORY OF RELIGION IN AMERICA, p. 230.
23 See W. B. McDonald, THE HISTORY OF THE CUMBERLAND PRESBYTERIAN CHURCH.
24 See W. E. McCleary, THE LIFE OF REV. JAMES O'KELLY, Raleigh, 1910.
25 W. W. Sweet, THE STORY OF RELIGION IN AMERICA, p. 238.
26 Barton W. Stone, 'A Short History of the Life of Barton W. Stone,' in J. R. Rogers, THE CANE RIDGE MEETING-HOUSE, pp. 119ff.

1   Baptists, Methodists and Presbyterians cooperated in the Concert of Prayer.
2   Devereux Jarratt, LIFE OF THE REV. DEVEREUX JARRATT, Baltimore, 1806.
3   Richard J. Hooker, editor, THE CAROLINA BACKCOUNTRY ON THE EVE OF THE REVOLUTION, p. 77.
4   Letter of Moses Waddel, 25 February 1832, William B. Sprague, LECTURES ON REVIVALS OF RELIGION, pp. 355ff.
5   W. H. Foote, SKETCHES OF VIRGINIA, pp. 413ff.
6   Cf. William Hill, AUTOBIOGRAPHICAL SKETCHES, pp. 7ff, 107ff. & W. H. Foote, SKETCHES OF VIRGINIA, pp. 408ff.
7   John B. Boles, THE GREAT REVIVAL, 1787–1805.
8   De la Rochefoucault, TRAVELS THROUGH THE UNITED STATES OF NORTH AMERICA, 1795–97, Volume II, pp. 50, 669.
9   W. E. Channing, MEMOIR OF WILLIAM ELLERY CHANNING, Volume I, p. 126.
10 Devereux Jarratt, LIFE OF THE REV. DEVEREUX JARRATT, p. 128.
11 See Isaac Weld, TRAVELS THROUGH THE STATES OF NORTH AMERICA AND PROVINCES OF UPPER AND LOWER CANADA.
12 Thomas Hugh Spence, THE PRESBYTERIAN CONGREGATION ON ROCKY RIVER, pp. 30 & 38.
13 W. H. Foote, SKETCHES OF NORTH CAROLINA, p. 227.
14 Letter of James Hall, in W. H. Foote, SKETCHES OF NORTH CAROLINA, pp. 382ff.
15 James Hall, A NARRATIVE OF A MOST EXTRAORDINARY WORK OF RELIGION IN NORTH CAROLINA, 1802.
16 George Howe, HISTORY OF THE PRESBYTERIAN CHURCH IN SOUTH CAROLINA, Volume II, pp. 106ff.
17 Letter of Richard Furman, 11 August 1802, quoted in Benedict's GENERAL HISTORY OF THE BAPTIST DENOMINATION, Volume II, p. 169.
18 George Howe, pp. 106ff.
19 W. H. Foote, SKETCHES OF NORTH CAROLINA, p. 404.
20 See A. M. Shipp, METHODISM IN SOUTH CAROLINA.
21 J. M. King, A HISTORY OF THE SOUTH CAROLINA BAPTISTS, p. 155.
22 Letter of Moses Waddel, 25 February 1832, Sprague, p. 355.
23 See METHODIST MAGAZINE, London, 1803, p. 521 (Letter of the Rev. Stith Mead, 11 May 1802)
24 Letter of Moses Waddel, 25 February 1832, Sprague, p. 356.
25 Jesse Lee, A SHORT HISTORY OF THE METHODISTS, pp. 292ff.
26 R. B. Semple, A HISTORY OF THE RISE AND PROGRESS OF THE BAPTISTS IN VIRGINIA, pp. 237ff.
27 Letter of Francis Asbury, in METHODIST MAGAZINE, 1802, pp. 217–218.
28 CONNECTICUT EVANGELICAL MAGAZINE, III, 1803, pp. 315ff.
29 cf. C. C. Sellers, LORENZO DOW, pp. 68–69.
30 THE JOURNAL OF FRANCIS ASBURY, Volume III, pp. 210–211.
31 Elmer T. Clark, editor, THE JOURNAL AND LETTERS OF FRANCIS ASBURY, Volume III, p. 253.
32 W. W. Sweet, 'The Churches as the Moral Courts of the Frontier,' in CHURCH HISTORY, 1933, II, pp. 3ff.
33 JOURNAL OF PRESBYTERIAN HISTORY, 1966, XL, pp. 89ff.

1   I. F. Mackinnon, SETTLEMENTS AND CHURCHES IN NOVA SCOTIA, 1749-1776, pp. 70-76; cf. Henry Alline, THE LIFE AND JOURNAL OF THE REV. MR. HENRY ALLINE, Boston, 1806.

2   S. D. Clark, CHURCH AND SECT IN CANADA, pp. 32-36, 69-70; cf. I. F. Mackinnon, pp. 70-76, 92.

3   J. Davis, LIFE AND TIMES OF REV. HARRIS HARDING, p. 229.

4   S. D. Clark, CHURCH AND SECT IN CANADA, p. 50.

5   I. E. Bill, FIFTY YEARS WITH THE BAPTIST MINISTERS AND CHURCHES OF THE MARITIME PROVINCES, p. 20.

6   J. Davis, LIFE AND TIMES OF REV. HARRIS HARDING, p. 30.

7   E. M. Saunders, A HISTORY OF THE BAPTISTS OF THE MARITIME PROVINCES, p. 36.

8   See Joseph Dimock's Diary, Acadia University, Wolfville, N.S., Baptist Historical Collection.

9   There were Methodists in Nova Scotia being supported by the British Conference as early as the middle 1780s.

10 Joshua Marsden, NARRATIVE OF A MISSION TO NOVA SCOTIA, NEW BRUNSWICK, AND THE SOMERS ISLANDS.

11 Joshua Marsden, NARRATIVE, pp. 216-217.

12 Samuel Codner, a Methodist pioneer still in Anglican membership, received support from the Society for the Propagation of the Gospel, see J. D. Mullins, OUR BEGINNINGS, Colonial and Continental Church Society, pp. 1-12.

13 Charles Inglis, THE JOURNAL OF BISHOP CHARLES INGLIS, 1785-1810.

14 J. E. Sanderson, THE FIRST CENTURY OF METHODISM IN CANADA, Volume I, p. 33.

15 The story of Major Neal is found in Sanderson, Volume I, p. 24.

16 J. E. Sanderson, p. 27.

17 Losee's career is cited in Sanderson, Volume I, pp. 27ff.

18 W. Gregg, THE HISTORY OF THE PRESBYTERIAN CHURCH IN CANADA, p. 187.

19 The Simcoe Papers, edited by Cruikshank, Volume III, pp. 91-93, quoted in S. D. Clark, CHURCH AND SECT IN CANADA, p. 109.

20 J. E. Sanderson, p. 35.

21 See S. D. Clark, CHURCH AND SECT IN CANADA, p. 93; & Sanderson, Volume I, pp. 36-37.

22 S. D. Clark, CHURCH AND SECT IN CANADA, p. 100.

23 J. E. Sanderson, p. 43.

24 See John Carroll, CASE AND HIS CONTEMPORARIES, A Biographical History of Methodism in Canada till 1855.

25 METHODIST MAGAZINE, London, 1811, Letter of William Case to Francis Asbury; cf. John Carroll, Volume I, pp. 182-186.

26 Stuart Ivison & Fred Rosser, THE BAPTISTS IN UPPER AND LOWER CANADA, p. 32.

27 J. L. Gilmour, 'The Baptists in Canada,' Volume XI, p. 362, in Shortt & Doughty, CANADA AND ITS PROVINCES.

28 Stuart Ivison & Fred Rosser, p. 156.

29 J. E. Sanderson, p. 97.

30 E. R. Fitch, editor, THE BAPTISTS OF CANADA, pp. 102ff.

31 C. B. Sissons, EGERTON RYERSON: HIS LIFE AND LETTERS, Toronto, 1937-1947.

1 C. P. Shedd, TWO CENTURIES OF STUDENT CHRISTIAN MOVEMENTS, pp. 37ff.
2 RECORD BOOK, Theological Society, 24 April 1808, Dartmouth College, MS.
3 Reuben Guild, EARLY RELIGIOUS HISTORY OF BROWN UNIVERSITY, Brown University, MS.
4 CONSTITUTION of the Saturday Evening Religious Society, 1802, Harvard University, MS.
5 Timothy Dwight, THE NATURE AND DANGER OF INFIDEL PHILOSOPHY, 1797; A DISCOURSE ON SOME EVENTS OF THE LAST CENTURY, New Haven, 1801.
6 Timothy Dwight, BACCALAUREATE SERMON, Yale College in 1796.
7 PRINCETON REVIEW, 1859, XXXI, p. 39; cf. Letter of 21 June 1815 from the Praying Society of Brown University to the students at Bowdoin College, Brown University, MS.
8 Careful scrutiny of primary and secondary sources has revealed not one instance of fanaticism reported in the awakenings of the collegiate communities.
9 F. G. Beardsley, A HISTORY OF AMERICAN REVIVALS, p. 89.
10 JOURNAL OF XLI ANNUAL CONVENTION OF THE PROTESTANT EPISCOPAL CHURCH IN THE DIOCESE OF OHIO, 1858, p. 28.
11 F. Rudolph, THE AMERICAN COLLEGE AND UNIVERSITY, pp. 79-80; in days of decline, the cynics called the day of prayer 'the day of whist.'
12 See Appendices, William B. Sprague, LECTURES ON REVIVALS OF RELIGION.
13 cf. PRINCETON REVIEW, 1859, XXXI, pp. 28ff; & Strickland, THE GREAT AMERICAN REVIVAL, pp. 133ff.
14 H. B. Wright, TWO CENTURIES OF CHRISTIAN ACTIVITY AT YALE, pp. 64-65.
15 C. Durfee, A HISTORY OF WILLIAMS COLLEGE, p. 117.
16 C. P. Shedd, pp. 74-80.
17 PRINCETON REVIEW, 1859, XXXI, p. 42.
18 cf. C. P. Shedd, TWO CENTURIES OF STUDENT CHRISTIAN MOVEMENTS, p. 77, & PRINCETON REVIEW, 1859, XXXI, p. 41.
19 PRINCETON REVIEW, 1859, XXXI, p. 39.
20 F. Rudolph, p. 53.

Notes on Chapter 12: UNDER THE SOUTHERN CROSS

1 J. du Plessis, THE LIFE OF ANDREW MURRAY OF SOUTH AFRICA, pp. 63ff.
2 See T. N. Hanekom, HELPERUS RITZEMA VAN LIER.
3 Graduated Ph. D., University of Groningen, May 1783.
4 W. Cowper, THE POWER OF GRACE ILLUSTRATED, (the biography of an unnamed minister, actually H. R. van Lier)
5 T. N. Hanekom, HELPERUS RITZEMA VAN LIER, pp. 135ff, 189ff.
6 See M. C. Vos, MERKWAARDIG VERHAAL.
7 W. J. van der Merwe, THE DEVELOPMENT OF MISSIONARY ATTITUDES IN THE DUTCH REFORMED CHURCH IN SOUTH AFRICA, pp. 73ff.

8 baptized Machtelt Combrink, 17 August 1749, as noted in the painstaking study in Afrikaans by Prof. Hanekom.
9 See John Philip, MEMOIR OF MRS. MATHILDA SMITH, LATE OF CAPE TOWN, London, 1824.
10 K. S. Latourette, A HISTORY OF THE EXPANSION OF CHRISTIANITY, Volume V, p. 339.
11 P. J. Blok, GESCHIEDENIS VAN HET NEDERLANDSCHE VOLK, Volume VI, pp. 501ff.
12 John Kendrick, MS Letter, 20 November 1810, at Cape Town, to Thomas Blanshard; in Archives of the Methodist Church of South Africa, Cory Library, Grahamstown.
13 WESLEYAN METHODIST MAGAZINE, 1810, p. 207.
14 George Middlemiss, Letter published in WESLEYAN METHODIST MAGAZINE, 1810, p. 446.
15 John Kendrick, Letter, 20 November 1810; also his journal, in THE JOURNAL OF THE METHODIST HISTORICAL SOCIETY of SOUTH AFRICA, Volume II, Number 4, p. 84.
16 Arthur Kitson, CAPTAIN JAMES COOK, THE NAVIGATOR.
17 Ernest Scott, A SHORT HISTORY OF AUSTRALIA, pp. 45ff.
18 J. B. Marsden, editor, MEMOIRS OF THE LIFE AND LABOURS OF THE REV. SAMUEL MARSDEN.
19 E. M. O'Brien, THE DAWN OF CATHOLICISM IN AUSTRALIA.
20 The various denominational histories detail their beginnings in the Australian Colonies.

Notes on Chapter 13: ORGANIZING FOR ADVANCE

1 K. S. Latourette, A HISTORY OF THE EXPANSION OF CHRISTIANITY, Volume IV, pp. 34–35.
2 K. S. Latourette, Volume IV, pp. 65–66.
3 W. Jones, A JUBILEE MEMORIAL OF THE RELIGIOUS TRACT SOCIETY, pp. 12ff.
4 See American Tract Society, ANNUAL REPORT, 1826.
5 G. R. Balleine, A HISTORY OF THE EVANGELICAL PARTY IN THE CHURCH OF ENGLAND, p. 133.
6 W. Canton, A HISTORY OF THE BRITISH AND FOREIGN BIBLE society, Volume I, pp. 1ff.
7 H. O. Dwight, CENTENNIAL HISTORY OF THE AMERICAN BIBLE SOCIETY, Volume I, pp. 7ff.
8 W. Roberts, MEMOIR OF THE LIFE OF HANNAH MORE.
9 D. Salmon, JOSEPH LANCASTER, passim; W. Corston, THE LIFE OF JOSEPH LANCASTER, pp. 11 & 16.
10 See J. H. Harris, ROBERT RAIKES: THE MAN AND HIS WORK; E. W. Rice, THE SUNDAY SCHOOL MOVEMENT, 1780–1917.
11 E. A. Payne, 'The Evangelical Revival and the Beginning of the Modern Missionary Movement,' CONGREGATIONAL QUARTERLY, 1943, XXI, pp. 223ff.
12 R. P. Beaver, 'The Concert of Prayer for Missions,' ECUMENICAL REVIEW, 1957-58, X, pp. 420ff.
13 E. A. Payne, THE CHURCH AWAKES, p. 31.
14 Eugene Stock, THE HISTORY OF THE CHURCH MISSIONARY SOCIETY, Volume I, p. 57.
15 See S. Pearce Carey, WILLIAM CAREY.
16 PROCEEDINGS OF THE WESLEY HISTORICAL SOCIETY, XXX, pp. 25-29.   17 S. Pearce Carey, WILLIAM CAREY, p. 83.
18 F. D. Walker, WILLIAM CAREY, MISSIONARY PIONEER.

19 William Carey, AN ENQUIRY INTO THE OBLIGATIONS OF CHRISTIANS TO USE MEANS FOR THE CONVERSION OF THE HEATHENS, Leicester, 1792.

20 R. Lovett, HISTORY OF THE LONDON MISSIONARY SOCIETY, Volume I, p. 5.

21 W. Carus, MEMOIRS OF THE LIFE OF THE REV. CHARLES SIMEON, p. 229.

22 Findlay & Holdsworth, HISTORY OF THE WESLEYAN METHODIST MISSIONARY SOCIETY, Volume I, p. 72.

23 D. Mackichan, THE MISSIONARY IDEAL IN THE SCOTTISH CHURCHES, pp. 74, 112ff.

24 See Charles Chaney, 'God's Glorious Work: The Theological Foundations of the Early Missionary Societies in America, 1787-1817.' University of Chicago, Ph.D. dissertation, 1972.

25 See J. D. Ibbotson, DOCUMENTARY HISTORY OF HAMILTON COLLEGE, pp. 25-103; Peter Thacher, BRIEF ACCOUNT OF THE SOCIETY FOR PROPAGATING THE GOSPEL AMONG THE INDIANS AND OTHERS IN NORTH AMERICA, Boston, 1798.

26 J. W. Alexander, THE LIFE OF ARCHIBALD ALEXANDER, pp. 48-81; & ACTS AND PROCEEDINGS OF THE GENERAL SYNOD OF THE REFORMED PROTESTANT DUTCH CHURCH IN NORTH AMERICA, (1859) p. 187.

27 C. G. Woodson, THE HISTORY OF THE NEGRO CHURCH, pp. 78ff.

28 C. H. Wesley, RICHARD ALLEN: APOSTLE OF FREEDOM, Washington, 1935.

29 See K. S. Latourette, A HISTORY OF THE EXPANSION OF CHRISTIANITY, Volume IV, pp. 335-336 for various sources on the subject of Negro education.

30 This handicap is evidenced by statistics of births and marriages of black citizens of the United States, up to date, regrettably, even in the 1970s.

31 Heman Humphrey, REVIVAL SKETCHES, pp. 286-287.

32 John M. Mason, 'Messiah's Throne,' a sermon preached before the London Missionary Society, 13 May 1802; in Ebenezer Mason, THE COMPLETE WORKS OF JOHN M. MASON, Volume III, pp. 270-271.

33 NEW YORK MISSIONARY MAGAZINE, January 1800, p. 9.

34 R. Pierce Beaver, PIONEERS IN MISSION, pp. 235ff.

35 John Blair Smith, THE ENLARGEMENT OF CHRIST'S KINGDOM, Schenectady, 1797.

36 ANNUAL BAPTIST REGISTER, III, pp. 535ff; CONNECTICUT EVANGELICAL MAGAZINE, Volume I, p. 14.

37 MASSACHUSETTS BAPTIST MISSIONARY SOCIETY, Volume I, pp. 5-12.

38 CONNECTICUT EVANGELICAL MAGAZINE, Volume I, p. 31.

39 S. B. Halliday, THE CHURCH IN AMERICA, pp. 515ff.

40 J. Tracy, HISTORY OF THE AMERICAN BOARD, pp. 24ff.

41 F. Wayland, MEMOIR OF ADONIRAM JUDSON.

42 J. M. Reid, MISSIONS AND MISSIONARY SOCIETY OF THE METHODIST EPISCOPAL CHURCH, Volume I, p. 17.

43 J. C. Emery, A CENTURY OF ENDEAVOR, pp. 29ff.

44 A. J. Brown, ONE HUNDRED YEARS, pp. 21ff.

45 George Drach, OUR CHURCH ABROAD, p. 23.

46 NEW YORK MISSIONARY MAGAZINE, Volume I, 1800, pp. 80-81.

47 THE PANOPLIST, Boston, Volume XI, January 1815, pp. 19-20.

1   THE PANOPLIST, XI, Boston, January & March 1815.
2   Letter of G. Gellard, METHODIST MAGAZINE, London, 1816, p. 462.
3   METHODIST MAGAZINE, 1816, p. 632.
4   METHODIST MAGAZINE, 1816, p. 632.
5   METHODIST MAGAZINE, 1816, p. 635.
6   W. E. Farndale, THE SECRET OF MOW COP, p. 48.
7   Primitive Methodist Conference, 1821-1824; cf. W. E. Farndale, THE SECRET OF MOW COP, p. 56.
8   See F. W. Bourne, BILLY BRAY, THE KING'S SON.
9   METHODIST MAGAZINE, London, 1821, pp. 294-295, 380ff, 457ff, 531ff.
10 George Smith, HISTORY OF WESLEYAN METHODISM, Volume III, p. 65.
11 See MINUTES OF THE METHODIST CONFERENCE, Volume V, London, 1820, p. 127; cf. George Smith, Volume III, p. 48.
12 See MINUTES OF THE METHODIST CONFERENCE, Volume V, p. 230;   Volume VII, p. 45.
13 George Smith, HISTORY OF WESLEYAN METHODISM, Volume III, p. 48; cf. W. W. Ward, THE EARLY CORRESPONDENCE OF JABEZ BUNTING, London, 1972.
14 T. P. Bunting, THE LIFE OF JABEZ BUNTING, p. 115.
15 METHODIST MAGAZINE, London, 1823, p. 43.
16 George Smith, HISTORY OF WESLEYAN METHODISM, Volume II, pp. 615ff; cf. METHODIST MAGAZINE, 1823, p. 322.
17 See R. W. Dale, HISTORY OF ENGLISH CONGREGATIONALISM, pp. 698-719.
18 W. T. Whitley, A HISTORY OF BRITISH BAPTISTS, pp. 266ff, BAPTIST MAGAZINE, London, 1815, p. 390.
19 J. W. Morris, RECOLLECTIONS OF REV. ROBERT HALL.
20 W. E. Carus, MEMOIRS OF THE LIFE OF CHARLES SIMEON, pp. 326ff.
21 G. R. Balleine, A HISTORY OF THE EVANGELICAL PARTY, p. 127; cf. G. C. B. Davies, THE FIRST EVANGELICAL BISHOP.
22 J. H. Overton, THE ENGLISH CHURCH IN THE NINETEENTH CENTURY, 1800-1833, pp. 150 & 156.
23 See R. P. Flindall, editor, THE CHURCH OF ENGLAND, 1815-1948, pp. 15-16; cf. R. A. Soloway, PRELATES AND PEOPLE.
24 J. O. Jones, COFIANT A GWEITHIAU Y PARCH: ROBERT ELLIS, YSGOLDY, Carnarvon, 1883, p. 223; Henry Hughes, DIWYGIADAU CREFYDDOL CYMRU, p. 252;
25 Henry Hughes, DIWYGIADAU CREFYDDOL CYMRU, p. 273; & J. O. Jones, ROBERT ELLIS, pp. 223-227;   cf. Henry Hughes, pp. 253-258 & 279.
26 John Hughes, METHODISTIAETH CYMRU, Volume III, p. 154.
27 Henry Hughes, DIWYGIADAU CREFYDDOL, pp. 293-294.
28 See Hugh Watt, THOMAS CHALMERS AND THE DISRUPTION, pp. 27ff; pp. 41ff.
29 Alexander Haldane, THE LIVES OF ROBERT AND JAMES ALEXANDER HALDANE, Chapter XX; W. J. Couper, SCOTTISH REVIVALS, p. 120.
30 Peter Bayne, THE FREE CHURCH OF SCOTLAND, Chapters IV & V; DICTIONARY OF NATIONAL BIOGRAPHY, XIX, p. 715.
31 W. J. Couper, SCOTTISH REVIVALS, p. 120.

32 Mary Duncan, HISTORY OF REVIVALS IN THE BRITISH ISLES, pp. 33ff; W. J. Couper, p. 120.
33 W. J. Couper, SCOTTISH REVIVALS, pp. 118-129.
34 See Alexander MacRae, REVIVALS IN THE HIGHLANDS AND ISLANDS, p. 80.
35 D. Beaton, DIARY OF REV. ALEXANDER MACLEOD, Inverness, 1925; Mary Duncan, HISTORY OF REVIVALS IN THE BRITISH ISLES, pp. 356ff; Alexander MacRae, pp. 80-89.
36 Alexander MacRae, pp. 96-97.
37 Alexander MacRae, pp. 98-99.
38 K. S. Latourette, CHRISTIANITY IN A REVOLUTIONARY AGE, Volume II, p. 425.
39 See W. A. Phillips, HISTORY OF THE CHURCH OF IRELAND, Volume III, p. 335; R. B. McDowell, PUBLIC OPINION IN IRELAND, 1801-1846, p. 33.
40 W. A. Phillips, Volume III, pp. 336ff.
41 See C. H. Crookshank, HISTORY OF METHODISM IN IRELAND, Volume III, passim.
42 See J. L. Porter, LIFE AND TIMES OF DR. COOKE, 1875.
43 H. A. Ironside, A HISTORICAL SKETCH OF THE BRETHREN MOVEMENT, p. 10.
44 DICTIONARY OF NATIONAL BIOGRAPHY, Volume V, pp. 493ff; also notices in various histories of the Brethren.
45 See A. T. Pierson, GEORGE MULLER OF BRISTOL.
46 Mrs. Oliphant, THE LIFE OF EDWARD IRVING.
47 See P. E. Shaw, THE CATHOLIC APOSTOLIC CHURCH.

Notes on Chapter 15: SWISS, FRENCH & DUTCH REVEIL

1 Alexander Haldane, THE LIVES OF ROBERT AND JAMES ALEXANDER HALDANE, pp. 401ff.
2 Letter of Robert Haldane, 4 September 1839, Haldane, pp. 388ff.
3 Ami Bost, MEMOIRES POUVENT SERVIR A L'HISTOIRE DU REVEIL RELIGIEUX DES EGLISES PROTESTANTES DE LA SUISSE ET DE LA FRANCE, p. 25.
4 Jean-Jacques Rousseau, letter quoted in Haldane, p. 395.
5 Ami Bost, MEMOIRES, pp. 76ff.
6 Alexander Haldane, pp. 402-408.
7 cf. Leon Maury, LE REVEIL RELIGIEUX DANS L'EGLISE REFORMEE, Volume I, pp. 20ff.
8 Alexander Haldane, p. 393.
9 See Malan, THE LIFE, LABOURS & WRITINGS OF CAESAR MALAN, London, 1869.
10 J. H. Merle D'Aubigne, HISTORY OF THE REFORMATION OF THE SIXTEENTH CENTURY, New York, 1844-53, 5 Volumes.
11 E. Rambert, ALEXANDRE VINET, Lausanne, 1930.
12 Felice & Bonifas, HISTOIRE DES PROTESTANTES DE FRANCE, pp. 597ff.
13 Alexander Haldane, pp. 434ff.
14 Continental Society for the Diffusion of Christian Knowledge, 1819 ANNUAL REPORT.
15 Continental Society, ANNUAL REPORTS, 1821-1823, 1831-1835.
16 George Smith, HISTORY OF WESLEYAN METHODISM, Volume III, pp. 339ff. See Alexander Haldane, pp. 411ff.
17 W. Canton, HISTORY OF THE BRITISH AND FOREIGN BIBLE SOCIETY, Volume I, pp. 185, 393, 402.

18 Jean Bianquis, LES ORIGINES DE LA SOCIETE DE MISSIONS EVANGELIQUES DE PARIS, 1822-1829, Paris, 1930-1931.
19 M. Elisabeth Kluit, HET REVEIL IN NEDERLAND, pp. 5ff.
20 See Isaak da Costa, BEZWAREN TEGEN DEN GEEST DER EEUW, 1823; cf. M. E. Kluit, pp. 40ff.
21 M. E. Kluit, HET REVEIL IN NEDERLAND, pp. 63ff.
22 G. G. van Prinsterer, ONGELOOF EN REVOLUTION; Kluit, pp. 123ff.
23 See W. P. Keijzer, VINET EN HOLLAND.
24 M. E. Kluit, HET REVEIL IN NEDERLAND, pp. 250ff, 171ff.

Notes on Chapter 15: THE GERMAN AWAKENING

1 L. Tiesmeyer, DIE ERWECKUNGSBEWEGUNG IN DEUTCHLAND, Volume VIII, pp. 15ff.
2 J. W. Goethe, JUNG-STILLINGS JUGEND, JUNGLINGSJAHRE, WANDERSCHAFT UND LEHRJAHRE.
3 Gustav Warnecke, ABRISS EINER GESCHICHTE DER PRO-TESTANTISCHEN MISSIONEN, p. 140.
4 See J. Gossner, MARTIN BOOS, 1831.
5 Alfred Ringwald, MENSCHEN VOR GOTT, Volume II, p. 350.
6 See L. Rott, ANFANGE DES WESLEYANISCHEN METHODISTUS, (Dissertation, Erlangen University).
7 Robert Steiner, 'Die Bibel in der Welt,' in JAHRBUCH DES VERBANDES DER EVANGELISCHEN BIBELGESELLSCHAFTEN IN DEUTSCHLAND, pp. 151ff.
8 Paulus Scharpff, GESCHICHTE DER EVANGELISATION, p. 114.
9 REALENCYCLOPADIE FUR PROTESTANTISCHE THEOLOGIE UND KIRCHE, Volume VIII, pp. 292ff; cf. Frau von Krüdener, EIN ZEITGEMALDE, Bern, 1868.
10 Paulus Scharpff, GESCHICHTE DER EVANGELISATION, p.139.
11 See F. W. Krummacher, GOTTFRIED DANIEL KRUMMACHER UND DIE NIEDER-RHEINISCHE ERWECKUNGSBEWEGUNG ZU ANFANG DES 19 JAHRHUNDERTS, Berlin, 1935.
12 L. Tiesmeyer, DIE ERWECKUNGSBEWEGUNG IN DEUTSCHLAND, Volume III, pp. 215ff.
13 F. W. Krummacher, SELBSTBIOGRAPHIE, Berlin, 1869.
14 F. W. Kantzenbach, DIE ERWECKUNGSBEWEGUNG, pp. 128ff.
15 E. Frommel, AUS DEM LEBEN DES DR. ALOYS HENHOFER.
16 See also K. F. Ledderhose, DR. ALOYS HENHOFER.
17 Heinrich Hermelink, DAS CHRISTENTUM IN DER MENSCH-HEITSGESCHICHTE VOR DER FRANZOSISCHEN REVOLUTION BIS ZUR GEGENWART; & G. Müller, CHRISTIAN GOTTLOB PREZIGER, Stuttgart, 1962.
18 Wilhelm Schlatter, GESCHICHTE DER BASLER MISSION, 1815-1915, Volume I, pp. 1-10.
19 F. W. Kantzenbach, DIE ERWECKUNGSBEWEGUNG, pp. 74ff.
20 Theodor Jäger, LUDWIG HOFACKER, Stuttgart, 1910.
21 Paulus Scharff, GESCHICHTE DER EVANGELISATION, p. 132.
22 L. Tiesmeyer, Volume VI, pp. 24ff, 32ff.
23 Alfred Ringwald, MENSCHEN VOR GOTT, Volume I, p. 296.
24 REALENCYCLOPADIE FUR PROTESTANTISCHE THEOLOGIE UND KIRCHE, Volume V, pp. 621ff.
25 L. Tiesmeyer, Volume IX, pp. 25ff.   26 Volume X, p. 83.
27 F. W. Kantzenbach, DIE ERWECKUNGSBEWEGUNG, p. 83. The Awakening movement enjoyed royal encouragement.

28 Gustav Warnecke, ABRISS EINER GESCHICHTE DER PRO-
   TESTANTISCHEN MISSIONEN, p. 140.
29 A. Jäckel, DER ALTE KOTTWITZ, Berlin, 1892.
30 REALENCYCLOPADIE FUR PROTESTANTISCHE THEOLOGIE
   UND KIRCHE, Volume X, pp. 447ff.
31 L. Witte, DAS LEBENS THOLUCKS, Leipzig, 1884.
32 L. Tiesmeyer, Volume XII, pp. 344ff.
33 L. Tiesmeyer, Volume XII, pp. 369ff.
34 J. W. Kantzenbach, DIE ERWECKUNGSBEWEGUNG, pp. 100ff.
35 L. Tiesmeyer, Volume XI, pp. 222ff.
36 L. Tiesmeyer, Volume XIV, pp. 159-169.
37 J. W. Kantzenbach, DIE ERWECKUNGSBEWEGUNG, p. 85.
38 Paulus Scharpff, GESCHICHTE DER EVANGELISATION, p. 159.
39 L. Tiesmeyer, Volume XIII, pp. 17ff.
40 Until the accession of Victoria, the British monarch was also king
   in Hanover.

Notes on Chapter 17: RENEWED AMERICAN REVIVAL, 1815—

1 Letter of Alexander Proudfit, 4 April 1832, William B. Sprague,
   LECTURES ON REVIVALS OF RELIGION, pp. 300-301.
2 See Bennet Tyler, MEMOIR OF THE LIFE AND CHARACTER
   OF REV. ASAHEL NETTLETON, Boston, 1850.
3 Heman Humphrey, REVIVAL SKETCHES, pp. 210-211.
4 Joshua Bradley, ACCOUNTS OF RELIGIOUS REVIVALS IN MANY
   PARTS OF THE UNITED STATES FROM 1815 TO 1818.
5 A. B. Strickland, THE GREAT AMERICAN REVIVAL, p. 114.
6 BAPTIST MISSIONARY MAGAZINE, IV, July 1816; March 1817.
7 Letter of Heman Humphrey, 10 April 1832, William B. Sprague,
   pp. 327ff; cf. Heman Humphrey, pp. 242ff.
8 Letter of Alvan Hyde, 22 March 1832, in Sprague, p. 275.
9 W. B. Sprague, LECTURES ON REVIVALS OF RELIGION, p. 276.
10 Heman Humphrey, REVIVAL SKETCHES, p. 259.
11 Letters of Noah Porter & Joel Hawes, 12 March 1832, William B.
   Sprague, pp. 279ff, 289ff.
12 AMERICAN BAPTIST MAGAZINE AND MISSIONARY INTELI-
   GENCER, Boston, 1817-1818, p. 307.
13 AMERICAN BAPTIST MAGAZINE, 1817-18, p. 341 & p. 383.
14 Letter of Joseph Dimock, AMERICAN BAPTIST MAGAZINE,
   1821-1822, p. 113.
15 Letter of Isaac Case, AMERICAN BAPTIST MAGAZINE, 1823-
   1824, pp. 347-348.
16 Letter of E. D. Griffin, 20 January 1832, in Sprague, p. 362.
17 Letter of John McDowell, 5 March 1832, Sprague, pp. 286-287.
18 William B. Sprague, LECTURES, p. 287.
19 Heman Humphrey, REVIVAL SKETCHES, pp. 213ff, Report of
   Gardiner Spring of New York City.
20 Letter of Alexander Proudfit, 4 April 1832, Sprague, pp. 300ff.
21 S. B. Halliday, THE CHURCH IN AMERICA AND ITS BAPTISMS
   OF FIRE, p. 205.
22 Whitney R. Cross, THE BURNED-OVER DISTRICT, pp. 9ff.
23 MINUTES OF THE ANNUAL CONFERENCES OF THE METHODIST
   EPISCOPAL CHURCH, Volume I, pp. 312ff.
24 J. H. Hotchkin, HISTORY OF THE SETTLEMENT OF WESTERN
   NEW YORK, pp. 132-133.
25 See G. F. Wright, CHARLES GRANDISON FINNEY, Boston, 1893.

26 C. G. Finney, MEMOIRS OF CHARLES G. FINNEY, pp. 61ff.
27 C. P. McIlvaine, BISHOP MCILVAINE ON THE REVIVAL OF RELIGION, New York, 1858; cf. Letter of C. P. McIlvaine, in William B. Sprague, pp. 306ff.
28 Letter of Nathan Lord, 12 March 1832, in Sprague, pp. 324ff.
29 Letter of E. D. Griffin, 20 January 1832, in Sprague, pp. 364ff.
30 Letter of Heman Humphrey, 10 April 1832, in Sprague, pp. 327ff.
31 Letter of Jeremiah Day, 2 March 1832, in Sprague, pp. 333ff.
32 Letter of Ashbel Green, 10 April 1832, in William B. Sprague, LECTURES ON REVIVALS OF RELIGION, p. 344.
33 See AMERICAN BAPTIST MAGAZINE, 1819-1820, p. 186; 1825, pp. 61 & 95.
34 S. D. Clark, CHURCH AND SECT IN CANADA, pp. 96-100.
35 W. M. Baker, LIFE AND LABOURS OF THE REV. DANIEL BAKER, Philadelphia, 1859.
36 AMERICAN BAPTIST MAGAZINE, 1818-1817, p. 273.
37 See Garnet Ryland, THE BAPTISTS OF VIRGINIA, Richmond, 1955; AMERICAN BAPTIST MAGAZINE, 1823-1824, p. 429.
38 AMERICAN BAPTIST MAGAZINE, 1823-1824, p. 419.
39 See J. M. King, HISTORY OF SOUTH CAROLINA BAPTISTS, AMERICAN BAPTIST MAGAZINE, 1823-1824, p. 227.
40 AMERICAN BAPTIST MAGAZINE, 1823-1824, p. 106.
41 Letter of Moses Waddel, 25 February 1832, Sprague, pp. 357ff.
42 J. H. Campbell, GEORGIA BAPTISTS, HISTORICAL AND BIO-GRAPHICAL, p. 193.
43 AMERICAN BAPTIST MAGAZINE, 1823-1824, p. 182.

Notes on Chapter 18: REVIVAL IMPACT ON MISSION FIELDS

1 R. Lovett, HISTORY OF THE LONDON MISSIONARY SOCIETY, Volume I, pp. 117-122.
2 See William Wilson, A MISSIONARY VOYAGE TO THE SOUTH PACIFIC OCEAN, PERFORMED IN THE YEARS 1796-1798, Chapter II; John Davies, THE HISTORY OF THE TAHITIAN MISSION; R. Lovett, Volume I, pp. 122ff.
3 John Davies, HISTORY OF THE TAHITIAN MISSION, pp. 90ff. William Ellis, POLYNESIAN RESEARCHES, Volume I, pp. 191ff.
4 MISSIONARY REGISTER, 1818, pp. 67ff.
5 See Alan R. Tippett, PEOPLE MOVEMENTS IN SOUTHERN POLYNESIA, p. 26.
6 Ebenezer Prout, MEMOIRS OF THE LIFE OF THE REV. JOHN WILLIAMS, pp. 263-264.
7 Gardiner Spring, MEMOIRS OF THE REV. SAMUEL J. MILLS, pp. 47ff.; cf. E. W. Dwight, MEMOIRS OF HENRY OBOOKIAH, New Haven, 1818.
8 H. Bingham, A RESIDENCE OF TWENTY-ONE YEARS IN THE SANDWICH ISLANDS, pp. 57ff.
9 See J. W. Burton, THE FIRST CENTURY: THE MISSIONARY ADVENTURE OF AUSTRALIAN METHODISM, 1855-1955, p. 18. Of course, three of the London missionaries had been murdered in Tonga in 1797, William Wilson, pp. 53-54. On New Zealand, see J. R. Elder, THE LETTERS AND JOURNALS OF SAMUEL MARSDEN, & Alexander Strachan, THE LIFE OF THE REV. SAMUEL LEIGH.
10 J. Rauws, Kraemer, Van Hasselt, and Slotemaker de Bruine, in THE NETHERLANDS INDIES, pp. 51ff.

11 J. Richter, DIE EVANGELISCHE MISSION IN NIEDERLANDISCH INDIEN, pp. 25-27.
12 R. Lovett, Volume I, pp. 675-676.
13 J. W. Pickett, CHRISTIAN MASS MOVEMENTS IN INDIA, pp. 39ff.
14 See J. C. Marshaman, THE LIFE AND TIMES OF CAREY, MARSHMAN & WARD.
15 See George Smith, HENRY MARTYN.
16 R. Lovett, Volume II, pp. 18ff.
17 W. E. Strong, THE STORY OF THE AMERICAN BOARD, p. 18.
18 Eugene Stock, HISTORY OF THE CHURCH MISSIONARY SOCIETY, Volume I, pp. 294ff; P. Cheriyan, THE MALABAR SYRIANS AND THE CHURCH MISSIONARY SOCIETY, 1816-1840.
19 Findley & Holdsworth, HISTORY OF THE WESLEYAN MISSION-ARY SOCIETY, Volume V, pp. 176ff.
20 A. Sutton, ORISSA AND ITS EVANGELISATION, pp. 101ff.
21 See J. A. Ewing, LANKA—THE BAPTIST MISSION IN CEYLON, pp. 16ff; & Findlay & Holdsworth, Volume V, pp. 15ff.
22 H. I. Root, A CENTURY IN CEYLON: A HISTORY OF THE AMERICAN BOARD IN CEYLON; Eugene Stock, Volume I, p. 216.
23 F. Wayland, MEMOIR OF THE LIFE OF ADONIRAM JUDSON.
24 J. du Plessis, A HISTORY OF CHRISTIAN MISSIONS IN SOUTH AFRICA, pp. 50ff, 73ff.
25 See W. J. van der Merwe, THE DEVELOPMENT OF MISSIONARY ATTITUDES IN THE DUTCH REFORMED CHURCH IN SOUTH AFRICA, pp. 73ff.
26 R. Lovett, Volume I, p. 481; A. D. Martin, Dr. VANDERKEMP.
27 C. Anshelm, BISKOP HANS PETER HALLBECK.
28 See R. Philip, THE ELIJAH OF SOUTH AFRICA: THE REV. JOHN PHILIP; cf. R. Lovett, Volume I, pp. 534ff.
29 D. J. Kotze, LETTERS OF THE AMERICAN MISSIONARIES, 1835-1838, p. 33.
30 LETTERS OF THE AMERICAN MISSIONARIES, p. 35.
31 TRANSACTIONS, London Missionary Society, Volume IV, pp. 28ff.
32 TRANSACTIONS, Volume IV, pp. 164ff.
33 Cf. QUARTERLY CHRONICLE & TRANSACTIONS of the London Missionary Society.
34 TRANSACTIONS, London Missionary Society, Volume IV, pp. 164ff.
35 QUARTERLY CHRONICLE, London Missionary Society, Volume I, p. 197.
36 See R. Moffat, MISSIONARY LABOURS AND SCENES IN SOUTH AFRICA, pp. 200ff; QUARTERLY CHROINCLE, Volume I, p. 197.
37 See J. Whiteside, HISTORY OF THE WESLEYAN METHODIST CHURCH IN SOUTH AFRICA, pp. 35ff.
38 R. Godlonton, MEMORIALS OF THE BRITISH SETTLERS OF SOUTH AFRICA, Grahamstown, 1844.
39 William Shaw, JOURNAL OF THE REV. WILLIAM SHAW, in the Cory Library, Rhodes University, Grahamstown.
40 Letter of William Shaw, 12 July 1822, WESLEYAN METHODIST MAGAZINE, London, 1822, p. 801.
41 G. E. Cory, THE RISE OF SOUTH AFRICA, Volume II, pp. 96ff.
42 E. A. Payne, FREEDOM IN JAMAICA, pp. 17-18.
43 Peter Duncan, A NARRATIVE OF THE WESLEYAN MISSION TO JAMAICA, pp. 8-10.
44 METHODIST MAGAZINE, London, 1803, pp. 133ff; 1816, pp. 473, 874 & 956.
45 E. A. Payne, FREEDOM IN JAMAICA, p. 19.

46 See Donald R. Mitchell, 'The Evangelical Contribution of James Thomson to South American Life, 1818-1825,' Th. D. Dissertation, Princeton Theological Seminary, 1972.
47 James Thomson, LETTERS ON THE MORAL AND RELIGIOUS STATE OF SOUTH AMERICA, London, 1827.
48 W. Canton, HISTORY OF THE BRITISH AND FOREIGN BIBLE SOCIETY, Volume II, pp. 347ff.

Notes on Chapter 19: AMERICAN OUTPOURING IN 1830

1 THE HOME MISSIONARY JOURNAL, 1831, p. 210.
2 Cf. AMERICAN BAPTIST MAGAZINE, Boston, 1830, p. 61; & HOME MISSIONARY JOURNAL, 1830-1831, p. 51.
3 HOME MISSIONARY JOURNAL, 1830-1831, p. 51.
4 The Congregationalists and Presbyterians were cooperating in the Plan of Union. HOME MISSIONARY JOURNAL, 1830-1831, p. 240. This journal served both denominations.
5 AMERICAN BAPTIST MAGAZINE, 1831, p. 155; 1832, p. 330; HOME MISSIONARY JOURNAL, 1830-1831, p. 4; 1831-1832, p. 75.
6 HOME MISSIONARY JOURNAL, 1831-1832, p. 5.
7 HOME MISSIONARY JOURNAL, 1830-1831, pp. 99 & 115.
8 HOME MISSIONARY JOURNAL, 1830-1831, p. 131.
9 HOME MISSIONARY JOURNAL, 1830-1831, pp. 99 & 115.
10 AMERICAN BAPTIST MAGAZINE, 1830, p. 157.
11 See Issues of 1830, p. 157, & 1831, pp. 26ff.
12 HOME MISSIONARY JOURNAL, 1830-1831, p. 4, & AMERICAN BAPTIST MAGAZINE, 1830, p. 184.
13 AMERICAN BAPTIST MAGAZINE, 1831, pp. 95, 125 & 276; cf. WESLEYAN METHODIST MAGAZINE, 1831, p. 239; 1832, p. 134.
14 NEW YORK EVANGELIST, 15 January 1831.
15 See AMERICAN BAPTIST MAGAZINE, 1831, p. 252; & HOME MISSIONARY JOURNAL, 1830-1831, pp. 151, 210-211; 1831-1832, pp. 14-18.
16 HOME MISSIONARY JOURNAL, 1830-1831, pp. 210ff.
17 William B. Sprague, LECTURES ON REVIVALS OF RELIGION, New York, 1833.
18 HOME MISSIONARY JOURNAL, 1830-1831, pp. 171 & 172; and AMERICAN BAPTIST MAGAZINE, 1830, p. 276.
19 See C. G. Finney, MEMOIRS OF REV. CHARLES G. FINNEY, Chapter XXI.
20 HOME MISSIONARY JOURNAL, 1831-1832, p. 4.
21 See C. G. Finney, MEMOIRS, p. 298, & Whitney R. Cross, THE BURNED-OVER DISTRICT, pp. 152ff.
22 C. G. Finney, MEMOIRS, p. 300.
23 See HOME MISSIONARY JOURNAL, 1830-1831, for reports of revival which began to increase in the early spring of 1830, while Finney's Rochester meetings ran from 10 September 1830 through 6 March 1831. Other journals confirm the dates.
24 C. G. Finney, LECTURES ON REVIVALS OF RELIGION, p. 30n.
25 Paulus Scharpff, GESCHICHTE DER EVANGELISATION, p. 119.
26 C. G. Finney, MEMOIRS, Chapter XXIII.
27 CHRISTIAN INDEX, Philadelphia, 19 February 1831.
28 C. G. Finney, MEMOIRS, pp. 238ff.
29 W. G. McLoughlin, MODERN REVIVALISM, p. 49, has noted the change of atmosphere in Philadelphia, but not the general revival—the cause of it.

30 HOME MISSIONARY JOURNAL, 1830-1831, p.234, & 1831-1832, p. 4, AMERICAN BAPTIST MAGAZINE, 1831, pp. 273, & 277; & 1834, pp. 167ff.
31 AMERICAN BAPTIST MAGAZINE, 1830, p. 62.
32 HOME MISSIONARY JOURNAL, 1829-1830, pp. 169ff.
33 HOME MISSIONARY JOURNAL, 1831-1832, pp. 171 & 195.
34 AMERICAN BAPTIST MAGAZINE, 1831, pp. 285 & 320.
35 J. M. King, A HISTORY OF SOUTH CAROLINA BAPTISTS, p. 246.
36 RELIGIOUS HERALD, Richmond, 20 September 1833.
37 HOME MISSIONARY JOURNAL, 1831-1832, p. 115.
38 Reports of meetings in 1801 and 1831 indicated different levels of excitement. HOME MISSIONARY JOURNAL, 1830-1831, p. 171.
39 See AMERICAN BAPTIST MAGAZINE, 1830, p. 124; & HOME MISSIONARY JOURNAL, 1830-1831, p. 171.
40 See J. M. King, A HISTORY OF SOUTH CAROLINA BAPTISTS; & AMERICAN BAPTIST MAGAZINE, 1830, p. 95.
41 J. H. Campbell, GEORGIA BAPTISTS, p. 194.
42 A. M. Shipp, METHODISM IN SOUTH CAROLINA, Columbia, 1883.
43 HOME MISSIONARY JOURNAL, 1829-1830, pp. 116, 184.
44 HOME MISSIONARY JOURNAL, 1830-1831, pp. 40, 171, 173, 177.
45 Issues of 1830-1831, p. 62; 1831-1832, p. 39.
46 HOME MISSIONARY JOURNAL, 1833, pp. 25 & 55.
47 BAPTIST HOME MISSION IN AMERICA, 1832-82, New York, 1883.
48 AMERICAN BAPTIST MAGAZINE, 1831, p. 277.
49 HOME MISSIONARY JOURNAL, 1831-1832, p. 3.
50 AMERICAN BAPTIST MAGAZINE, 1831, p. 155.
51 HOME MISSION JOURNAL, 1833, p. 155.
52 AMERICAN BAPTIST MAGAZINE, 1834, pp. 167 & 203.
53 J. H. Jones, OUTLINE OF A WORK OF GRACE IN THE PRESBYTERIAN CONGREGATION at NEW BRUNSWICK, NEW JERSEY, DURING THE YEAR 1837, Philadelphia, 1839, pp. 13ff.
54 J. H. Jones, OUTLINE OF A WORK OF GRACE, pp. 51ff.
55 J. H. Jones, OUTLINE OF A WORK OF GRACE, p. 117.
56 J. H. Jones, OUTLINE OF A WORK OF GRACE, p. 121.
57 AMERICAN BAPTIST MAGAZINE, 1831, p. 270.
58 David Benedict, A HISTORY OF THE BAPTIST DENOMINATION IN AMERICA, Volume I, p. 366.
59 Nathan Bangs, A HISTORY OF THE METHODIST EPISCOPAL CHURCH, Volume IV, p. 74.
60 Nathan Bangs, Volume IV, p. 151.
61 Nathan Bangs, Volume IV, pp. 20, 55, 60, 70 & 140.
62 G. L. Curtiss, MANUAL OF METHODIST EPISCOPAL HISTORY, pp. 148-149.
63 See H. C. Weber, PRESBYTERIAN STATISTICS THROUGH ONE HUNDRED YEARS, Philadelphia, 1927; & 'Narrative of the State of Religion,' General Assembly, Presbyerian Church, 1832.
64 W. E. Garrison, RELIGION FOLLOWS THE FRONTIER, pp. 70ff.
65 See R. Richardson, MEMOIRS OF ALEXANDER CAMPBELL.
66 A. R. Wentz, THE LUTHERAN CHURCH IN AMERICAN HISTORY, p. 82.
67 E. J. Wolf, THE LUTHERANS IN AMERICA, p. 354.
68 See R. W. Albright, HISTORY OF THE EVANGELICAL CHURCH, & A. W. Drury, HISTORY OF THE CHURCH OF THE UNITED BRETHREN IN CHRIST.
69 W. W. Sweet, THE STORY OF RELIGION IN AMERICA, p. 266.
70 CHRISTIAN REVIEW, Boston, 1836, p. 67.

1 R. W. Church, THE OXFORD MOVEMENT: 1833-45, pp. 82ff.
2 J. H. Overton, THE ANGLICAN REVIVAL, p. 119.
3 G. R. Balleine, A HISTORY OF THE EVANGELICAL PARTY, p. 122.
4 Paulus Scharpff, GESCHICHTE DER EVANGELISATION, p. 91.
5 See William Haslam, FROM DEATH UNTO LIFE, 1841-1861.
6 George Smith, HISTORY OF WESLEYAN METHODISM, Volume II, pp. 615ff.   Wesleyan Methodist Conference, 1840.
7 WESLEYAN MAGAZINE, 1834, p. 446.
8 MINUTES OF THE METHODIST CONFERENCES, Volume VII, pp. 45, 152, 274, 389, 517; Volume VIII, pp. 55, 192, 324, 475.
9 F. G. Beardsley, HISTORY OF AMERICAN REVIVALS, p. 202.
10 See James Caughey, METHODISM IN EARNEST.
11 Robert Sandall, THE HISTORY OF THE SALVATION ARMY, Volume I, pp. 3-4.
12 Cf. James Caughey, METHODISM IN EARNEST & SHOWERS OF BLESSING.
13 James Caughey, SHOWERS OF BLESSING, p. 14.
14 James Caughey, SHOWERS OF BLESSING, p. 16.
15 James Caughey, SHOWERS OF BLESSING, p. 17.
16 James Caughey, pp. 80ff.   17 pp. 80ff & 98.
18 James Caughey, p. 302.   19 pp. 407-409.
20 MINUTES OF THE METHODIST CONFERENCES, 1840-1849; George Smith, Volume III, pp. 452ff.
21 See K. S. Inglis, CHURCHES AND THE WORKING CLASSES IN VICTORIAN ENGLAND, pp. 9-13, 85ff.
22 T. P. Bunting, THE LIFE OF JABEZ BUNTING; 'Uncrowned king of the Wesleyans,' K. S. Inglis, p. 11.
23 T. P. Bunting, THE LIFE OF JABEZ BUNTING, Volume I, p. 115.
24 See W. R. Ward, THE EARLY CORRESPONDENCE OF JABEZ BUNTING, Introduction.
25 K. S. Inglis, CHURCHES AND THE WORKING CLASSES, p. 10.
26 W. E. Farndale, THE SECRET OF MOW COP, p. 57.
27 John Hughes, METHODISTIAETH CYMRU, Volume II, pp. 435ff.
28 Henry Hughes, DIWYGIADAU CREFYDDOL CYMRU, pp. 326-327.
29 Henry Hughes, pp. 326ff & p. 353.
30 J. O. Jones, ROBERT ELLIS, YSGOLDY, p. 248.
31 Thomas Rees, HISTORY OF PROTESTANT NONCONFORMITY IN WALES, p. 430.
32 See Hugh Watt, THOMAS CHALMERS AND THE DISRUPTION.
33 A. A. Bonar, THE LIFE OF THE REV. ROBERT MURRAY McCHEYNE, Edinburgh. (Many editions)
34 W. J. Couper, SCOTTISH REVIVALS, pp. 118ff.
35 Islay Burns, MEMOIR OF THE REV. WILLIAM C. BURNS.
36 W. J. Couper, SCOTTISH REVIVALS, p. 120.
37 See A. A. Bonar, ROBERT MURRAY McCHEYNE; & W. J. Couper.
38 RELIGIOUS LIFE IN SCOTLAND, pp. 189ff.
39 Report of the Aberdeen Presbytery, May 1841.
40 RELIGIOUS LIFE IN SCOTLAND, pp. 189ff.
41 W. J. Couper, SCOTTISH REVIVALS, pp. 128-129.
42 W. J. Couper, SCOTTISH REVIVALS, pp. 128-129.
43 MEMOIR OF THE REV. JOHN CAMPBELL, cited in Alexander MacRae, REVIVALS IN THE HIGHLANDS AND ISLANDS, p. 53.
44 Alexander MacRae, REVIVALS, pp. 52-53.

45 See MEN OF SKYE; Alexander MacRae, REVIVALS IN THE HIGHLANDS AND ISLANDS, pp. 75ff; pp. 58ff; pp. 64ff.
46 Report to Aberdeen Presbytery, 1840, cited in Alexander MacRae, pp. 142-145. See Report of the Aberdeen Presbytery, May 1841.
47 Alexander MacRae, pp. 99-100.
48 See James Bryce, TEN YEARS OF THE CHURCH OF SCOTLAND, FROM 1833 to 1843, Two Volumes, Edinburgh, 1850.
49 David Woodside, THE SOUL OF A SCOTTISH CHURCH: THE CONTRIBUTION OF THE UNITED PRESBYTERIAN CHURCH TO SCOTTISH LIFE AND RELIGION, Edinburgh, n. d.
50 Oliphant Smeaton, PRINCIPAL JAMES MORISON, pp. 137-163.
51 W. T. Whitley, A HISTORY OF BRITISH BAPTISTS, pp. 293ff.
52 John Campbell, MEMOIRS OF DAVID NASMITH, London, 1844.
53 W. D. Killen, ECCLESIASTICAL HISTORY OF IRELAND, Volume II, p. 463.
54 Mrs. Dallas, THE LIFE AND MINISTRY OF THE REV. A. R. C. DALLAS, London, 1871.
55 MINUTES OF THE METHODIST CONFERENCE, Volume VII, pp. 52, 274, 389.
56 C. H. Crookshank, HISTORY OF METHODISM IN IRELAND, Volume III, p. 111.
57 See James Caughey, METHODISM IN EARNEST.
58 MINUTES OF THE GENERAL SYNOD OF ULSTER, 1833.
59 W. H. Crookshank, Volume III, pp. 422-430.

Notes on Chapter 21: REVIVALS IN SCANDINAVIA, 1830—

1 Gunnar Westin, GEORGE SCOTT OCH HANS VERKSAMHET I SVERIGE, Stockholm, 1927.
2 George Smith, HISTORY OF WESLEYAN METHODISM, Volume III, pp. 352-353.
3 See Karl A. Olsson, BY ONE SPIRIT, pp. 42-46.
4 G. M. Stephenson, THE RELIGIOUS ASPECTS OF SWEDISH IMMIGRATION, p. 142.
5 There is much documentary evidence in Sweden for this statement. See also G. M. Stephenson, p. 17.
6 Karl A. Olsson, BY ONE SPIRIT, pp. 40-42.
7 Sven Lodin, CARL OLOF ROSENIUS I UNGA AR, 1816-1842, Stockholm, 1933.
8 See John Wordsworth, THE NATIONAL CHURCH OF SWEDEN, pp. 373-375.
9 See Sven Lodin, CARL OLOF ROSENIUS, HANS LIV OCH GARNING, Stockholm, 1956, p. 62.
10 KUNGELIKE GAZETTE, Stockholm, 17 November 1838.
11 G. M. Stephenson, p. 29.
12 E. J. Ekman, INRE MISSIONENS HISTORIA, Volume II, pp. 197ff, revision by N. P. Ollen, Jönköping, 1921.
13 C. O. Rosenius, editor, PIETISTEN, Stockholm, May 1850.
14 There are several biographies of Jenny Lind, the incomparable singer, in Swedish and English, besides an appreciative article in ENCYCLOPEDIA BRITANNICA.
15 G. W. Schroeder, HISTORY OF THE SWEDISH BAPTISTS; cf. Gunnar Westin, DEN KRISTNA FRIFORSAMLING I NORDEN, and H. C. Vedder, A SHORT HISTORY OF THE BAPTISTS, pp. 400ff.
16 G. M. Stephenson, p. 45.

17 Sam Ronegard, PRAIRIE SHEPHERD, LARS PAUL EJBJORN, AND BEGINNINGS OF THE AUGUSTANA LUTHERAN CHURCH, translated by G. E. Arden.

18 See Einar Molland, FRA HANS NIELSEN HAUGE TIL EIVIND BERGGRAV, pp. 10ff; cf. Andreas Aarflot, NORSKE KIRKE-HISTORIE, p. 267, noting a sweeping revival in Sunnmøre.

19 Andreas Aarflot, NORSKE KIRKEHISTORIE, p. 269.

20 See Einar Molland, FRA HANS NIELSEN HAUGE TIL EIVIND BERGGRAV, p. 32.

21 Andreas Aarflot, NORSKE KIRKEHISTORIE, p. 476.

22 G. Ousland, EN KIRKEHOVDING: PROFESSOR GISLE JOHNSON.

23 M. W. Montgomery, A WIND FROM THE HOLY SPIRIT IN SWEDEN AND NORWAY; Einar Molland, CHURCH LIFE IN NORWAY.

24 Hal Koch, DEN DANSKE KIRKES HISTORIE, Volume VI, pp. 211ff.

25 J. O. Andersen, SURVEY OF THE HISTORY OF THE CHURCH IN DENMARK, pp. 44–46.

26 Hal Koch, GRUNDTVIG, translated by Llewellyn Jones, 1952.

27 Walter Lowrie, A SHORT LIFE OF KIERKEGAARD, 1938.

28 H. Nyman, PAAVO RUOTSALAINEN, Helsinki, 1949.

29 W. Schmidt, FINLANDS KYRKA, pp. 218ff.

30 W. Schmidt, pp. 221–222.

31 F. Siegmund–Schultze, editor, DIE KIRCHE IN FINLAND, p. 52.

Notes on Chapter 22: THE ISLANDS AWAKENINGS

1 Letter of John Thomas, 8 August 1832, in MISSIONARY NOTICES, London, 1833; for Peter Vi's account, Thomas West, pp. 360ff.

2 Thomas West, TEN YEARS IN SOUTH–CENTRAL POLYNESIA, pp. 365–368; cf. Letter of Peter Turner, 26 January 1833, in MISSIONARY NOTICES.

3 Taufa'ahau, quoted in Basil Thomson, DIVERSIONS OF A PRIME MINISTER, pp. 346–348.

4 James Colwell, editor: A CENTURY IN THE PACIFIC, p. 420.

5 MISSIONARY NOTICES, London, VII & VIII, Letter of Charles Tucker, Habaii, 10 August 1834; Letter of Peter Turner, Vavau, 1 August; Letter of John Thomas, Nuku'alofu, 6 December 1834.

6 See Letters of Turner and Tucker, MISSIONARY NOTICES; also article by W. Butler, in Harvey Newcomb, CYCLOPEDIA OF MISSIONS, pp. 678ff.

7 Basil Thomson, DIVERSIONS OF A PRIME MINISTER, p. 349.

8 A. R. Tippett, PEOPLE MOVEMENTS IN SOUTHERN POLYNESIA, p. 88.   9 Robert Young, THE SOUTHERN WORLD, pp. 258ff.

10 Peter Turner, quoted in Robert Young's Report to the Wesleyan Methodist Conference in London.

11 John Williams, A NARRATIVE OF MISSIONARY ENTERPRISES IN THE SOUTH SEA ISLANDS, pp. 141ff.

12 James Colwell, editor: A CENTURY IN THE PACIFIC, pp. 483ff.

13 WESLEYAN CHRONICLE, Melbourne, 11 February 1864.

14 Martin Dyson, MY STORY OF SAMOAN WESLEYANISM, p. 27.

15 AUSTRALIAN WESLEYAN CONFERENCE MINUTES, 1856.

16 See MISSIONARY REGISTER, 1831, p. 90; 1832, pp. 98ff; 1833, p. 100.   17 MISSIONARY REGISTER, 1836, pp. 534ff.

18 MISSIONARY HERALD, Boston, 1836, p. 106.

19 Letter of Titus Coan, 19 March 1838, in MISSIONARY HERALD, 1839, p. 197.

20 O. H. Gulick, THE PILGRIMS OF HAWAII, pp. 315ff.
21 Letter of Titus Coan, 26 September 1838, MISSIONARY HERALD, 1840, pp. 246ff; and further correspondence.
22 MINUTES OF THE DELEGATE MEETING OF THE SANDWICH ISLANDS MISSION, June 1838, Honolulu 1839.
23 Report of Titus Coan, 6 June 1839; see LIFE IN HAWAII, by the same writer, published in New York, 1882.
24 Letter of H. R. Hitchcock, MISSIONARY HERALD, 1839, pp. 306ff.
25 Letter of Lowell Smith, MISSIONARY HERALD, 1839, p. 151.
26 B. M. Brain, THE TRANSFORMATION OF HAWAII, pp. 113ff.
27 Letter of Titus Coan, 26 September 1838, MISSIONARY HERALD, pp. 246ff.
28 B. M. Brain, THE TRANSFORMATION OF HAWAII, pp. 113ff.
29 R. Anderson, HISTORY OF THE SANDWICH ISLANDS, pp. 315ff.
30 G. C. Henderson, FIJI AND THE FIJIANS, 1836-1856, pp. 50ff.
31 Findlay & Holdsworth, THE HISTORY OF THE WESLEYAN METHODIST MISSIONARY SOCIETY, Volume III, pp. 371-372.
32 G. C. Henderson, FIJI AND THE FIJIANS, pp. 168ff.
33 Williams & Calvert, FIJI AND THE FIJIANS, Volume II, pp. 269ff.
34 See Joseph Waterhouse, THE KING AND PEOPLE OF FIJI, pp. 251ff; cf. WESLEYAN METHODIST MISSIONARY SOCIETY, Report of 1856, p. 114; 1857, p. 126.
35 N. Grundemann, JOHANN FRIEDRICH REIDEL, 1873.
36 C. J. Bunyon, MEMOIRS OF FRANCIS T. McDOUGALL, 1889.
37 William Ellis, THE MARTYR CHURCH, pp. 114-197.

Notes on Chapter 23: AWAKENINGS IN SOUTH AFRICA

1 Letter of William Shaw, 19 December 1831, in the Archives of the Methodist Missionary Society, London.
2 Letter of Samuel Young, 24 July 1831, Methodist Archives.
3 Minutes of the Methodist District Meeting, Grahamstown, 1831, Cory Library, Rhodes University.
4 J. du Plessis, THE LIFE OF ANDREW MURRAY, pp. 12-16.
5 William Douglas, ANDREW MURRAY AND HIS MESSAGE, p. 15.
6 J. du Plessis, THE LIFE OF ANDREW MURRAY, pp. 34ff, 55ff.
7 E. A. Walker, A HISTORY OF SOUTHERN AFRICA, p. 150.
8 G. E. Cory, THE DIARY OF THE REV. FRANCIS OWEN, p. 4.
9 See T. V. Bulpin, TO THE SHORES OF NATAL.
10 MISSIONARY NOTICES, London, Volume VII, pp. 6-7.
11 W. Eversleigh, THE SETTLERS AND METHODISM, p. 101.
12 B. F. Holt, JOSEPH WILLIAMS AND THE SOUTHEASTERN BANTU, Lovedale, 1954.
13 J. S. Moffat, THE LIVES OF ROBERT AND MARY MOFFAT, London, 1886.
14 Robert Moffat, MISSIONARY LABOURS AND SCENES IN SOUTH AFRICA, p. 496.
15 J. du Plessis, A HISTORY OF CHRISTIAN MISSIONS IN SOUTH AFRICA, p. 163.
16 Minutes of the Methodist District Meeting, 1832, Archives, Cory Library, Rhodes University, Grahamstown.
17 MISSIONARY NOTICES, 1832-1834, Volume VII, p. 9.
18 MISSIONARY NOTICES, 1838, p. 13; cf. William Shaw, THE STORY OF MY MISSION IN SOUTHEASTERN AFRICA, p. 186.
19 Minutes, 14th Annual Methodist District Meeting, 5 February 1838 at Butterworth; Archives, Cory Library, Rhodes University.

20 M. E. Appleyard, University of Cape Town, Bibliography on David Livingstone.
21 R. H. W. Shepherd, LOVEDALE, SOUTH AFRICA, 1841-1941; cf. G. E. Cory, THE RISE OF SOUTH AFRICA, Volume II, p. 96.
22 C. F. Pascoe, TWO HUNDRED YEARS OF THE S. P. G., pp. 269ff.
23 W. E. Strong, THE STORY OF THE AMERICAN BOARD, pp. 132ff.
24 C. W. Mackintosh, COILLARD OF THE ZAMBESI, pp. 3ff.
25 J. du Plessis, A HISTORY OF CHRISTIAN MISSIONS IN SOUTH AFRICA, pp. 200ff.
26 J. du Plessis, p. 273.
27 Andrew Burgess, UNKULUNKULU IN ZULULAND, pp. 104ff.
28 See W. Claus, DR. LUDWIG KRAPF, Missionar in Ostafrika, Basel, n. d.

Notes on Chapter 24: STIRRINGS IN THE EAST, 1830—

1 Rufus Anderson, HISTORY OF THE MISSION OF THE AMERICAN BOARD TO THE ORIENTAL CHURCHES, Volume I, Chapter I.
2 MISSIONARY HERALD, Boston, 1838, pp. 117ff.
3 See E. D. G. Prime, FORTY YEARS IN THE TURKISH EMPIRE: MEMOIRS OF REV. WILLIAM GOODELL.
4 J. L. Barton, DAYBREAK IN TURKEY, pp. 163ff.
5 H. G. O. Dwight, CHRISTIANITY IN TURKEY: A NARRATIVE OF THE REFORMATION IN THE ARMENIAN CHURCH.
6 J. L. Barton, DAYBREAK IN TURKEY, pp. 174-175.
7 MISSIONARY HERALD, Boston, 1844, p. 225.
8 J. P. Thompson, MEMOIR OF DAVID TAPPAN STODDARD.
9 MISSIONARY HERALD, 1845, pp. 351, 407, 419.
10 D. T. Stoddard, NARRATIVE OF THE LATE REVIVAL AMONG THE NESTORIANS, Boston, 1847.
11 MISSIONARY HERALD, 1846, pp. 234ff, 248.
12 MISSIONARY HERALD, 1846, pp. 253ff, 1847, p. 6.
13 Rufus Anderson, HISTORY OF THE MISSION OF THE AMERICAN BOARD TO THE ORIENTAL CHURCHES, Volume I, pp. 164-223, Volume II, pp. 107-149; Anonymous, A CENTURY OF MISSION WORK IN IRAN, p. 113.
14 Eugene Stock, THE HISTORY OF THE CHURCH MISSIONARY SOCIETY, Volume I, pp. 350-351.
15 Samuel Gobat, JOURNAL OF A THREE YEARS' RESIDENCE IN ABYSSINIA, London, 1834.
16 P. Cherian, THE MALABAR SYRIANS AND THE CHURCH MISSIONARY SOCIETY, 1816-1840, Kottayam, 1935.
17 George Smith, THE LIFE OF ALEXANDER DUFF, 1899.
18 George Smith, THE LIFE OF JOHN WILSON, 1879.
19 George Smith, STEPHEN HISLOP: PIONEER MISSIONARY.
20 MADRAS CHRISTIAN COLLEGE MAGAZINE, October 1923.
21 Mrs. Groves, MEMOIR OF ANTHONY NORRIS GROVES, 1856.
22 Robert Jeffrey, THE INDIAN MISSION OF THE IRISH PRESBY-TERIAN CHURCH, pp. 29ff, 131ff.
23 J. H. Morris, THE STORY OF OUR FOREIGN MISSION.
24 Mrs. Chamberlain, FIFTY YEARS IN FOREIGN FIELDS, pp. 9ff.
25 Ronald Bryan, ALL IN A DAY'S WORK, pp. 26ff.
26 Drach & Kuder, THE TELUGU MISSION OF THE EVANGELICAL LUTHERAN CHURCH.
27 Hermann Karsten, DIE GESCHICHTE DER EVANGELISCH-LUTHERISCHEN MISSION IN LEIPZIG.

28 Wilhelm Schlatter, GESCHICHTE DER BASLER MISSION, 1815-1915, Basel, 1916.
29 Stephen Neill, A HISTORY OF CHRISTIAN MISSIONS, pp. 277ff.
30 G. M. Thomssen, SAMUEL HEBICH OF INDIA, pp. 186ff.
31 R. Lovett, HISTORY OF THE LONDON MISSIONARY SOCIETY, Volume II, pp. 18-21; J. A. Ewing, LANKA: THE RESPLENDENT ISLE, pp. 16ff; Findlay & Holdsworth, THE HISTORY OF THE WESLEYAN METHODIST MISSIONARY SOCIETY, Vol. V, pp. 15ff.
32 C. F. Pascoe, TWO HUNDRED YEARS OF THE S.P.G., p. 660.
33 H. I. Root, A CENTURY IN CEYLON: THE AMERICAN BOARD, 1816-1916. MISSIONARY HERALD, 1825, pp. 27, 60, 79, 348.
34 Alonzo King, MEMOIR OF GEORGE DANA BOARDMAN; & Francis Mason, THE KAREN APOSTLE: KO THAH-BYU.
35 J. C. Marshman, THE LIFE AND TIMES OF CAREY, MARSHMAN AND WARD, Volume I, pp. 18-19.
36 Eliza Morrison, MEMOIR OF THE LIFE AND LABOURS OF ROBERT MORRISON; William Milne, A RETROSPECT OF THE FIRST TEN YEARS OF PROTESTANT MISSIONS TO CHINA, pp. 100ff.
37 REPORT OF THE AMERICAN BOARD, 1828 & 1829.
38 A. J. Brown, ONE HUNDRED YEARS, pp. 274-275.
39 John Kesson, THE CROSS AND THE DRAGON, 1854.
40 Islay Burns, REV. WILLIAM C. BURNS.
41 W. J. Hail, THE TAIPING REBELLION.
42 K. S. Latourette, A HISTORY OF THE EXPANSION OF CHRISTIANITY, Volume VI, p. 336.
43 Karl Gützlaff, JOURNAL OF THREE VOYAGES ALONG THE COAST OF CHINA, 1831, 1832 & 1833.

Notes on Chapter 25: SOCIAL OUTCOME OF REVIVAL

1   See J. W. Bready, ENGLAND BEFORE AND AFTER WESLEY, London, 1938.
2   Cf. T. Clarkson, THE RISE, PROGRESS AND ACCOMPLISHMENT OF THE ABOLITION OF THE AFRICAN SLAVE TRADE BY THE BRITISH PARLIAMENT.
3   John Wesley, THOUGHTS UPON SLAVERY, 1774.
4   J. C. Colquhoun, WILBERFORCE: HIS FRIENDS AND HIS TIMES.
5   G. M. Trevelyan, ENGLISH SOCIAL HISTORY, p. 495.
6   See C. W. Stubbs, CONSTITUTIONAL HISTORY OF ENGLAND.
7   Congress of Vienna, November 1814.
8   Thomas Clarkson, THE ABOLITION OF THE SLAVE TRADE.
9   John Harris, A CENTURY OF EMANCIPATION, pp. 3ff.
10 See G. H. Barnes, THE ANTI-SLAVERY IMPULSE, 1830-1844, pp. 10-12, 39, 69, 79-87, 104-105.
11 J. Field, THE LIFE OF JOHN HOWARD, passim.
12 See A. R. C. Gardner, THE PLACE OF JOHN HOWARD IN PENAL REFORM.
13 J. W. Bready, THIS FREEDOM—WHENCE? pp. 251ff.
14 See J. Whitney, ELIZABETH FRY, QUAKER HEROINE.
15 Fliedner's Autobiography is found only in his native German; see AUS MEINEN LEBEN, ERINNERUNGEN UND ERFAHRUNGEN.
16 A. B. Wentz, FLIEDNER, THE FAITHFUL, p. 13.
17 G. Fliedner, THEODOR FLIEDNER, (3rd Edition, 1892).
18 A. B. Wentz, FLIEDNER, THE FAITHFUL, p. 25.
19 (Translated from the German by A. B. Wentz, p. 29.)

20 C. Woodham-Smith, FLORENCE NIGHTINGALE, bibliography, New York, 1951.

21 Sir Edward Cook, THE LIFE OF FLORENCE NIGHTINGALE, Volume I, p. 479; Volume II, p. 366.

22 R. F. Wearmouth, METHODISM AND THE WORKING CLASS MOVEMENTS OF ENGLAND, 1800-1850.

23 E. Hodder, THE LIFE AND WORK OF THE SEVENTH EARL OF SHAFTESBURY, Volume III, p. 3.

24 R. G. Cowherd, THE POLITICS OF ENGLISH DISSENT, pp. 143ff; E. Hodder, Volume III, pp. 76-90.

25 J. W. Bready, THIS FREEDOM—WHENCE? pp. 264ff.

26 K. S. Latourette, A HISTORY OF THE EXPANSION OF CHRISTIANITY, Volume IV, p. 155.

27 J. W. Bready, THIS FREEDOM—WHENCE? pp. 265-266.

28 See K. S. Inglis, CHURCHES AND THE WORKING CLASSES IN VICTORIAN ENGLAND, p. 10.

29 See H. U. Faulkner, CHARTISM AND THE CHURCHES; also R. F. Wearmouth, pp. 226ff.

30 DURHAM CHRONICLE, 20 August 1831.

31 Cited in W. E. Farndale, THE SECRET OF MOW COP, pp. 63-64.

32 See Sidney & Beatrice Webb, HISTORY OF TRADE UNIONISM.

33 J. W. Bready, THIS FREEDOM—WHENCE? p. 275.

34 E. D. Branch, THE SENTIMENTAL YEARS, 1836-1860.

35 W. W. Sweet, REVIVALISM IN AMERICA, p. 159.

36 G. H. Barnes, THE ANTI-SLAVERY IMPULSE, pp. 18-28.

37 W. W. Sweet, REVIVALISM IN AMERICA, p. 159.

38 K. S. Latourette, Volume IV, p. 416.

39 D. G. Tewkesbury, THE FOUNDING OF AMERICAN COLLEGES AND UNIVERSITIES BEFORE THE CIVIL WAR, p. 69.

40 Gardiner Spring, MEMOIRS OF SAMUEL J. MILLS, pp. 132ff.

41 Charles Buxton, editor, MEMOIRS OF SIR THOMAS FOWELL BUXTON, pp. 100-108.

42 Fairholme & Pain, A CENTURY OF WORK FOR ANIMALS.

43 Massachusetts enacted legislation against brutal sports in 1836; see G. M. Trevelyan, ENGLISH SOCIAL HISTORY, p. 504.

44 See J. H. Hutton, CASTE IN INDIA.

45 J. Bateman, THE LIFE OF DANIEL WILSON, Volume I, pp. 381ff.

46 Kenneth Ingham, REFORMERS IN INDIA, p. 34.

47 See MISSIONARY REGISTER, 1831, pp. 31-32.

48 S. Pearce Carey, WILLIAM CAREY, 5th edition, p. 209.

49 MISSIONARY REGISTER, 1824, pp. 238 & 278; Parliamentary Debates, Volume LXII, May–June 1813.

50 Philip Hartog, SOME ASPECTS OF INDIAN EDUCATION, r 6.

51 Cf. H. Sharp, SELECTION FROM EDUCATIONAL RECORDS, Part I, 1781-1839; Nurullah & Naik, A HISTORY OF EDUCATION IN INDIA, p. 165; M. A. Sherring, THE HISTORY OF PROTESTANT MISSIONS IN INDIA, pp. 442-447.

52 William Paton, ALEXANDER DUFF: PIONEER OF MISSIONARY EDUCATION, p. 59.

53 See A. D. Martin, DOCTOR VANDERKEMP.

54 J. E. Hutton, A HISTORY OF MORAVIAN MISSIONS, pp. 266ff.

55 David Livingstone, MISSIONARY TRAVELS AND RESEARCHES IN SOUTH AFRICA, London, 1857.

56 See Sir Philip Mitchell, Essay on 'Africa and the West in Historical Perspective,' quoted in TROPICAL AFRICA, Time & Life Books.

57 Rufus Anderson, HISTORY OF THE HAWAIIAN MISSION, pp. 48ff.

SPECIAL NOTE:

'History,' declared Prof. William G. McLoughlin, 'has not dealt fairly with American revivals.' This, in my opinion, has been chiefly due to a sorry addiction of American church historians to an illogical philosophy of 'revivalism.' 'Revivalism' used to be applied to the study of revivals of religion, and still is outside the United States where it is defined as 'professional mass evangelism'—McLoughlin, MODERN REVIVALISM, p. 11. Dr. Roy Eckhard, THE SURGE OF PIETY IN AMERICA, New York, 1958, (p. 115n), elected to define the word 'adjectivally'—as in 'revival meeting,' itself a misuse of the word, recalling the words of a Texan pastor who declared: 'We have just had a revival, but nobody got revived!' Dr. Winthrop Hudson, AMERICAN PROTESTANTISM, 1961, asserted that 'revivalism was a technique developed to induce that experience' (conversion). Mass evangelism has developed techniques but the general revivals of religion were not techniques but rather spontaneous movements. This confusion of revival with mass evangelism may be traced to Finney who said that 'a revival is the result of the right use of the appropriate means,' a notion valid in evangelism but utterly false regarding the three general awakenings of Finney's lifetime—1792, 1830, and 1858—which were neither planned, promoted nor programmed.

Encyclopedists have echoed a popular view, that the second great national awakening . . . began in the camp meetings of Kentucky and Tennessee . . . Actually, it began in New England ten years earlier. Why should historians be so enchanted by the extravagances of a tiny minority in the backwoods and ignore the major drive of a great revival without extravagance? Take, for example, the reports of the 'barking.' F. M. Davenport, in PRIMITIVE TRAITS IN RELIGIOUS REVIVALS, (p. 80) written a century after the event, referred to 'barking' or 'treeing the devil' as not so common, but cited no authority whatsoever. Alice Tyler, in FREEDOM'S FERMENT, (pp. 35ff), claimed another forty years later that the 'barking' seemed to have been common, citing no authority. Francis X. Curran, S.J., MAJOR TRENDS IN AMERICAN HISTORY, wrote later still and denounced the 'barking,' citing Tyler and Davenport—which serves to show that the farther removed from the event, the more dogmatic one may become; also cited was John B. McMaster, HISTORY OF THE PEOPLE OF THE UNITED STATES, Volume II, p. 52, claiming that Kentucky men fancied themselves dogs, went down on all fours, and barked till they grew hoarse—'no uncommon sight'! Grover Loud, EVANGELIZED AMERICA, p. 102, claimed that 'jerkers' barked like dogs, but cited no authority. Weisberger, in THEY GATHERED AT THE RIVER, cited Davenport, who cited no authority; credit was given to Charles A. Johnston, THE FRONTIER CAMP MEETING, pp. 61-62, who cited J. B. McMaster, but admitted that the story had been rebutted. Again, David Benedict, excusing the Baptists and blaming it upon the Methodists and Presbyterians, also reported it on hearsay, as did Robert Davidson, a Presbyterian enemy of the Revival. Only Richard McNemar, later a Shaker, affirmed it but without authority. F. R. Cossitt's LIFE AND TIMES OF FINIS EWING (a founder of the Cumberland Presbyterian Church) rebutted the story, as did Barton Stone, another eye-witness, who attributed the legend to the involuntary gasps of people afflicted with the 'jerks.' (pp. 69ff). An aged Presbyterian minister, involuntarily jerking, grasped a tree for support—and a wisecracker started a legend now gleefully endorsed.

BIBLIOGRAPHY

Periodicals:

AMERICAN BAPTIST MAGAZINE & MISSIONARY INTELLIGENCER, Boston, 1817—
ARMINIAN MAGAZINE, London, 1780—
ARMINIAN MAGAZINE, Philadelphia, 1790—
AUSTRALIAN WESLEYAN CONFERENCE MINUTES, Sydney, 1856.
BAPTIST ANNUAL REGISTER, London, 1790—
BAPTIST MISSIONARY MAGAZINE, London, 1800—
CHRISTIAN INDEX, Phialdelphia, 1830—
CHRISTIAN OBSERVER, London, 1802—
CHURCH HISTORY, Chicago, 1933.
CONGREGATIONAL QUARTERLY, Volume XXI, London, 1943.
CONNECTICUT EVANGELICAL MAGAZINE AND RELIGIOUS INTELLIGENCER, Hartford, 1800—
DURHAM CHRONICLE, Durham, England, 1830—
EVANGELICAL MAGAZINE AND MISSIONARY CHRONICLE, London, 1800—
HOME MISSIONARY JOURNAL, New York, 1830—
JOURNAL OF PRESBYTERIAN HISTORY, XL, 1966.
MADRAS CHRISTIAN COLLEGE MAGAZINE, Madras, 1883—
MASSACHUSETTS BAPTIST MISSIONARY MAGAZINE, 1803—
METHODIST MAGAZINE, New York, 1818—
METHODIST MAGAZINE, London, 1800—
MINUTES OF THE ANNUAL CONFERENCE OF THE METHODIST EPISCOPAL CHURCH, Volume I, (1773-1828), 1840.
MINUTES OF THE DELEGATES MEETING OF THE SANDWICH ISLANDS MISSION, Honolulu, 1835—
MINUTES OF THE METHODIST CONFERENCE, Volume I, 1800.
MINUTES OF THE METHODIST DISTRICT MEETING, Grahamstown, South Africa, 1830—
MISSIONARY NOTICES, Wesleyan Methodist Missionary Society, London.
MISSIONARY HERALD, Boston, 1821—
MISSIONARY MAGAZINE, Edinburgh, 1796—
MISSIONARY REGISTER, London, 1830—
NEW YORK EVANGELIST, New York, 1830—
NEW YORK MISSIONARY MAGAZINE, 1900—
THE PANOPLIST, Boston, 1806—
PRINCETON REVIEW, Volume XXXI, Princeton, 1859.
QUARTERLY CHRONICLE, London Missionary Society, Volume I, London, 1821 (1815-1819).
RELIGIOUS HERALD, Richmond, 1833.
REPORT OF THE AMERICAN BOARD, Boston, 1811—
TRANSACTIONS, London Missionary Society, London, 1820—
WELCH PIETY, (accounts of the Circulating Schools in Wales), 1740-1750.
WELSH MAGAZINE, Bala, 1825—
WESLEYAN CHRONICLE, Melbourne, 1860—
WESLEYAN METHODIST MAGAZINE, London, 1810—
WESLEYAN METHODIST MISSIONARY SOCIETY, London, 1800—

Aarflot, Andreas, NORSKE KIRKEHISTORIE, Oslo, 1967.

Albright, Raymond W., A HISTORY OF THE EVANGELICAL CHURCH, Harrisburg, 1942.

Alexander, J. W., THE LIFE OF ARCHIBALD ALEXANDER, New York, 1854.

Alline, Henry, THE LIFE AND JOURNAL OF THE REV. HENRY ALLINE, Boston, 1806.

Anderson, J. O., SURVEY OF THE HISTORY OF THE CHURCH IN DENMARK, Copenhagen, 1930.

Anderson, Rufus, THE HAWAIIAN ISLANDS: MISSIONARY LABORS, Boston, 1865.

Anderson, Rufus, HISTORY OF THE MISSION OF THE AMERICAN BOARD OF COMMISSIONERS FOR FOREIGN MISSIONS TO THE ORIENTAL CHURCHES, Boston, 2 Volumes, 1872.

Anderson, Rufus, HISTORY OF THE SANDWICH ISLANDS MISSION, Boston, 1870.

Anonymous, A CENTURY OF MISSION WORK IN IRAN, 1834-1934, Beirut, 1935.

Anshelm, C., BISKOP HANS PETER HALLECK, Lund, 1927.

Appleyard, M. E., BIBLIOGRAPHY, DAVID LIVINGSTONE, University of Cape Town.

Armitage, Thomas, A HISTORY OF THE BAPTISTS, New York, 1887.

Bacon, Leonard W., A HISTORY OF AMERICAN CHRISTIANITY, New York, 1900.

Baird, Robert, RELIGION IN THE UNITED STATES OF AMERICA, Glasgow, 1844.

Baker, W. M., LIFE AND LABOURS OF THE REV. DANIEL BAKER, Philadelphia, 1859.

Balleine, G. R., A HISTORY OF THE EVANGELICAL PARTY IN THE CHURCH OF ENGLAND, London, 1908.

Bangs, Nathan, A HISTORY OF THE METHODIST EPISCOPAL CHURCH, New York, 4 Volumes, 1845.

BAPTIST HOME MISSIONS IN AMERICA, 1832—, New York, 1883.

Barnes, Gilbert Hobbs, THE ANTI-SLAVERY IMPULSE, 1830-1844, New York, 1933.

Barton, James L., DAYBREAK IN TURKEY, Boston, 1908.

Bateman, J., THE LIFE OF DANIEL WILSON, BISHOP OF CALCUTTA AND METROPOLITAN OF INDIA, Boston, 1860.

Bayne, Peter, THE FREE CHURCH OF SCOTLAND, Edinburgh, 1894.

Beard, A. F., THE STORY OF JOHN FREDERIC OBERLIN, Boston, 1909.

Beardsley, Frank G., A HISTORY OF AMERICAN REVIVALS, New York, 1904.

Beecher, Charles, AUTOBIOGRAPHY OF LYMAN BEECHER, New York, 2 Volumes, 1864-1865.

Belden, Albert D., GEORGE WHITEFIELD, THE AWAKENER, New York, 1930.

Benedict, David, A GENERAL HISTORY OF THE BAPTIST DENOMINATION IN AMERICA AND OTHER PARTS OF THE WORLD, New York, 1848.

Bianquis, Jean, LES ORIGINES DE LA SOCIETE DE MISSIONS EVANGELIQUES DE PARIS, 1822-1829, Paris, 1930.

Bill, I. E., FIFTY YEARS WITH THE BAPTIST MINISTERS AND CHURCHES OF THE MARITIME PROVINCES, Saint John, New Brunswick, 1880.

Bilmanis, Alfred, THE CHURCH IN LATVIA, New York, 1935.

Bingham, Hiram, A RESIDENCE OF TWENTY-ONE YEARS IN THE SANDWICH ISLANDS, Hartford, 1848.

Boles, John B., THE GREAT REVIVAL, 1787-1805: THE ORIGINS OF THE SOUTHERN EVANGELICAL MIND, Lexington, 1972.

Bonar, Andrew A., THE LIFE AND REMAINS, LETTERS, LECTURES AND POEMS OF THE REV. ROBERT MURRAY McCHEYNE, Edinburgh, 21st edition, 1860.

Bost, Ami, MEMOIRES POUVENT SERVIR A L'HISTOIRE DU REVEIL RELIGIEUX DES EGLISES PROTESTANTES DE LA SUISSE ET DE LA FRANCE, Paris, 1854.

Bourne, F. W., BILLY BRAY, THE KING'S SON, London, 1890.

Branch, E. D., THE SENTIMENTAL YEARS, 1836-1860, New York, 1934.

Bradley, Joshua, ACCOUNTS OF RELIGIOUS REVIVAL IN MANY PARTS OF THE UNITED STATES FROM 1815 TO 1818, Albany, New York, 1819.

Brain, B. M., THE TRANSFORMATION OF HAWAII, New York, 1898.

Bready, J. Wesley, ENGLAND BEFORE AND AFTER WESLEY: THE EVANGELICAL REVIVAL AND SOCIAL REFORM, London, 1938.

Bready, J. Wesley, THIS FREEDOM—WHENCE?, London, 1942.

Brown, Arthur Judson, ONE HUNDRED YEARS. A HISTORY OF THE FOREIGN MISSIONARY WORK OF THE PRESBYTERIAN CHURCH IN THE U. S. A., New York, 1937.

Bryan, Ronald, ALL IN A DAY'S WORK, London, 1954.

Bryce, James, TEN YEARS OF THE CHURCH OF SCOTLAND FROM 1833 TO 1843, Edinburgh, 2 Volumes, 1850.

Buell, Samuel, A BRIEF ACCOUNT OF THE REVIVAL OF RELIGION IN BRIDGHAMPTON AND EASTHAMPTON IN 1799 AND 1800, Sag Harbor, Long Island, 1808.

Bunyon, C. J., MEMOIRS OF FRANCIS T. McDOUGALL, BISHOP OF LABUAN AND SARAWAK, London, 1889.

Burgess, Andrew, UNKULUNKULU IN ZULULAND, Minneapolis, 1932.

Burns, Islay, MEMOIR OF REV. WILLIAM C. BURNS, London, 1885.

Burton, J. W., THE FIRST CENTURY: THE MISSIONARY ADVEN-TURE OF AUSTRALIAN METHODISM, 1855-1955, Sydney, 1955.

Buxton, Charles, MEMOIRS OF SIR THOMAS FOWELL BUXTON, London, 1848.

Campbell, J. H., GEORGIA BAPTISTS, HISTORICAL AND BIO-GRAPHICAL, Richmond, 1847.

Campbell, John, MEMOIRS OF DAVID NASMITH, London, 1844.

Canton, William, A HISTORY OF THE BRITISH AND FOREIGN BIBLE SOCIETY, London, 5 Volumes, 1904-1910.

Carey, S. Pearce, WILLIAM CAREY, FELLOW OF THE LINNAEAN SOCIETY, New York, 1923.

Carey, William, AN ENQUIRY INTO THE OBLIGATION OF CHRISTIANS TO USE MEANS FOR THE CONVERSION OF THE HEATHENS, Leicester, 1792.

Carroll, John, CASE AND HIS CONTEMPORARIES, Toronto, 1867–1877, 2 Volumes.

Carus, William, MEMOIRS OF THE LIFE OF THE REV. CHARLES SIMEON, London, 1847.

Caughey, James, METHODISM IN EARNEST, Richmond, 1852.

Caughey, James, SHOWERS OF BLESSING, Boston, 1857.

Chamberlain, Mrs. W. I., FIFTY YEARS IN FOREIGN FIELDS, CHINA, JAPAN, INDIA, ARABIA, New York, 1925.

Chaney, Charles, 'God's Glorious Work: The Theological Foundations of the Early Missionary Societies in America,' Th.D. Dissertation, University of Chicago, 1972.

Channing, W. H., MEMOIR OF WILLIAM ELLERY CHANNING, Boston, 3 Volumes, 1848.

Cheriyan, P., THE MALABAR SYRIANS AND THE CHURCH MISSIONARY SOCIETY, 1816–1840, Kottayam, 1935.

Church, R. W., THE OXFORD MOVEMENT, 1833–1845, London, 1891.

Clark, Elmer T., editor, JOURNAL AND LETTERS OF FRANCIS ASBURY, Nashville, 3 Volumes, 1958.

Clark, S. D., CHURCH AND SECT IN CANADA, Toronto, 1948.

Clarkson, Thomas, THE RISE, PROGRESS AND ACCOMPLISHMENT OF THE ABOLITION OF THE AFRICAN SLAVE TRADE BY THE BRITISH PARLIAMENT, London, 1808.

Claus, W., DR. LUDWIG KRAPF, Basel, n. d.

Cleveland, Catharine C., THE GREAT REVIVAL IN THE WEST, 1797–1805, Chicago, 1916.

Coan, Titus, LIFE IN HAWAII, New York, 1882.

Colquhoun, John Campbell, WILBERFORCE: HIS FRIENDS AND HIS TIMES, London, 1867.

Colwell, James, editor, A CENTURY IN THE PACIFIC: SCIENTIFIC, SOCIOLOGICAL, HISTORICAL, MISSIONARY, GENERAL, London, 1914.

Cook, Sir Edward, THE LIFE OF FLORENCE NIGHTINGALE, London, 2 Volumes, 1913.

Cornish, F. W., THE ENGLISH CHURCH IN THE NINETEENTH CENTURY, London, 2 Volumes, 1910.

Cory, G. E., THE DIARY OF THE REV. FRANCIS OWEN, Cape Town, 1926.

Cory, G. E., THE RISE OF SOUTH AFRICA, London, 1930.

Cossitt, F. R., THE LIFE AND TIMES OF THE REV. FINIS EWING, Louisville, 1853.

Couper, W. J., SCOTTISH REVIVALS, Dundee, 1918.

Cowan, James, THE NEW ZEALAND WARS, Wellington, 2 Volumes, 1956.

Cowherd, R. G., THE POLITICS OF ENGLISH DISSENT: THE RELIGIOUS ASPECTS OF LIBERAL AND HUMANITARIAN REFORM MOVEMENTS FROM 1815 TO 1842, New York, 1956.

Cowper, William, THE POWER OF GRACE ILLUSTRATED, (the Life of Helperus Ritzema van Lier, unnamed), Edinburgh, 1792.

Crookshank, C. H., HISTORY OF METHODISM IN IRELAND, London, 3 Volumes, 1888.

Cross, Whitney R., THE BURNED-OVER DISTRICT, THE SOCIAL AND INTELLECTUAL HISTORY OF ENTHUSIASTIC RELIGION IN WESTERN NEW YORK, 1800–1850, Ithaca, 1950.

Curran Francis X., MAJOR TRENDS IN AMERICAN HISTORY, New York, 1946.

Dale, R. W., HISTORY OF ENGLISH CONGREGATIONALISM, 2nd edition, London, 1907.

Dallas, Mrs., THE LIFE AND MINISTRY OF THE REV. A. R. C. DALLAS, London, 1871.

D'Aubigne, J. H. Merle, HISTORY OF THE REFORMATION OF THE SIXTEENTH CENTURY, New York, 5 Volumes, 1844–1853.

Davenport, Frederick M., PRIMITIVE TRAITS IN RELIGIOUS REVIVALS, New York, 1905.

Davidson, Robert, HISTORY OF THE PRESBYTERIAN CHURCH IN THE STATE OF KENTUCKY, New York, 1847.

Davies, G. C. B., THE FIRST EVANGELICAL BISHOP, London, 1958.

Davies, John, THE HISTORY OF THE TAHITIAN MISSION, 1799–1830, New York, 1961.

Davis, J., THE LIFE AND TIMES OF REV. HARRIS HARDING, Charlottetown 1866.

De la Rochefoucault, Duc, TRAVELS THROUGH THE UNITED STATES OF NORTH AMERICA, IN THE YEAR 1795, 1796 & 1797. London, 2 Volumes, 1799.

DICTIONARY OF NATIONAL BIOGRAPHY, London, 63 Volumes, 1885–1900.

Dorchester, Daniel, THE PROBLEM OF RELIGIOUS PROGRESS, New York, 1881.

Douglas, William M., ANDREW MURRAY AND HIS MESSAGE, London, 1926.

Dow, Lorenzo, HISTORY OF COSMOPOLITE, New York, 1814.

Drach, George, editor, OUR CHURCH ABROAD: THE FOREIGN MISSIONS OF THE LUTHERAN CHURCH IN AMERICA, Philadelphia, 1926.

Drach, George, & Kuder, C. F., THE TELUGU MISSION OF THE EVANGELICAL LUTHERAN CHURCH IN NORTH AMERICA, Philadelphia, 1914.

Drury, A. W., HISTORY OF THE CHURCH OF THE UNITED BRETHREN IN CHRIST, Dayton, 1931.

Duncan, Mary, HISTORY OF REVIVALS OF RELIGION IN THE BRITISH ISLES, Edinburgh, 1836.

Du Plessis, J., A HISTORY OF CHRISTIAN MISSIONS IN SOUTH AFRICA, New York, 1911.

Du Plessis, J., THE LIFE OF ANDREW MURRAY OF SOUTH AFRICA, London, 1919.

Durfee, C., A HISTORY OF WILLIAMS COLLEGE, Boston, 1860.

Dwight, E. W., MEMOIRS OF HENRY OBOOKIAH, A NATIVE OF OWHYHEE, New Haven, 1818.

Dwight, H. O., CENTENNIAL HISTORY OF THE AMERICAN BIBLE SOCIETY, New York, 1916.

Dwight, A. G. O., CHRISTIANITY IN TURKEY: A NARRATIVE OF THE PROTESTANT REFORMATION IN THE ARMENIAN CHURCH, London, 1854.

Dwight, Timothy, A DISCOURSE ON SOME EVENTS OF THE LAST CENTURY, New Haven, 1801.

Dwight, Timothy, lecture, THE NATURE AND DANGER OF INFIDEL PHILOSOPHY, New Haven, 1798.

Dyson, M., STORY OF SAMOAN WESLEYANISM, Melbourne, 1875.

Edwards, A. G., LANDMARKS IN THE HISTORY OF THE WELSH CHURCH, London, 1912.

Edwards, Jonathan, THE WORKS OF PRESIDENT EDWARDS, New York, 4 Volumes, 1844.

Elder, J. R., LETTERS AND JOURNALS OF SAMUEL MARSDEN, Dunedin, 1932.

Elliott-Binns, L. E., THE EARLY EVANGELICALS, London, 1961.

Ellis, William, THE MARTYR CHURCH, A NARRATIVE OF CHRISTIANITY IN MADAGASCAR, London, 1870.

Ellis, William, POLYNESIAN RESEARCHES . . . IN THE SOCIETY AND SANDWICH ISLANDS, London, 4 Volumes, 1831.

Emery, Julia C., A CENTURY OF ENDEAVOR, 1821-1921: A RECORD OF THE MISSIONARY SOCIETY OF THE PROTESTANT EPISCOPAL CHURCH, New York, 1921.

Etheridge, J. W., THE LIFE OF THE REV. ADAM CLARKE, London, 1859.

Evans, Eifion, WHEN HE IS COME, Bala, 1959.

Eversleigh, W., THE SETTLERS AND METHODISM, Cape Town, 1920.

Ewing, J. A., LANKA—THE RESPLENDENT ISLE: THE BAPTIST MISSION IN CEYLON, London, 1912.

Fairholme, E. G., & Pain, Wellesley, A CENTURY OF WORK FOR ANIMALS: THE R.S.P.C.A., 1824-1924, London, 1924.

Farndale, W. E., THE SECRET OF MOW COP, London, 1950.

Faulkner, H. U., CHARTISM AND THE CHURCHES: A STUDY IN DEMOCRACY, New York, 1916.

Felice, G. de, & Bonifas, F., HISTOIRE DES PROTESTANTES DE FRANCE, Toulouse, 6th edition, 1874.

Field, J., THE LIFE OF JOHN HOWARD, London, 1850.

Findlay, G. G., & Holdsworth, W. W., THE HISTORY OF THE WESLEYAN METHODIST MISSIONARY SOCIETY, London, 5 Volumes, 1921-1924.

Finney, Charles G., LECTURES ON REVIVALS OF RELIGION, New York, 1835, (Edinburgh, 1928).

Finney, Charles G., MEMOIRS OF REV. CHARLES G. FINNEY, New York, 1876.

Fish, H. C., HANDBOOK OF REVIVALS, London, 1873.

Fitch, E. R., editor, THE BAPTISTS OF CANADA, Toronto, 1911.

Flindall, R. P., editor, THE CHURCH OF ENGLAND, 1815-1948, London, 1972.

Foote, W. H., SKETCHES OF NORTH CAROLINA, HISTORICAL AND BIOGRAPHICAL, New York, 1846.

Foote, W. H., SKETCHES OF VIRGINIA, HISTORICAL AND BIOGRAPHICAL, Philadelphia, 2 Volumes, 1850-1855.

Frommel, E., AUS DEM LEBEN DES DR. ALOYS HENHOFER, Karlsruhe, 1865.

Gardner, A. R. C., THE PLACE OF JOHN HOWARD IN PENAL REFORM, London, 1926.

Garrison, W. E., RELIGION FOLLOWS THE FRONTIER: A HISTORY OF THE DISCIPLES OF CHRIST, New York, 1931.

Glasgow Tract Society, NARRATIVES OF REVIVALS OF RELIGION IN SCOTLAND, IRELAND AND WALES, Glasgow, 1839.

Gobat, Samuel, JOURNAL OF A THREE YEARS' RESIDENCE IN ABYSSINIA, London, 1834.

Godlonton, R., MEMORIALS OF THE BRITISH SETTLERS OF SOUTH AFRICA, Grahamstown, 1844.

Goethe, J. W., JUNG-STILLINGS JUGEND, JUNGLINGSJAHRE, WANDERSCHAFT UND LEHRJAHRE, Giessen, 1954.

Gregg, William, THE HISTORY OF THE PRESBYTERIAN CHURCH IN THE DOMINION OF CANADA, Toronto, 1885.

Groves, Mrs., MEMOIR OF ANTHONY NORRIS GROVES, London, 1856.

Gulick, Orramel Hinckley, THE PILGRIMS OF HAWAII, New York, 1918.

Gutzlaff, Karl, JOURNAL OF THREE VOYAGES ALONG THE COAST OF CHINA, IN 1831, 1832, 1833, London, 1834.

Hägglund, H., HENRIC SCHARTAU, Stockholm, 1924.

Hail, William James, TSENG KUO-FAN AND THE TAIPING RE-BELLION, New Haven, 1927.

Haldane, Alexander, THE LIVES OF ROBERT HALDANE OF AIRTHREY AND OF HIS BROTHER, JAMES ALEXANDER HALDANE, Edinburgh, 5th edition, 1855.

Hall, James, A NARRATIVE OF A MOST EXTRAORDINARY WORK OF RELIGION IN NORTH CAROLINA, Philadelphia, 1802.

Halliday, S. B. & D. S. Gregory, THE CHURCH IN AMERICA AND ITS BAPTISMS OF FIRE, New York, 1896.

Hanekom, T. N., HELPERUS RITZEMA VAN LIER, Cape Town, 1959.

Hansen, Maurice G., THE REFORMED CHURCH IN THE NETHER-LANDS, FROM 1340 TO 1840, New York, 1884.

Harris, John, A CENTURY OF EMANCIPATION, London, 1933.

Hartog, Philip, SOME ASPECTS OF INDIAN EDUCATION, PAST AND PRESENT, London, 1939.

Haslam, William, FROM DEATH UNTO LIFE, London, 1880.

Henderson, G. C., FIJI AND THE FIJIANS, 1835-1856, Sydney, 1931.

Hermelink, Heineich, DAS CHRISTENTUM IN DER MENSCHHEITS-GESCHICHTE VON DER FRANZOSISCHEN REVOLUTION BIS ZUR GEGENWART, Stuttgart, 1951.

Hill, William, AUTOBIOGRAPHICAL SKETCHES, Richmond, 1968.

Hodder, Edwin, THE LIFE AND WORK OF THE SEVENTH EARL OF SHAFTESBURY, London, 1887.

Holmquist, Hjalmar, HANDBOK I SVENSK KYRKOHISTORIA, Stockholm, 3 Volumes, 1952.

Holt, Basil F., JOSEPH WILLIAMS AND THE PIONEER MISSION TO THE SOUTHEASTERN BANTU, Lovedale, 1954.

Hood, Paxton, CHRISTMAS EVANS, THE PREACHER TO WILD WALES, London, 1883.

Hooker, Richard J., THE CAROLINA BACKCOUNTRY ON THE EVE OF THE REVOLUTION: THE JOURNAL AND OTHER WRITINGS OF CHARLES WOODMASON, Chapel Hill, 1953.

Hotchkin, J. H., HISTORY OF THE SETTLEMENT OF WESTERN NEW YORK, New York, 1848.

Hovey, Alvah, A MEMOIR OF THE LIFE AND TIMES OF THE REV. ISAAC BACKUS, Boston, 1854.

Howe, George, HISTORY OF THE PRESBYTERIAN CHURCH IN SOUTH CAROLINA, Columbia, 1883.

Hughes, Henry, DIWYGIADU CREGYDDOL CYMRU, Carnarvon, 1906.

Hughes, John, METHODISTAETH CYMRU, Wrexham, 3 Volumes, 1851-1856.

Humphrey, Heman, REVIVAL SKETCHES, New York, 1859.

Hutton, J. E., A HISTORY OF MORAVIAN MISSIONS, London, 1923.

Ingham, Kenneth, REFORMERS IN INDIA, 1783-1833, London, 1956.

Inglis, K. S., CHURCHES AND THE WORKING CLASS IN VIC-TORIAN ENGLAND, London, 1963.

Ironside, H. A., A HISTORICAL SKETCH OF THE BRETHREN MOVEMENT, Grand Rapids, 1942.

Jäckel, A., DER ALTE KOTTWITZ, Berlin, 1892.

Jacobs, Henry Eyster, HISTORY OF THE EVANGELICAL LUTHERAN CHURCH IN THE UNITED STATES, New York, 1893.

Jager, Theodor, LUDWIG HOFACKER, Stuttgart, 1910.

Jarratt, Devereux, THE LIFE OF THE REVEREND DEVEREUX JARRATT, Baltimore, 1806.

Jeffrey, Robert, THE INDIAN MISSION OF THE IRISH PRESBYTERIAN CHURCH, London, 1890.

Jenkins, D. E., THE LIFE OF THOMAS CHARLES OF BALA, Denbigh, 1908.

Johnston, Charles A., THE FRONTIER CAMP MEETING: RELIGIOUS HARVEST TIME, Dallas, 1955.

Jones, David, THE LIFE AND TIMES OF GRIFFITH JONES, London, 1902.

Jones, J. H., OUTLINE OF A WORK OF GRACE IN THE PRESBYTERIAN CONGREGATION AT NEW BRUNSWICK, NEW JERSEY, DURING THE YEAR 1837, Philadelphia, 1839.

Jones, J. O., COFIANT A GWEITHIAU Y PARCH: ROBERT ELLIS, YSGOLDY, Carnarvon, 1883.

Jonzon, Bengt, STUDIER I PAAVO RUOTSULAINENS FROMHET, Stockholm, 1935.

JOURNAL OF XLI ANNUAL CONVENTION OF THE PROTESTANT EPISCOPAL CHURCH, DIOCESE OF OHIO, Cincinnati, 1858.

Kantzenbach, F. W., DIE ERWECKUNGSBEWEGUNG, Neuendettelsau, 1957.

Karsten, Hermann, DIE GESCHICHTE DER EVANGELISCH LUTHERISCHEN MISSION IN LEIPZIG, Leipzig, 1893.

Keijzer, W. P., VINET EN HOLLAND, Wageningen, 1941.

Keller, Charles Roy, THE SECOND GREAT AWAKENING IN CONNECTICUT, New York, 1942.

Kendall, H. B., A HISTORY OF THE PRIMITIVE METHODIST CHURCH, London, 1919.

Kennedy, John, THE APOSTLE OF THE NORTH, LIFE AND LABOURS OF THE REV. DR. McDONALD, London, 1867.

Kesson, John, THE CROSS AND THE DRAGON: THE FORTUNES OF CHRISTIANITY IN CHINA, London, 1854.

Killen, W. D., ECCLESIASTICAL HISTORY OF IRELAND, London, 1875.

King, Alonzo, MEMOIR OF GEORGE DANA BOARDMAN, Boston, 1834.

King, J. M., A HISTORY SOUTH CAROLINA BAPTISTS, Columbia, 1964.

Kjaer, Jens Christian, HISTORY OF THE CHURCH OF DENMARK, Blair, Nebraska, 1945.

Kluit, M. Elisabeth, HET REVEIL IN NEDERLAND, Amsterdam, 1936.

Knight, Helen, LADY HUNTINGTON AND HER FRIENDS, London, 1852.

Koch, Hal, DANMARKS KIRKE GJENNOM TIDERNE, Copenhagen, 1949.

Koch, Hal & Kornerup, Bjorn, DEN DANSKE KIRKES HISTORIE, Copenhagen, 1949.

Koch, Hal, GRUNDTVIG, translated by Llewellyn Jones, Yellow Springs, Ohio, 1952.

Kotze, D. J., LETTERS OF THE AMERICAN MISSIONARIES, 1832-1834, Cape Town, 1950.

Krummacher, F. W., GOTTFRIED DANIEL KRUMMACHER UND DIE NEIDER RHEINISCHE ERWECKUNGSBEWEGUNG ZU ANFANG DES 19 JAHRHUNDERTS, Berlin, 1935.

Krummacher, F. W., SELBSTBIOGRAPHIE, Berlin, 1869.

Lacy, Benjamin R., REVIVALS IN THE MIDST OF THE YEARS, Richmond, 1943.

Latourette, Kenneth Scott, CHRISTIANITY IN A REVOLUTIONARY AGE, 5 VOLUMES, New York, 1950.

Latourette, Kenneth Scott, A HISTORY OF THE EXPANSION OF CHRISTIANITY, New York, 7 Volumes, 1937-1945.

Lee, Jesse, A SHORT HISTORY OF THE METHODISTS IN THE UNITED STATES OF AMERICA, Baltimore, 1810.

Ledderhose, K. F., DR. ALOYS HENHOFER, Karlsruhe, 1865.

Leflon, Jean, LA CRISE REVOLUTIONNAIRE, 1789-1846, Paris, 1949.

Livingstone, David, MISSIONARY TRAVELS AND RESEARCHES IN SOUTH AFRICA, London, 1857.

Lodin, Sven, CARL OLOF BOSENIUS I UNGA AR, 1816-1842, Stockholm, 1933.

Loud, Grover, EVANGELIZED AMERICA, New York, 1928.

Lovett, Richard, THE HISTORY OF THE LONDON MISSIONARY SOCIETY, 1795-1895, London, 1899.

Lowrie, Walter, A SHORT LIFE OF KIERKEGAARD, Princeton, 1944.

Lumsden, James, SWEDEN: ITS RELIGIOUS STATE AND PROSPECTS, London, 1855.

McCleary, W. E., THE LIFE OF REV. JAMES O'KELLY, Raleigh, 1910.

McDonagh, M., THE LIFE OF BISHOP DOYLE, Dublin.

McDonald, W. B., THE HISTORY OF THE CUMBERLAND PRESBYTERIAN CHURCH, Nashville, 1888.

McDowell, R. B., PUBLIC OPINION IN IRELAND, 1801-1846, Dublin, 1957.

McIlvaine, C. P., BISHOP McILVAINE ON THE REVIVAL OF RELIGION, New York, 1858.

Macinnes, John, EVANGELICAL MOVEMENT IN THE HIGHLANDS OF SCOTLAND, Aberdeen, 1951.

Mackinnon, I. F., SETTLEMENTS AND CHURCHES. IN NOVA SCOTIA, 1749-1776, Montreal, 1930.

Mackichan, D., THE MISSIONARY IDEAL IN THE SCOTTISH CHURCHES, London, 1927.

McLoughlin, W. G., MODERN REVIVALISM: CHARLES GRANDISON FINNEY TO BILLY GRAHAM, New York, 1959.

MacRae, Alexander, REVIVALS IN THE HIGHLANDS AND ISLANDS IN THE 19TH CENTURY, Stirling, 1906.

Malan, THE LIFE, LABOURS AND WRITINGS of CAESAR MALAN, London, 1869.

Marsden, Joshua, NARRATIVE OF A MISSION TO NOVA SCOTIA, NEW BRUNSWICK, AND THE SOMERS ISLANDS, Plymouth, England, 1816.

Marshman, John Clark, THE LIFE AND TIMES OF CAREY, MARSHMAN AND WARD, London, 2 Volumes, 1859.

Mason, Ebenezer, THE COMPLETE WORKS OF JOHN M. MASON, New York, 4 Volumes, 1849.

Mason, Francis, THE KAREN APOSTLE: KO THAH-BYU, Boston, 1843.

Maury, Leon, LE REVEIL RELIGIEUX DANS L'EGLISE REFORMEE A GENEVE ET EN FRANCE (1810-1850), Paris, 1892.

Milne, William, A RETROSPECT OF THE FIRST TEN YEARS OF THE PROTESTANT MISSION TO CHINA, Malacca, 1820: —largely the work of his associate, Robert Morrison.

Mitchell, Donald R., 'The Evangelical Contribution of James Thomson to South American Life, 1818-25,' Th.D. Dissertation, Princeton Theological Seminary, 1972.

Moffat, John S., THE LIVES OF ROBERT AND MARY MOFFAT, London, 1886.

Moffat, Robert, MISSIONARY LABOURS AND SCENES IN SOUTH AFRICA, London, 1842.

Molland, Einar, CHURCH LIFE IN NORWAY, 1800-1950, Minneapolis, 1957.

Molland, Einar, FRA HANS NIELSEN HAUGE TIL EIVIND BERG-GRAV, Oslo, 1951.

Montgomery, M. W., A WIND FROM THE HOLY SPIRIT IN SWEDEN AND NORWAY, New York, 1884.

Morison, S. E., THREE CENTURIES AT HARVARD, 1636-1936, Cambridge, 1936.

Morgan, H. D., RELIGIOUS PRINCIPLES AND PRACTICES OF THE AGE, Bampton Lecture, Oxford, 1819.

Morgan, James, MY LIFE AND TIMES, Belfast, 1874.

Morris, John Hughes, THE STORY OF OUR FOREIGN MISSION (Presbyterian Church of Wales), Liverpool, 1930.

Morrison, Eliza, MEMOIRS OF THE LIFE AND LABOURS OF ROBERT MORRISON, London, 1839.

Moulton, J. Egan, MOULTON OF TONGA, London, 1921.

Muller, G., CHRISTIAN GOTTLOB PREZIGER, Stuttgart, 1962.

Mullins, J. D., OUR BEGINNINGS: HISTORY OF THE COLONIAL AND CONTINENTAL CHURCH SOCIETY, London, 1923.

Murray, T., THE LETTERS OF DAVID HUME, Edinburgh, 1841.

Neill, Stephen, A HISTORY OF CHRISTIAN MISSIONS, London, 1964.

Newcomb, Harvey, A CYCLOPEDIA OF MISSIONS, New York, 1854.

Newman, A. H., A MANUAL OF CHURCH HISTORY, 2 Volumes, Philadelphia, 1931.

Newton, John, THE WORKS OF JOHN NEWTON, London, 1808, 6 Volumes; 1827, 1 Volume.

Norborg, Sverre, HANS NIELSEN HAUGE, 1771-1804, Oslo, 1966.

Nurullah, Syed & Naik, J. P., A HISTORY OF EDUCATION IN INDIA, Bombay, 1951.

Nyman, H., PAAVO RUOTSALAINEN: DEN BIDANDE TRON, Helsinki, 1949.

Oliphant, Mrs., THE LIFE OF EDWARD IRVING, New York, 1862.

Olsson, Karl A., BY ONE SPIRIT, Chicago, 1962.

Overton, J. H., THE ENGLISH CHURCH IN THE NINETEENTH CENTURY, 1800-1833, London, 1894.

Overton, J. H., THE ANGLICAN REVIVAL, London, 1897.

Overton, J. H., THE EVANGELICAL REVIVAL IN THE EIGH-TEENTH CENTURY, London, 1886.

Ousland, G., EN KIRKEHOVDING: PROFESSOR GISLE JOHNSON, Oslo, 1950.

Pascoe, C. F., TWO HUNDRED YEARS OF THE S. P. G., 1701-1900, London, 1901.

Paton, William, ALEXANDER DUFF: PIONEER OF MISSIONARY EDUCATION, London, 1923.

Patton, J. M., A POPULAR HISTORY OF THE PRESBYTERIAN CHURCH IN THE U.S.A., New York, 1900.

Payne, Ernest A., FREEDOM IN JAMAICA, London, 1933.

Philip, R., THE ELIJAH OF SOUTH AFRICA: THE REV. JOHN PHILIP, London, 1951.

Phillips, C. S., THE CHURCH IN FRANCE, 1769-1848: A STUDY IN REVIVAL, London, 1929.

Phillips, Walter Allison, editor, HISTORY OF THE CHURCH OF IRELAND FROM THE EARLIEST TIMES TO THE PRESENT DAY, London, 3 Volumes, 1933-1939.

Pickett, J. W., CHRISTIAN MASS MOVEMENTS IN INDIA, New York, 1933.

Pierson, A. T., GEORGE MULLER OF BRISTOL, New York, 1905.

Poland, B. C., FRENCH PROTESTANTISM AND THE FRENCH REVOLUTION, Princeton, 1957.

Porter, J. L., THE LIFE AND TIMES OF HENRY COOKE, Belfast, 1875.

Prime, E. D. G., FORTY YEARS IN THE TURKISH EMPIRE, MEMOIRS OF REV. WILLIAM GOODELL, New York, 1876.

Prout, Ebenezer, MEMOIRS OF THE LIFE OF THE REV. JOHN WILLIAMS, New York, 1843.

Purviance, Levi, BIOGRAPHY OF ELDER DAVID PURVIANCE, Dayton, 1848.

Rambert, E., ALEXANDRE VINET, Lausanne, 1930.

Rauws, J., Kraemer, H., Van Hasselt, F. J. F., & Slotemaker de Bruine, N. A. C., THE NETHERLANDS INDIES, London, 1935.

REALENCYCLOPEDIA FUR PROTESTANTISCHE THEOLOGIE UND KIRCHE, Leipzig, 22 Volumes, 1896-1909.

Rees, Thomas, HISTORY OF PROTESTANT NONCONFORMITY IN WALES, FROM ITS RISE TO THE PRESENT TIME, London, 1861.

Reid, J. M., MISSIONS AND MISSIONARY SOCIETY OF THE METHODIST EPISCOPAL CHURCH, New York, 3 Volumes, 1895-1896.

Reid, J. S., HISTORY OF THE PRESBYTERIAN CHURCH IN IRELAND, Belfast, 1867.

REPORT OF THE ABERDEEN PRESBYTERY, Aberdeen, 1841.

Rice, Edwin Wilbur, THE SUNDAY SCHOOL MOVEMENT AND AMERICAN SUNDAY SCHOOL UNION, Philadelphia, 1927.

Rice, David, A SERMON ON THE PRESENT REVIVAL OF RELIGION IN KENTUCKY, Lexington, 1803.

Richards, T. C., THE LIFE OF SAMUEL J. MILLS, Boston, 1906.

Richardson, R., MEMOIRS OF ALEXANDER CAMPBELL, New York, 1868.

Richter, Julius, DIE EVANGELISCHE MISSION IN NIEDERLAND-ISCH-INDIEN, Gutersloh, 1932.

Ringwald, Alfred, MENSCHEN VOR GOTT, 3 Volumes, Stuttgart, 1958.

Ritson, Joseph, THE ROMANCE OF PRIMITIVE METHODISM, London, 1909.

Roden, R. J., PROGRESS OF THE REFORMATION IN IRELAND, London, 1852.

Rogers, James, R., CANE RIDGE MEETING-HOUSE, Cincinnati, 1910.

Ronegard, Sam, LARS PAUL ESBJORN AND THE BEGINNINGS OF THE AUGUSTANA LUTHERAN CHURCH, Rock Island, 1952.

Root, H. I., A CENTURY IN CEYLON: A HISTORY OF THE AMERICAN BOARD IN CEYLON, 1816-1916, Boston, 1916.

Rosenqvist, G. O., FINLANDS KYRKA, Lund, 1946.

Rott, L., DIE ANFANGE DES WESLEYANISCHEN METHODISMUS, Frankfurt.

Rudolph, Frederick, THE AMERICAN COLLEGE AND UNIVERSITY, New York, 1962.

Ryerson, Egerton, THE STORY OF MY LIFE, Toronto, 1883.

Ryland, Garnet, THE BAPTISTS OF VIRGINIA, Richmond, 1955.

Ryland, John, THE LIFE AND DEATH OF ANDREW FULLER, London, 1816.

Sandall, Robert, THE HISTORY OF THE SALVATION ARMY, 1865-1878, London, 1947.

Sanderson, J. E., THE FIRST CENTURY OF METHODISM IN CANADA, Toronto, 2 Volumes, 1908.

Saunders, E. M., A HISTORY OF THE BAPTISTS OF THE MARITIME PROVINCES, Halifax, 1902.

Scharpff, Paulus, GESCHICHTE DER EVANGELISATION, Giessen, 1964.

Schlatter, Wilhelm, GESCHICHTE DER BASLER MISSION, 1815-1915, Basel, 3 Volumes, 1916.

Schmidt, Wolfgang, FINLANDS KYRKA GJENNOM TIDERNE, Stockholm, 1940.

Schroeder, G. W., HISTORY OF THE SWEDISH BAPTISTS IN SWEDEN AND AMERICA, New York, 1898.

Scott, Alfred Russell, 'The Ulster Revival of 1859,' Ph.D. Dissertation, University of Dublin, 1962.

Sellers, C. C., LORENZO DOW, New York, 1928.

Semple, R. B., A HISTORY OF THE RISE AND PROGRESS OF THE BAPTISTS IN VIRGINIA, Richmond, 1810.

Sharp, H., SELECTIONS FROM EDUCATIONAL RECORDS, 1781-1839, London, 1920.

Shaw, P. E., THE CATHOLIC APOSTOLIC CHURCH, SOMETIMES CALLED IRVINGITE, New York, 1946.

Shaw, William, THE STORY OF MY MISSION IN SOUTHEASTERN AFRICA, London, 1860.

Shedd, Clarence P., TWO CENTURIES OF STUDENT CHRISTIAN MOVEMENTS, New York, 1934.

Shepherd, R. H. W., LOVEDALE, SOUTH AFRICA, 1841-1941, Lovedale, 1941.

Sherring, M. A., THE HISTORY OF PROTESTANT MISSIONS IN INDIA, London, 1884.

Shipp, Albert M., METHODISM IN SOUTH CAROLINA, Columbia, 1883.

Shortt, Adam, & Doughty, Arthur, editors, CANADA AND ITS PROVINCES, Toronto, 23 Volumes, 1914-1917.

Siegmund Schultze, F., editor, DIE KIRCHE IN FINNLAND, Leipzig, 1838.

Sievewright, J., MEMOIR OF ALEXANDER STEWART, Edinburgh, 1822.

Sigston, James, A MEMOIR OF THE LIFE AND MINISTRY OF WILLIAM BRAMWELL, London, 1820.

241

Simon, J. S., THE REVIVAL OF RELIGION IN THE EIGHTEENTH CENTURY, London, 1907.

Sissons, C. B., EGERTON RYERSON, HIS LIFE AND LETTERS, Toronto, 2 Volumes, 1937-1947.

Smeaton, Oliphant, PRINCIPAL JAMES MORISON: THE MAN AND HIS WORK, Edinburgh, 1902.

Smith, George, HENRY MARTYN, London, 1892.

Smith, George, HISTORY OF WESLEYAN METHODISM, London, 3 Volumes, 1862.

Smith, George, THE LIFE OF ALEXANDER DUFF, London, 1899.

Smith, George, THE LIFE OF JOHN WILSON, London, 1879.

Smith, George, STEPHEN HISLOP: PIONEER MISSIONARY, London, 1879.

Smith, G. G., THE LIFE AND LABOURS OF FRANCIS ASBURY, Nashville, 1898.

Smith, John Blair, THE ENLARGEMENT OF CHRIST'S KINGDOM, Schenectady, 1797.

Smith, Timothy L., REVIVALISM AND SOCIAL REFORM IN MID-NINETEENTH CENTURY AMERICA, Nashville, 1947.

Soloway, R. A., PRELATES AND PEOPLE, London, 1969.

Speer, William, THE GREAT REVIVAL OF 1800, Philadelphia, 1872.

Spencer, J. H., A HISTORY OF THE KENTUCKY BAPTISTS FROM 1769 TO 1885, 2 Volumes, Cincinnati, 1886.

Spence, Thomas Hugh, THE PRESBYTERIAN CONGREGATION ON ROCKY RIVER, Concord, N. C., 1954.

Sprague, William B., LECTURES ON REVIVALS OF RELIGION, New York, 1833.

Spring, Gardiner, MEMOIRS OF THE REV. SAMUEL J. MILLS, New York, 1820.

Stephens, Abel, THE LIFE AND TIMES OF NATHAN BANGS, New York, 1863.

Stephenson, George M. THE RELIGIOUS ASPECTS OF SWEDISH IMMIGRATION, Minneapolis, 1932.

Stewart, Alexander, AN ACCOUNT OF THE LATE REVIVAL OF RELIGION AT MOULIN, Edinburgh, 1801.

Stewart, David, THE SECEDERS IN IRELAND, Belfast, 1950.

Stock, Eugene, THE HISTORY OF THE CHURCH MISSIONARY SOCIETY: ITS ENVIRONMENT, ITS MEN AND ITS WORK, London, 4 Volumes, 1899-1916.

Stoddard, D. T., NARRATIVE OF THE LATE REVIVAL AMONG THE NESTORIANS, Boston, 1847.

Stone, Barton Warren, THE BIOGRAPHY OF ELDER BARTON WARREN STONE, edited by John Rogers, Cincinnati, 1847.

Strachan, Alexander, THE LIFE OF THE REV. SAMUEL LEIGH, London, 1870.

Strickland, A. B., THE GREAT AMERICAN REVIVAL, Cincinnati, 1934.

Strickland, W. B., editor, THE AUTOBIOGRAPHY OF PETER CARTWRIGHT, THE BACKWOODS PREACHER, New York, 1856.

Strong, William Elsworth, THE STORY OF THE AMERICAN BOARD: AN ACCOUNT OF THE FIRST HUNDRED YEARS OF THE AMERICAN BOARD OF COMMISSIONERS FOR FOREIGN MISSIONS, Boston, 1910.

Sutton, A., ORISSA AND ITS EVANGELIZATION, Derby, 1850.

Sweet, William Warren, REVIVALISM IN AMERICA: ITS RISE, PROGRESS, AND DECLINE, New York, 1945.

Sweet, William Warren, THE STORY OF RELIGION IN AMERICA, New York, 1950.

Tewkesbury, Donald G., THE FOUNDING OF AMERICAN COLLEGES AND UNIVERSITIES BEFORE THE CIVIL WAR, New York, 1932.

Thacher, Peter, A BRIEF ACCOUNT OF THE SOCIETY FOR PROPAGATING THE GOSPEL AMONG INDIANS AND OTHERS IN NORTH AMERICA, Boston, 1790.

Thompson, C. L., TIMES OF REFRESHING: A HISTORY OF AMERICAN REVIVALS FROM 1740 TO 1877, Chicago, 1877.

Thompson, Basil, DIVERSIONS OF A PRIME MINISTER, Edinburgh, 1894.

Thomson, James, LETTERS ON THE MORAL AND RELIGIOUS STATE OF SOUTH AMERICA, London, 1830.

Thomssen, G. M., SAMUEL HEBICH OF INDIA, Mangalore, 1915.

Tiesmeyer, L., DIE ERWECKUNGSBEWEGUNG IN DEUTCHLAND, Kassel, 1901.

Tiffany, Charles C., A HISTORY OF THE PROTESTANT EPIS- COPAL CHURCH IN THE UNITED STATES OF AMERICA, New York, 1895.

Tippet, Alan R., PEOPLE MOVEMENTS IN SOUTHERN POLYNESIA, Chicago, 1971.

Tracy, J., HISTORY OF THE AMERICAN BOARD OF COMMIS- SIONERS FOR FOREIGN MISSIONS, New York, 1842.

Trail, H. D. & Mann, J.S., editors, SOCIAL ENGLAND, 5 Volumes, London, 1904.

Trevelyan, George Macauley, ENGLISH SOCIAL HISTORY, London, 1944.

Turner, J. E., THE PIONEER MISSIONARY: REV. NATHANIEL TURNER, London, 1872.

Tyler, Alice F., FREEDOM'S FERMENT, Minneapolis, 1944.

Tyler, Bennet, MEMOIR OF THE LIFE AND CHARACTER OF REV. ASAHEL NETTLETON, Hartford, 1844.

Tyler, Bennet, NEW ENGLAND REVIVALS AT THE CLOSE OF THE EIGHTEENTH AND THE BEGINNING OF THE NINE- TEENTH CENTURIES, Boston, 1846.

Uustalu, Evald, HISTORY OF THE ESTONIAN PEOPLE, London, 1952.

Van der Merwe, W. J., THE DEVELOPMENT OF MISSIONARY ATTITUDES IN THE DUTCH REFORMED CHURCH IN SOUTH AFRICA, Cape Town, 1936.

Various Authors, RELIGIOUS LIFE IN SCOTLAND FROM THE REFORMATION TO THE PRESENT DAY, London, 1888.

Vedder, Henry C., A SHORT HISTORY OF THE BAPTISTS, Philadelphia, 1907.

Von Krüdener, Frau, EIN ZEITGEMALDE, Bern, 1868.

Walsh, H. H., THE CHRISTIAN CHURCH IN CANADA, Toronto, 1956.

Ward, W. W., THE EARLY CORRESPONDENCE OF JABEZ BUNTING, London, 1972.

Warnecke, Gustav, ABRISS EINER GESCHICHTE DER PROTES- TANTISCHEN MISSIONEN, Berlin, 10th edition, 1913.

Waterhouse, Joseph, THE KING AND PEOPLE OF FIJI, London, 1866.

Watt, Hugh, THOMAS CHALMERS AND THE DISRUPTION, Edin- burgh, 1943.

Wayland, F., MEMOIR OF THE LIFE OF ADONIRAM JUDSON, Boston, 1853.

Wearmouth, R. F., METHODISM AND THE WORKING-CLASS MOVEMENTS OF ENGLAND, 1800-1850, London, 1937.

Webb, Sidney & Beatrice, A HISTORY OF TRADE UNIONISM, London, 1894.

Weber, H. C., PRESBYTERIAN STATISTICS THROUGH ONE HUNDRED YEARS, 1826-1926, Philadelphia, 1927.

Weisberger, Bernard A., THEY GATHERED AT THE RIVER, Boston, 1958.

Weld, Isaac, TRAVELS THROUGH THE STATES OF NORTH AMERICA AND PROVINCES OF UPPER AND LOWER CANADA DURING THE YEARS 1795, 1796 and 1797, London, 1799.

Wentz, A. R., FLIEDNER, THE FAITHFUL, Philadelphia, 1936.

Wentz, A. R., THE LUTHERAN CHURCH IN AMERICAN HISTORY, Philadelphia, 1933.

Wertenbaker, T. J., PRINCETON: 1746-1896, Princeton, 1896.

Wesley, Charles H., RICHARD ALLEN: APOSTLE OF FREEDOM, Washington, 1935.

West, Thomas, TEN YEARS IN SOUTH-CENTRAL POLYNESIA, London, 1865.

Westin, Gunnar, DEN KRISTNA FRIFORSAMLINGEN I NORDEN, Stockholm, 1956.

Westin, Gunnar, GEORGE SCOTT OCH HANS VERKSAMHET I SVERIGE, Stockholm, 2 Volumes, 1928-1929.

Whiteside, J., HISTORY OF THE WESLEYAN METHODIST CHURCH IN SOUTH AFRICA, London, 1906.

Whitley, W. T., A HISTORY OF BRITISH BAPTISTS, London, 2nd edition, 1932.

Whitney, J., ELIZABETH FRY, QUAKER HEROINE, Boston, 1936.

Williams, John, A NARRATIVE OF MISSIONARY ENTERPRISE IN THE SOUTH SEA ISLANDS, New York, 1837.

Wilson, William, A MISSIONARY VOYAGE TO THE SOUTH PACIFIC OCEAN, PERFORMED 1796-1798, London, 1799.

Witte, L., DAS LEBENS THOLUCKS, Leipzig, 1884.

Wolf, Edmund Jacob, THE LUTHERANS IN AMERICA: A STORY OF STRUGGLE, PROGRESS, INFLUENCE AND MARVELOUS GROWTH, New York, 1889.

Wolff, Christian, EIGEN LEBENSBESCHREIBUNG, Berlin, 1841.

Woodham-Smith, C., FLORENCE NIGHTINGALE, New York, 1951.

Woods, Nathan S., A HISTORY OF THE FIRST BAPTIST CHURCH OF BOSTON, Boston, 1920.

Woodside, David, THE SOUL OF A SCOTTISH CHURCH, Edinburgh, no date given.

Woodson, Carter G., THE HISTORY OF THE NEGRO CHURCH, Washington, 2nd edition, 1921.

Woodward, W. W., SURPRISING ACCOUNTS OF THE REVIVAL OF RELIGION IN THE UNITED STATES, Philadelphia, 1802.

Wordsworth, John, THE NATIONAL CHURCH OF SWEDEN, London 1911.

Wright, G. F., CHARLES GRANDISON FINNEY, Boston, 1893.

Wright, H. B., TWO CENTURIES OF CHRISTIAN ACTIVITY AT YALE, New Haven, 1925.

Young, Robert, THE SOUTHERN WORLD, London, 1858.

Zorn, H. M., BARTHOMAEUS ZIEGENBALG, St. Louis, 1933.

INDEX

55384